Africana Jewish Journeys

Africana Jewish Journeys:

Studies in African Judaism

Edited by

Marla Brettschneider, Edith Bruder and Magdel Le Roux

Cambridge Scholars Publishing

Africana Jewish Journeys: Studies in African Judaism

Edited by Marla Brettschneider, Edith Bruder and Magdel Le Roux

This book first published 2019

Cambridge Scholars Publishing

Lady Stephenson Library, Newcastle upon Tyne, NE6 2PA, UK

British Library Cataloguing in Publication Data
A catalogue record for this book is available from the British Library

ISBN (10): 1-5275-2213-X
ISBN (13): 978-1-5275-2213-8

Some of the articles in this book come from papers presented at the Third International Conference of the International Society for the Study of African Jewry (www.issaj.com) “The Surge of Judaism across Africa, the African Diaspora and Asia in the Twenty-first Century” at The Museum of Jewish History and Art Paris, France, 10-11 November 2015.

TABLE OF CONTENTS

ACKNOWLEDGEMENTS

We would like to thank at the University of New Hampshire the College of Liberal Arte, the Center for the Humanities, Women's Studies, and Political Science as well as Tali Cherim, Elisabeth Lohmueller, Bethany Kaminsky, and Nina Judith Katz.

INTRODUCTION

MARLA BRETTSCHNEIDER, EDITH BRUDER, AND MAGDEL LE ROUX

In recent decades, we have witnessed a new global phenomenon. Throughout the world, tens of thousands of individuals have chosen to become part of the Jewish people, adopting Jewish religious identity either through self-identification or religious conversion. This remarkable phenomenon occurs in areas where Judaism has not historically been known to be present and at a time when anti-Zionism and anti-Semitism are on the upsurge in Europe and elsewhere. In West, East, Central, and Southern Africa, several ethnic groups have chosen to embrace Judaism and proclaim that they are returning to long-forgotten Jewish roots. Many clans trace their lineage back to ancient Israel or speak in the trope of the "Lost Tribes of Israel", affirming that they were among the outposts of Israel in Africa. Many of these communities and individuals want to understand their diasporic history, and the majority are seeking to further their religious education and connection with global Jewry. This phenomenon is developing somewhat in tandem with a growing number of African American Jews and Jewish communities in the United States since the mid-twentieth-century.

We see a similar situation in Asia. There are historic Jewish communities in India. At the same time, some additional ethnic groups in India are newly adopting or sometimes rediscovering a Judaic religious identity and have emerged, for a variety of reasons, as members of the Jewish/Israelite global people. This growth in new expressions of Jewish identity and new geographical areas of Jewish influence marks a significant transition in the history of the Jewish people. These communities' entry or re-entry into the world as Jews implies the necessity of reshaping the standard accounts of collective Jewish experience, both in the contemporary period and historically.

Until recently, this history of Judaism in Africa and Asia has been underestimated. The overall phenomenon, which constitutes an unprecedented turning point in the history of Jewish collectivity, was considered almost nonexistent by scholars and most community religious leaders of the Global North. The first intention of this book is to examine this phenomenon in both global and local contexts and to challenge the way standard accounts of African—and in some related ways, Asian—Judaism must be reshaped. Our second intention is that the different trajectories to and affiliations with Judaism be perceived from as many angles as possible.

Through the various chapters, drawn from a wide variety of disciplinary backgrounds, we examine the multiple sources, reasons, and meanings for this shaping or reshaping of modern Jewish identities in a world marked by political upheaval, economic uncertainty, ecological crises, and ethnic and religious conflicts.

This book is made all the more crucial by its commitment to contemporary history and recent events such as group conversion of communities in Africa and mass emigration to Israel of some groups in India. The work here allows for a greater historical understanding of a new reality and a more informed dialogue between scholars of religious boundaries. Scholars' contributions cross borders and break free of constraints prioritizing the Global North and the perspectives of elites from among the centers of the historic Atlantic slave trade and European Christian missionizing. As a book on identity, history, and religion written from diverse disciplinary backgrounds, it reflects the profound changes and endogenous and exogenous controversies aroused by the new reality of affiliation to Judaism. Such a study is undeniably of a political nature.

The net impact of this collective project is to bring cohesion to a disparate and dispersed field of study and to bring together scholars and members of the communities in question working in the fields of Jewish studies and African and Asian studies—disciplines that until now have had very little in common. To grapple with the complexity in this phenomenon and developing field of study, the essays in this book employ a wide variety of methodological approaches from anthropology, phenomenology, history, archaeology, linguistics, political philosophy, genetics, and religious and cultural studies. They offer a network of theoretical suggestions about the religious and cultural aspects of African and Indian Jewish development, in both continents as well as in the African diaspora.

A variety of audiences will likely find the contents herein helpful: members of the various communities discussed, as well as scholars and students interested in the study of the History of Religion, African History, Political Theory, Post-Colonial Studies, Ethnology, Modern Jewish Studies, and Cultural Studies.

Part One: Myths and Misinterpretations

We begin this volume with an exploration of the circulation of myths and scientific or pseudo-scientific misrepresentations that gave birth to polymorphic racial stereotypes, sporadically contradicting or supplementing one another. This first section offers a brief overview of the developments of racial myths and misrepresentations that have permeated the history of the relations between Blackness and Jewishness, their circulation in the history of ideas, and the way people in Africa and India have dealt with them as they have been embracing Judaism.

Opening this section, readers will find an article by Edith Bruder, "Black Philo-Semitism versus Racial Myths", that examines the interrelations between Black people and Judaism and how they have been inextricably entangled with biblical myths. In this essay, Bruder offers a critical overview of the developments of the myths that have permeated the history of the relations between Blackness and Jewishness, and the way people of African descent have dealt with them to embrace Judaism regardless of any racial consideration. She explores interpretations of these biblical myths that are as diverse as they are paradoxical and wonders about how the negative dimension of these racial myths connected to slavery and White supremacy could have been overcome by Black Philo-Semites.

Sar Ahmadiel Ben Yehuda's "Make Way for the New Normative: A New Paradigm for Approaching African Judaism" takes a critical look at this field. Ben Yehuda notes that the social sciences were deeply influenced by social Darwinism with the presumption that the ancient Israelites were white. Essentially unchallenged for more than a century, this skewed worldview has been virtually enshrined in Western social thought by anthropologists and ethnographers engaged in the investigation of African Hebrew Israelites/Jews/Judeans and their intersections, interactions, and influences. Neither the exigencies of "political correctness" nor compelling DNA studies have resulted in a change of course. While the fundamentally Eurocentric definition of "normative" Judaism continues to predominate, Ben Yehuda offers a wide range of evidentiary information that challenges the existing paradigm and addresses the question: "What will it take to overcome this flawed approach?"

Professor Emerita Carol Conaway brings the testimony of her personal experience related to Ben Yehuda's essay. Conaway's paper chronicles her journey as an African American to Judaism from the 1960s to the late 1990s. As an African American Jew by choice, she was surprised that, after her conversion, being accepted as a Jew by white Jews was difficult and painful. Her treatment by white Jews in the US contradicted her long-held, idealistic image of Jews—the one that she had developed during the 1960s when white Jews participated in such large numbers in the Black Civil Rights Movement. In this article, Conaway discusses her conversion to Judaism and her acceptation by the larger Jewish community, considering these both in light of the relationships between urban Blacks and white Jews in the US in that fraught historical moment.

We close this section with Barbara C. Johnson's "Misrepresentation of Jewish Social Organization in Kerala, India through Models of Race, Caste, and Slavery." Johnson looks back on the ancient and changing community of the Indian Jews of Cochin. She frames for readers the politics of scholarship, how easy it can be for "outsiders" to impose presumptions on subjects, and the latter's implications. In this work, Johnson argues that outdated and inaccurate paradigms of race, caste, and slavery continue to distort the historical understanding of "Cochin" Jewish social organization in Kerala (southwestern India) and Israel. She criticizes research and analysis by many twentieth-century Western scholars—including her own early work—for over-emphasizing and exoticizing past social divisions among these Indian Jews. In this work, Johnson points out that the former categories of "Black", "white", and "freed slave" Jews ceased to have practical social significance more than half a century ago—noting that outsider emphasis on these labels has had a negative impact on the Kerala Jews themselves.

Part Two: Islands and Insularity

In Part Two, three case studies contribute to the growing body of scholarship on divergent perceptions of Jewishness among emerging communities from the islands of Madagascar and Cabo Verde. Taken together, these contributions propose new conceptualizations of Jewish identity in Africa.

Sub-Saharan Africa today is still undergoing a long process of throwing off the yoke of colonialism; yet, in "Anti-Colonialism and Jewish Women in Madagascar" Marla Brettschneider notes that many male leaders of communities on the ground have not spoken in this way and have been rather offended at this Global Northern, academic analysis. In her experience, the male leaders with whom she has worked have also shied away from discussing the history of European Christian missionizing in their regions in political terms. At the same time, almost no Global Northern academics have worked with groups of women in communities on the ground. Brettschneider discusses the origins of Malagasy Jewish life as understood by groups of women in the capital city Antananarivo and connects these women's experiences to concrete statistics of life in the country in terms of politics, economics, and gendered power dynamics. These women's continued assertion that Christian missionizing was a tool of European colonialism makes sense in this gendered, political, and economic rendering. Brettschneider grounds this radical analysis in a discussion of Michel Foucault's conceptualization that in the modern Christian West the soul is in fact the prison of the body, and not—as commonly discussed—the reverse.

Nathan Devir's essay uses a mixed-methods approach (discourse analysis, socio-historical research, ethnographic fieldwork, and communicative interaction studies) to highlight several major trends in the prevalent belief that Madagascar's indigenous inhabitants stem from an Israelite pedigree. Through an exploration of these trends as they appear in association or community-based manifestos or creeds, supposed oral histories, and popular journalistic and social media outlets, this study shows how the Israelite model has taken center stage in the identity paradigms of select individuals, communities, and religious associations in Madagascar. The particular groups Brettschneider discusses have publicly proclaimed and advocated such an Israelite identity, and Devir's contribution compliments Brettschneider's work.

Next in this section, we present the work of Alma Gottlieb on the example of Cabo Verde. In "Recapturing Jewish Roots in Cabo Verde: Changing Diasporic Identities," Alma Gottlieb asks: What happens when a long-ago, suppressed history of Jewish practice is newly remembered? To answer this question, Gottlieb's chapter explores the Sephardic Jewish history of the nine West African islands of Cabo Verde from the perspective of contemporary Cabo Verdeans (both on and off the islands) who are now exploring—and sometimes embracing—the Jewish identity of their nation and, in many cases, their own families.

The final chapter in this section, "Concentric Circles of Jewish/Israelite Identity in sub-Saharan Africa" by William F. S. Miles, proposes a conceptualization of Jewish identity in Africa in terms of three concentric circles: an outer ring ("vague Israelitism"), a middle ring of pseudopraxy ("Hebraic eclecticism"), and finally a normative core (characterized by "orthopraxis"). Miles applies this model to Jewish and Hebraic/Israelite-identifying communities in Nigeria and Madagascar, with some reference to Cameroon. The budding phenomenon of sub-Saharan Judaism poses challenges to First World notions of Jewish identity. Future engagement between those in what Miles calls a normative core with Jewish Africans will likely induce increasing numbers of Western Jews to re-examine what "being Jewish" means to them.

Part Three: New Directions in Lemba Studies

In Section Three, we offer new research on the Lemba tribe in Southern Africa. The Lemba have a significant place in the growing Jewish phenomenon in sub-Saharan Africa. They are an ancient tribe in the region, with rich histories and traditions. In the contemporary period, these traditions continue to be in transition, and scholars continue to examine the range of histories.

Magdel Le Roux advances her pivotal research on the Lemba with her work here: "Lemba and Other Perspectives on Great Zimbabwe and Mapungubwe." The Lemba (in Southern Africa) came by boat to Africa as traders, from a place called Sena on the other side of the Phusela, and they are "children of Abraham." Many reports and traditions confirm that they were known as builders, miners, and smelters of gold, iron, copper, and other minerals. Scant archaeological or other remains of their involvement in Great Zimbabwe, Mapungubwe, and other parts of Southern Africa are available. Le Roux investigates various accounts and sources that bear witness to Lemba activities on the East Coast of Africa and the interior, while Lemba oral traditions also add valuable information to their involvement and journeys into Africa.

In his work, "Naming Practices among Vhalemba/Basena of South Africa," Tom Sengani addresses controversies that continue to rage among scholars on the origin of Vhalemba or Basena found in South Africa, Zimbabwe, and other parts of Africa. Whereas some scholars associate these groups with Jews, there are others who allege that they are of Arab origin, with some African scholars linking them with Africa. Members of the Lemba claim that they are of Jewish origin. In this contribution (as a Lemba), Sengani uses critical discourse analysis, as well as Colonial and Post-Colonial discourse theories, to look into factors that have been part of the practice of Lemba members keeping their Jewish-Arabic clan names. Additionally, he analyzes how Lemba people also adopted other names from other cultures and languages. This analysis demonstrates that these languages show traces of tribal travel from Judea, Yemen, and East as well as Southern Africa.

Finally, in this section, we hear from a leader in a Lemba cultural youth organization. Oded Hams Maramwidze is a member of the Dumah House of the Lemba people. In this chapter, he shares his concerns for current trends in Lemba practice, focusing on dietary traditions, Sabbath observance, and the ways in which many Lemba today combine multiple religious traditions. Maramwidze seeks increased interaction between his Lemba community and global Jewish communities as well as transitions in tribe leadership structures to include expertise as a criterion in addition to the more long-standing reliance on seniority.

Section Four: Politics and Resistance

While the contributions to this volume and the Jewish phenomenon in sub-Saharan Africa itself are political, struggling with power dimensions historically and today, in this section we specifically look at additional examples of politics and resistance.

We open this section with Yvonne Crenshaw's "The Politics of Relocation of Ethiopian Jews". Crenshaw notes that people have argued for over a hundred years about the details of the long history of Jews in ancient and twentieth-century Ethiopia, including their origins and the historical events concerning their interactions with foreign travelers. The Ethiopian Jews (Beta Israel) languished in poverty and remained the victims of genocidal government policies in their ancient homeland while European Jews argued over their right to be accepted as Jews. This chapter explores the question: Why did it take until the mid-1980s for the Jewish world to launch a serious mission to relocate Ethiopian Jews to Israel? Racism and politics led the Ethiopian government, the Israeli government, and the world community to postpone helping them. Concerned Jewish laypeople, rabbis, and Jewish humanitarian agencies worked to highlight this urgent situation, but help did not arrive until global politics shifted. Racism may have played a part in this, but, Crenshaw argues, the primary reason for the delay was political. Already struggling to absorb a vast number of non-observant Soviet immigrants, Israel ascribed no urgency to the needs of this Third World population seeking its shores until an outcry erupted from the West and it became politically advantageous for numerous global parties to arrange the Ethiopian Aliyah.

We bring in here the work of Cornet Alexandre Zouko of the Beit Israel community in Côte d'Ivoire. In "Judaism is Home to Africans," Zouko examines the relationships between the histories of oppression and resistance in both the African and Jewish contexts. He explores primary examples from the long histories of both contexts, noting similarities and divergences. In sum, Zuoko argues that despite some difficult differences, the centrality of both oppression and resistance makes Judaism recognizable for many in sub-Saharan Africa. These political vectors promote a draw to Jewishness for many across the continent in the contemporary period.

In "The Tradition of Israelite Descent among the Pashtuns in India and its Contemporary Ramifications", Navras J. Aafreedi explores the rapidly eroding tradition of Israelite descent of some tribes of Pashtuns/Pathans.

The Pashtuns/Pathans are a large network of tribes, comprised of approximately 41 million people. Aafreedi describes these tribes generally as a warlike people in northeast Afghanistan and northwest Pakistan with a diaspora in India. Many Pashtuns are unaware of or uninterested in the notion of an Israelite origin for their people; however, there has been much interest in Israel in them. In this work, Aafreedi examines the complexities of the Jewish (particularly Israeli) political and also scholarly interest in this tradition. He then clarifies the current trends in the Pashtun/Pathan response to this Jewish, Israeli, and scholarly attention.

This collection of essays contributes new methodological and theoretical paradigms for the study of the Jewish and Jewish-related phenomena in sub-Saharan Africa and Asia and demonstrates that Judaism is going through profound changes. Serious attention is needed to what these developments have to offer to the study of the history of religions, historical and contemporary Christianity, Islam, Jewishness, and the myriad local and ancient cultural and religious traditions of these regions. Certainly, this field also contributes to controversial questions regarding "who is a Jew", global Jewish identities, and a range of potentially productive issues in Jewish diversity studies. The blossoming of African and Indian Judaism challenges and redefines conventional Western understandings of what constitutes Jewish identity and ethnicity in a globalized world. A new analytical light is cast by these new trajectories on the evolving reality of contemporary Judaism and may force Western Jews to re-examine what "being Jewish" means to them.

The role of Israel in this arena is crucial in the management of both policy and identity development. In March 2018, the publication of a report appointed by Israel's Diaspora Affairs Ministry considering Israel's policies towards the various kinds of people wishing to affiliate themselves with the Jewish collective in recent years pointed out the important consequences for Israeli domestic and international politics represented by these communities. The recommendations put forward in the report suggested educating members of these communities in Judaism, Hebrew, and Jewish culture as well as providing them with information about Israel, though they did not include any further recommendations specifically encouraging their conversion or immigration to Israel.[1] It is clear that African, African American, and Indian Jews may no longer remain merely the objects of Western recognition but must assume the role of active stakeholders of what it means to claim to be a Jew, anywhere, in the twenty-first century.

Notes

[1] Noa Landau and Chaim Levinson, "Israel Ministry Sets Sights on Millions of 'Potential Jews' to Improve Country's Image and Fight BDS", *Haaretz*, March 27, 2018
https://www.haaretz.com/israel-news/MAGAZINE-israeli-ministry-sets-sights-on-millions-of-potential-jews-1.5954692

CONTRIBUTORS

Dr. Navras J. Aafreedi is an Indo-Judaic Studies scholar employed as Assistant Professor of History at Presidency University, Kolkata, India, where he teaches several self-designed courses, including the only undergraduate course in Jewish history taught in Asia outside of China and Israel. He is the author of a number of publications, which include *Jews, Judaizing Movements and the Traditions of Israelite Descent in South Asia* (New Delhi, 2016). He has published extensively advocating the introduction of Jewish Studies in India. He has made significant contributions to Jewish Studies in Urdu, the lingua franca of almost all South Asian Muslims, though he writes primarily in English. Aafreedi has been a Visiting Fellow at Tel Aviv University, Woolf Institute, (Cambridge, UK) and the University of Sydney and has spoken at scholarly forums in Africa, Asia, Australia, Europe, and North America. During his two-year tenure (2008–2010) as a Fellow of the Centre for Communication & Development Studies, and under its youth outreach programme, Open Space, he organized fifty-six events in his hometown Lucknow with the aim of bringing about a positive change in Muslim attitudes towards Jews. Aafreedi sits on the editorial boards of the peer-reviewed journals *The Journal of Indo-Judaic Studies* and *The Social Ion*, on the international advisory board of *Asian Jewish Life*, and is referee to several peer-reviewed journals.

Ahmadiel Ben Yehuda is the Minister of Information and National Spokesman of the African Hebrew Israelites of Jerusalem, which numbers nearly three thousand men, women, and children and is based in Dimona, Israel, with satellite communities of thousands across the US, the Caribbean, and Africa. Ben Yehuda did his undergraduate work at Virginia Wesleyan University and American University. He interned and later worked as a legislative assistant on Capitol Hill on both sides of the partisan aisle before answering to his spiritual calling and relocating to Israel in 1978. He received advanced degrees in History and Diplomacy at the School of the Prophets Institute at Jerusalem. In 1993, Ben Yehuda established the African/Edenic Heritage Museum, a traveling photographic and research exhibition with the theme "Exploring the African Presence in the Promised Land". Identical exhibitions operate in the US, Ghana, South

Africa, the UK, and Israel. Widely traveled, he conducts "Sacred Visitation" tours of Israel, with an emphasis on the African presence, and has presented at universities and conferences across the US, the UK, Europe, the Caribbean, and Africa, including a series of seminars documenting the migration patterns and cultural parallels to the ancient Israelites found among various West African ethnic groups, in association with Ghana's National Commission for Culture. He currently serves as advisor to the South African jurisdictions of the African Hebrew Israelites and is also a member of the International Society for the Study of African Judaism (ISSAJ).

Marla Brettschneider is Professor of Political Philosophy with a joint appointment in Political Science and Women's Studies at the University of New Hampshire. She has taught, lectured, and published widely on issues of Jewish diversity politics. The article for this volume emerged from research conducted after Brettschneider published her 2015 *The Jewish Phenomenon in Sub-Saharan Africa: The Politics of Conflicting Discourses*. She has published numerous award-winning books and is currently working on her tenth book and fifth special issue of select academic journals.

Edith Bruder, PhD is a French ethnologist who has an academic multi-disciplinary background in the History of Art and Clinical Psychology. The focus of her research is on the documentation and analysis of the history and the contemporary phenomena of Jewish practices across sub-Saharan Africa, Judaising movements, contemporary diasporas, and particular Jewish identities. Her book, *The Black Jews of Africa: History, Identity, Religion* (Oxford University Press, 2008 and 2012), offers an overview of both past and present Jewish activities across Africa. She founded in 2010 an international scholarly organization—of which she serves as President—the International Society for the Study of African Jewry (http://issaj.com). Her own scholarship and the collective project she is sponsoring through the ISSAJ aim to promote understanding of the global context of Jewish history and practice, and to help bringing together scholars and others working in the fields of Jewish Studies and African Studies—two disciplines that, until now, have had very little in common. Bruder is a research associate at the French National Center for Scientific Research (CNRS) and a research fellow at Unisa—the University of South Africa. She is the author of *Black Jews, Les Juifs noirs d'Afrique et le mythe des Tribus perdues* (Albin Michel 2014), co-editor of *African Zion, Studies in*

Black Judaism (Cambridge Scholars Publishing 2012) with Tudor Parfitt, and has written many articles and chapters in books.

Carol Conaway, PhD is an Associate Professor Emerita of Women's Studies in the Women's Studies Program at the University of New Hampshire (Durham, NH). Her interests are media studies as they pertain to gender, race, class, and sexual orientation; African American women feminists of the nineteenth century; African and African American Jewry; and Jewish feminism. She currently is writing a personal memoir of her life as a Jew by choice who is also an African American woman. Her degrees are from the Massachusetts Institute of Technology and Bryn Mawr College. She is co-editor of *Black Women Intellectual Traditions: Speaking their Minds* (2007).

Cornet Alexandre Zouko is an Ivorian Jew (Ivory Coast) with a master's degree in English from the Civilizations, Languages and Literature Department of Abidjan University. Since 2000, he has played a pivotal role in the development and advancement of local Jewish life in the Ivory Coast by establishing and supporting Jewish communities including Beta Israel and the Danite Consistory of Ivory Coast.

Yvonne M. Crenshaw, diverse in life experiences, spent twenty-five years working and communicating with diverse populations. She was one of the first female patrol officers in the Flint Police Division, graduating top of her rookie class, and was one of the first to pass the Sergeants exam. Over a twenty-year period, she wrote grants, secured government funding, designed programs, supervised and trained staff, and oversaw business operations of social service programs. While at Frank Lynn & Associates, an international industrial consulting firm, she spent four years interviewing, researching, collecting and assessing data. While there, she recruited Fortune 500 companies for project management seminars and assisted with presentations. She did artist promotion, sales, and fan management for Art Porter, jazz artist, until his untimely death. Crenshaw's writing positions include: Staff Writer for East Village Magazine Flint, MI; Columnist for MOBETTER News Chicago, IL; and Editor of Northeastern Illinois University student magazine, MWANAFUNZI Newsletter Chicago, IL. Crenshaw has been a guest speaker on African and African American History and Religion for student groups at the University of Illinois, Malcolm X College, Northeastern Illinois University (NEIU) and the University of Michigan. She has received numerous volunteer and community awards, in addition to membership in the NEIU Academic

Honor Society, University Scholars Award NEIU, Presidential Scholars NEIU, Alpha Kappa Alpha Sorority Inc., Association for the Study of Classical African Civilization, and African Studies Association. Crenshaw attended the University of Illinois, Champaign-Urbana; Mott College, Flint, MI; Restoration Bible Institute, Detroit, MI; Midwest Police Training Academy, Flint, MI; Northeastern Illinois University, Chicago, IL; and is currently pursuing graduate degrees in African History at Wayne State University.

Nathan P. Devir is Assistant Professor of Jewish Studies, Religious Studies, and Comparative Literary and Cultural Studies at the University of Utah, where he also serves as Director of the Middle East Center and Religious Studies Program. His published work includes a monograph, *New Children of Israel: Emerging Jewish Communities in an Era of Globalization* (University of Utah Press, 2017), as well as essays on Jewish Studies in *Biblical Reception*, *Jewish Culture and History*, *Journal of Feminist Studies in Religion*, *Journal of Modern Jewish Studies*, *Nashim*, *Religion and the Arts*, *Studies in American Jewish Literature*, and *Journal of the Middle East and Africa*. He has received numerous honors for his research on worldwide Judaizing movements, including awards from the Association for the Study of the Middle East and Africa, the Center for Advanced Holocaust Studies, the Council of American Overseas Research Centers, the Earhart Foundation, the Lucius N. Littauer Foundation, the National Endowment for the Humanities, the Posen Foundation, the Reed Foundation, and the Tauber Institute for the Study of European Jewry.

Alma Gottlieb is a cultural anthropologist who has (co-)authored or (co-) edited nine books (three, award-winning) about religion, diaspora, gender issues, anthropology, and Africa; her work has been translated into French, Portuguese, and German. Her book-in-progress developing from her current research is tentatively titled *Across the Seder Table: Jewish Identity in the Cape Verdean Diaspora*. Committed to listening to the multiple stories that define the human condition, Gottlieb is past president of the Society for Humanistic Anthropology. In support of her research and writing, Gottlieb has received grants from the Guggenheim Foundation, Social Science Research Council, National Endowment for the Humanities, Wenner-Gren Foundation, and other agencies. Gottlieb has held teaching and research appointments at Princeton University, École des Hautes Études (Paris), Catholic University of Leuven (Belgium), Instituto Superior de Ciências Sociais e Políticas/Universidade Técnica de Lisboa (Lisbon), National University of Ivory Coast, and elsewhere. She is currently Professor Emerita at the University of Illinois at Urbana-Champaign (US) and a Visiting Scholar in Anthropology at Brown University (US).

Barbara C. Johnson is a Professor Emerita from Ithaca College, where she was founder and coordinator of the Jewish Studies Program. She lived four years in South India during the 1960s, after graduating from Oberlin College, and then began her long-term research on the Jews of Kerala during the next decade, completing her anthropology degree at the University of Massachusetts. In addition to many published articles on the Kerala Jewish communities of India and Israel, she is co-author with Ruby Daniel of the memoir *Ruby of Cochin: An Indian Jewish Woman Remembers* (Jewish Publication Society, 1995). Her book on the Malayalam-language songs preserved and performed by Kerala Jewish women, with translations, transcriptions, and commentary on seventy-nine of these songs, is forthcoming from the Jewish Music Research Centre, Hebrew University, Jerusalem. She edited the 2004 CD *Oh, Lovely Parrot: Jewish Women's Songs from Kerala*, also published by the Jewish Music Research Center.

Magdel Le Roux is Professor in the Department of Biblical and Ancient Studies at the University of South Africa. She specializes in the Old Testament and specifically on the "tribes of Israel". Le Roux has published widely on the Lemba of Southern Africa and her recent publications include *The Lemba: A Lost Tribe of Israel in Southern Africa? The case of the Lemba* (Second edition with correction, Pretoria: University of South Africa Press, 2015); "Sing, eat, pray: Transmission of tradition in Lemba communities in Southern Africa," in a special issue of *Africa and Black diaspora: An international journal* entitled *Tastes and tunes of Black Israeli(te)s*, edited by F. Markowitz (Chicago: Routledge, Taylor & Francis Group, November 2017). https://orchid.org/0000-0002-0770-7303

Thomas Maitakhole Sengani was born in Lady Selborne, Pretoria and completed his primary and secondary school education in Venda and Pretoria. He obtained his BA and his teachers' diploma at the University of the North, his Honors degree and Masters' degree (cum laude) at Unisa in 1988, and his PhD at the University of Limpopo in 2008. He is an Associate Professor in the Department of African languages at the Unisa. His research interests are in Oral Literature, Contextual Grammar, Critical Discourse Analysis, Critical Language Awareness and Eco-Linguistics. He has presented papers both nationally and internationally and has published articles in numerous accredited journals.

Oded Hams Maramwidze is a member of the Dumah House of the Lemba people with a vision towards the revival of the Lemba tribe. Maramwidze is an enthusiast of Jewish religious scholarship, having been inspired by Rashi the exegete, Maimonides the philosopher, and Josephus the historian. He also has a command of both Classical and Modern Hebrew, which he learned at the Unisa Old Testament Department and at the Yeshiva College of Johannesburg.

William F. S. Miles is a Professor of Political Science at Northeastern University in Boston, US, where he teaches on religion and politics and on Third World development. From 1998–2002 he was also the Stotsky Professor of Jewish Historical and Cultural Studies at Northeastern. Professor Miles is the author of *Afro-Jewish Encounters from Timbuktu to the Indian Ocean* and two American National Jewish Book Award finalists: *Zion in the Desert* and *Jews of Nigeria: An Afro-Judaic Odyssey.* Along with Daniel Lis and Tudor Parfitt, Miles is co-editor of *In the Shadow of Moses: New Jewish Movements in Africa and the Diaspora*. In addition to publishing on the Jewish experience in the French Antilles, William Miles convened the first international symposium on Third World Views of the Holocaust. He is the recipient of four Fulbright research awards and is past winner of the National Bible Contest, from which he went on to represent North America in the International Bible Contest in Israel.

PART ONE:

MYTHS AND MISREPRESENTATIONS

CHAPTER ONE

BLACK PHILO-SEMITISM VERSUS RACIAL MYTHS

EDITH BRUDER

As I have demonstrated elsewhere, since the colonial era many African Christians have expressed a general feeling of sympathy towards the Jewish people as well as the idea of having a spiritual relationship with them.[1] Some have taken this idea of a relationship with the Jews a stage further than a spiritual brotherhood, and in the course of the twentieth century more than a dozen disparate ethno-religious groups throughout Africa have begun to identify themselves as descendants of the Jewish people and to claim Hebrew or Israelite ancestry.[2] The evidence for a Black philo-Semitism widely predates this recent upsurge of Judaism in Africa. As early as the nineteenth century, in the United States African American individuals and groups incorporated resources from the Old Testament for the construction of their own religious identities. In African American religious discourse, the rhetoric of deliverance of the Children of Israel, the Exodus, and the concepts of chosenness and diaspora were powerfully invested as their own historical destiny and helped forge their self-renewal. The identification with the Jews of the Old Testament was particularly significant to African Americans who were fighting against racial injustice and for the civil rights of their people.[3] The first organized communities of African American Jews with structured ideologies appeared between the 1920s and 1930s, when several African American synagogues were built in the cities of New York, Washington, Philadelphia, and Chicago, paving the way for a wider surge of an African American Judaism that has been developing and growing ever since. African American Jews now occupy a cultural religious space in both communities, and they challenge the imposed categories of "Black" and "Jewish" that can alternatively refer to ethnic, racial, religious, and sometimes politics issues.

This message of the Old Testament presented similar revelation and significance in Africa in the context of the struggle for physical and spiritual liberation from colonial alienation. From the 1980s, throughout Africa, various communities identified themselves as the authentic descendants of the Lost Tribes of Israel and assert that, prior to the arrival of colonial missionaries, they had already practiced a form of Judaism. One can say that in the African psyche the idealization of the Jewish people associated with great antiquity, learning, and a determination to preserve a religious and cultural cohesion is combined with the belief that Africans are themselves the ethnic heirs of biblical Israel. The development of philo-semitic trends in Africa appear to be the outcome of a long historical and anthropological process and is considered part of the colonial or post-colonial situation.[4] With the production of the translations in local languages, the Old Testament began to play a key role in the cultural, social, and political life of African Christians who identified with it. African Christians recognized within it their cultural traditions and they used it as an affirmation of their own religious heritage. John S. Mbiti, the prominent African theologian, writes: "[We] opened the scriptures in our own languages and saw the Jewish people in the Bible as a mirror in which we viewed ourselves… We could find anthropological refuge and protection within the pages of the Bible, and nowhere else".[5]

Religions and the religious are deeply involved in globalization, which itself redraws boundaries of various kinds—political, economic, religious, and ethnic.[6] It is conjectured that the current recombination of cultural and religious experience is connected with growing worldwide interconnectedness and coincides with the deregulation of the cultures of the regional blocks in post-colonial Africa. Lehmann notes: "Modernity and globalization are changing the definition of religion itself, at least the definition which has been assumed in Western Europe, of a heritage, a culture imbued in childhood".[7]

Currently, Africans and African Americans who embraced Judaism identify themselves with contemporary Jews, and most claim that they are members of a larger worldwide Jewish community. In asserting a contemporary Jewish identity, they heralded the phenomenon of African philo-Semitism that follows the typologies of philo-Semitism usually presented by scholars that intertwine religious, cultural, and political strands.[8] As noted by Karp, "The key philosemitic act is not to preserve an image of Jews drawn exclusively from scripture but to reconcile the biblical heritage with the disjunctive reality of modern Jewishness".[9]

It is well known that these theological affinities between Black people and the Jews did not prevent palpable tensions and antagonisms—specifically, harsh polemics on Jewish slave trading, anti-Black racism and Black anti-Semitism that developed from the 1940s.[10] These antagonisms emerged from the social context and were in competition with the spiritual affinities and the idealization of biblical paradigms of Jewish chosenness. The considerations of Black-Jewish relations are already being extensively examined in scholarly and non-scholarly discussions. In this essay I will leave aside the issue of contemporary social and political tensions between the two communities in order to focus on the symbolic system of racial myths and their interactions at work within the philo-Semitic momentum. For Africans or people of African descent, the scriptures favored the rationale of a common theological and historical provenance with Jews. Interrelations between Black people and Judaism are thus inextricably entangled with the biblical myths—whose process of production is as complex as it is shifting while, at the same time, they all exist synchronically in parallel systems.[11] These pages reveal my personal fascination with the circulation of racial myths that gave birth to polymorph stereotypes, sporadically contradicting or supplementing one another in the elaboration of an African Jewish religious identity. What Goldenberg names "etiological myths" and Pepper "roots metaphor" combine notions of skin color and race associated with complex interpretations that lead to the elaboration of stereotypes of the Other.[12] Black philo-Semitism, as it manifests itself today, has somehow overcome the paradoxes of this relationship, making its own path and choices.

In this essay, I will try to offer a brief overview of the developments of racial myths that permeated the history of the relations between Blackness and Jewishness, their circulation in the history of ideas, and the way people of African descent have dealt with them to embrace Judaism. The sets of views, opinions, and beliefs regarding Blackness and Judaism have a mutable development that is constantly shifting within the cultural history of ideas—which makes the theoretical scope of this article expansive. After a brief exploration of the misguided modes of the blackening of Ham, attributed to the scriptures and ancient rabbinic attitudes, I will examine how the Hamitic myth, a racial myth born in post-medieval Europe, became part of an "African genesis" by considering that African "Hamites" were a degenerated branch of the "Caucasian" race related to the Hebrews. In parallel, I will briefly examine how the confusion of ideas linking skin color and Jews, Judaism, or Jewishness ironically reached a peak with the claim of the blackness of the Jews that was incorporated into the theory of racialism by eighteenth- and nineteenth-century "scientists". In this essay, I attempt to analyze the way in which Black philo-Semites operated personal and collective transformations in bypassing or amending the paradoxes that coexisted throughout the mythical history of dark skin and the Jews.

The Curse of Ham: an "Etiological Myth"

How did the biblical text and its interpretations really develop racial myths associated with skin color and the Curse of Ham? And, more specifically, how was the negative dimension of the Curse of Ham connected to slavery incorporated by Black philo-Semites? In fact, the biblical text does not describe anyone as Black—most references to *Kush* (the land) or *Kushim* (the people) are descriptive and contain no judgment.[13] Isaiah describes the people who live "beyond the rivers of Cush" as "tall" (*memushah*) and "shining" (*memorah*), only suggesting that their complexion differed from the majority group.[14] Over time, it is the passage of Genesis (Gen 9:18–25) where Ham found Noah drunk and naked in his tent that has functioned as a building block for racist representations of the Black African in the history of ideas. When Noah awoke, he learned of the disrespect of his son Ham about his nakedness and pronounced a curse not against him but against his son Canaan: "Cursed be Canaan; a slave of slaves he shall be to his brothers" (Gen 9:18–25).

From the beginning, the passage stigmatizing the Curse of Ham is fraught with contradictions. Why is the apparently innocent Canaan cursed, and not his guilty father Ham? There is no reason given as to why Ham's actions should result in the cursing of his son and Noah's grandson Canaan. Kush's brother is punished by eternal slavery for the sin of his father Ham against his grandfather Noah—in fact, there is no reference to skin color in the Old Testament. *Kush* himself is not mentioned, nor is there any reference to Canaan's skin color. Researchers of African origin and theologians of Judaism leaned on such textual problems to assume that the identification of Ham and his sons as dark skinned and destined to slavery was post-biblical. The so-called Curse of Ham appears to be the result of later etymological interpretations and shifts that gave these passages the negative connotation it subsequently took on. There is a general consensus among scholars that this tradition grew out of a socio-political context fraught with linguistic problems. Ephraim Isaac, for example, notes:

> There is little doubt that the story of the curse of Canaan was invented to explain the feeling of the Israelites towards the Canaanites and the reason of their struggles with the people with whom they were perpetually at odds…. Thus, the Canaanites were said to be cursed because their father Canaan violated the divine ordinance of land distribution and usurped the dwelling and inheritance of the Israelites, and later generations elaborated upon this curse.[15]

Goldenberg's and Melamed's examinations of the rabbinic works confirm that the pejorative image of Africans was developed from the biblical text in rabbinic literature. In *The Curse of Ham*, Goldenberg demonstrates that the origin of the relation between blackness, race, and slavery is at least in part based on erroneous etymology and interpretation.[16] Melamed comments: "The identification of Ham and his sons as dark skinned and naturally destined to slavery is post-biblical—the result of later historical and cultural circumstances—and is by no means to be projected anachronistically onto the Bible itself".[17] This idea permeated African American circles. Charles Copher, a Professor of Old Testament in Atlanta and a minister in the United Methodist Church, wrote in 1993: "Racial myths [were] created and employed by the first interpreters of the so-called Old Testament, the ancient Jewish rabbis. They then continue through the use of myths inherited from the rabbis".[18]

What is interesting is that the rabbinic view of the curse of God rests upon a crucial statement: blackness is seen as divine punishment for disobedience. Ham and the *Aethiops*, as descendants of Adam through Noah, could only have a White ancestor, and therefore they became Black through their own doing. Having created an "etiological myth", namely that Black people will descend from non-Black people, rabbinic exegesis attempts to offer an explanation.[19] Another biblical etiological statement is based on the legend of the prohibition of sexual intercourse committed in the ark during the flood—though there is no direct biblical support for it.[20] The prohibition by God, and consequently the sin, are inferred from enigmatic interpretations about the entrance in the ark by pairs, male and female, specially broadcast by Tannaitic traditions from the third century. These traditions transmitted that God prohibited Noah and all the creatures in the ark from having sex and that three creatures transgressed—the dog, the raven, and Ham son of Noah—and were punished. The connection of the punishment to the crime is that the dog and the raven were punished in sexual ways for their sexual sins and that Ham "went forth blackened (*mefuham*)", as mentioned in the *Jerusalem Talmud Ta'anit* 1:6.

David Aaron, an expert in rabbinic literature, explains the choice of the word *mefuham* for "Black'" in this passage from a linguistic and semantic point of view as a "paronomasia".[21] The word Ham—he demonstrates—is not etymologically related to the Hebrew root for "hot" and does not mean "dark" or "Black", the confusion deriving from the fact that "Ham" and "hot" are identical in the Hebrew script. If versions of the dog and the raven's punishment vary from one tradition to another, the punishment of Ham is systematically seen as the darkening of his skin, and one can remark that interpretation of texts led over time to a reinforcement of skin stigmas associating sin with blackness. Moreover, because Ham's sin took place in the dark, he became dark, according to the "measure-for-measure" principle very common in rabbinic literature. The interpretation of Ham's blackness can thus be considered the result of later historical and cultural circumstances—mean-deviations bending paronomasia and the measure-for-measure principle, none of them bent on establishing a racial policy.[22]

If the slow revelation of these textual manipulations could convince some of the innocence of this passage of the text of Genesis, how have Africans' philo-Semite aspirations been able to counter the charge by the negative etiological statements of the earlier Talmudic-midrashic corpus? They have done this by radically reversing the situation, claiming the "Black blood" of the Hebrews and emphasizing some passages of the biblical text. From the nineteenth century, Afrocentrist texts provided a theoretical basis and recurring themes for African American Jews' doctrine during its formative period. The identification with a great Egyptian or Ethiopian civilization provided the paradigm and the impetus for the eclectic strategies that were utilized by African Americans in their search for a Hebrew/Jewish heritage and the creation of new traditions. In 1915 in Philadelphia, for example, the prophet F. S. Cherry, leader of one of the first Black Jewish groups, the Church of the Living God, the Pillar Ground of Truth for All Nations, elaborated a racial theology asserting the primacy of Blacks in Judaism.[23] Cherry assured his followers that, in a vision, God had called him to bring the message that the true descendants of the biblical Hebrews were African Americans. Citing confused interpretations of the Old Testament, Cherry concluded that God and Jesus were Black and that Blacks were the true original Jewish race.[24]

In the 1920s, Wentworth A. Matthew, a Black man from Harlem who would later be known as Rabbi Matthew, described how, according to the Bible, "Jacob was a black man because he had smooth skin".[25] Black Jews considered that American Blacks were in fact African Hebrews torn from their origins and religion by slavery and who had lost the knowledge of their ancestral heritage: "During slavery they took away our name, language, religion and science, as they were the only possessions the slaves had, and they were pumped full of Christianity, to make them more docile".[26] A new definition of themselves as "Hebrews of Ethiopian descent", which pointed to a common origin and reunification, was proposed by Rabbi Matthew. This phenomenon was accelerated by the spread of information by Jacques Faitlovitch about a Black Jewish Diaspora in Ethiopia, the "Falasha", which reinforced the issue of Black Jewish identity.[27] Brotz emphasized that the knowledge of the existence of the Jews of Ethiopia was "the missing link", which for some African Americans symbolically settled the question of their

Jewish identity in response to skepticism about the plausibility of an original Black Judaism.[28]

African American authors from the Caribbean currents such as Marcus Garvey, J. A. Rogers, George G. M. James, and later figures as diverse as Yosef Ben-Jochannen, Ivan Van Sertima, and Louis Farrakhan, put these conventional themes in more polemic and popularly accessible form.[29] In these groups, the assertion of "great cultural heritage", claiming ties to a biblical lineage, led to the assimilation of Judaism as a source of Black identity. Garvey's ideas reflected the various themes of Black and African history expressed earlier and distilled them into a mythologizing but extremely influential synthesis proclaiming that all Africans were Hebrews, and thus that Hebrews were Black.[30]

African Hermeneutics

From the 1970s, as Africa developed its pride and its "Africanness" through the voice of its intellectuals, the correction of the negative image of Africans in the mythical Curse of Ham evolved in concert. The change of vision operated by African hermeneutics started to mobilize Africans on the presence of Africa in the scriptures showing that Africa and Africans occupy a prominent place in the world of the Bible. New interpretations were developed, in part as a way of establishing African historical and geographical links with the biblical world and in part to correct the tendency in Western scholarship that minimized Africa's presence.[31] African theologians focused on the contribution of Africa in the biblical story and argued that ancient Hebrew society was influenced by foreign nations including ancient African cultures.[32] These themes were discussed in conferences that took place in the 1970s and focused on African hermeneutics. At the Jerusalem Congress of Black Africa and the Bible, held in 1972 in Jerusalem, E. Mveng, a theologian from Cameroon, affirmed the lack of foundation of the myth of Ham and that the Africans of the ancient world were thus neither a cursed race nor an inferior form of humanity. In developing the idea that *Kush* represented one of the great powers of antiquity, together with Egypt, Mveng asserted that the Bible is the legacy of Africans who have been creators of civilizations. He writes: "Since Genesis, Africa and black Africans are present in the Bible, the Bible's message is our message and the people of the Bible are our people".[33] The African reading of the Old Testament—which intersects with biblical narratives and prophecies that mentioned the existence of Jews in the land of *Kush* and the account of the Lost Tribes in Africa—continued to shape the thinking of the African common reader and to render the Old

Testament an African heritage. African readers' awareness of the so-called African texts played a fundamental role in strengthening and legitimizing the importance of Africa in the story of Israel, consequently supporting their philo-Semite aspirations.

Africans as "Caucasoids", Jews as Blacks

Gilman's formula "It is a truism that skin-colour has mythic qualities" finds its full expression in the mythology of relations between Blacks and Jews, Judaism, and Jewishness.[34] The best illustration is the Hamitic hypothesis—a racial theory derived from the scriptures that gained academic currency from the beginning of the nineteenth to the mid-twentieth century.[35] This theory argues that anything of value found in Africa was brought there by the White Hamites, inherently superior to the native populations. The so-called Hamites were so politically civilized that they organized the conquered territories into complex states with themselves as the running elites—a high intellectual development necessarily signifying "Caucasian" blood. These "Caucasians" were brought to Africa with their skills in iron-making and were described as pastors, with Blacks allegedly being farmers.

Hamitic hypotheses were widely accepted as authoritative among missionaries, reinforcing a long tradition of identifying African peoples as descendants of Jews, and filled a generalized explanatory function that no contradiction could weaken. Within a total confusion of ideas, the beliefs and practices of African peoples were considered by colonists and missionaries, through various semantic shifts, as deriving from the religion of the Hebrews from antiquity. Joseph Williams's *Hebrewisms of West Africa: From the Nile to the Niger with the Jews* (1930) represents probably the earliest and most famous compilation of comparative studies between African and Jewish traditions.[36] Williams, a Jesuit and member of both the Royal Geographical Society and the American Geographical Society, published this study with the help of eminent scientists, historians, anthropologists, and colonial officers of his day. In this work he established numerous parallels of sub-Saharan tribes' cultural traits with Hebraic influence dating back to antiquity. The customs, religions, and cultures of the Igbo from Nigeria, Ashanti from Ghana, Masaï from Kenya and northern Tanzania, and Peuls from the Senegal and Niger basins, as well as those of the Lemba, Zulu, "Hottentots", and Xhosa from South Africa, and many others were compared to those of the Jews.[37]

How did the Africans themselves react to the notion of Black Hamite? In the African ethnology of the beginning of the twentieth century, such concepts led to the idea that the continent was inhabited by two groups, the

"Caucasoids" and the "Negroids", as well as mixtures of the two. "Caucasoid" and "Negroid" "types" were considered as absolute and universal, represented in the same way in biology, linguistics, and the cultural and political aspects of the Black individual. Deep mental structures were mobilized within African societies with, on the one hand, the nostalgia of one's origins and, on the other, the resonance of the Aryan myth generating the recurrent concept of "white with a black skin". In his work *Ibos: Hebrew Exiles from Israel* (1999), Professor Alaezi, a renowned Igbo historian, wrote: "An estimated number of 400,000 Hebrews arrived in the apparent safe territory of Nigeria in about 686 BCE". He explains the most cogent reason for this settlement during this period: "Nigeria was safer in terms of freedom of religious practice…the Hebrews…more than any other things wanted a safe place for their practice of Judaism, monotheism, worshipping…the god of Abraham, Isaac and Jacob, as the only God".[38] This sentiment is shared by various African Jewish communities such as the House of Israel in Ghana, the Lemba of South Africa and Zimbabwe, the Baluba in Congo, the Abayudaya of Uganda, the Tutsi-Hebrews of Rwanda and Burundi, the recently emerging Jewish communities of Kenya and Madagascar, and many others who affirm that their ancestors came from elsewhere.[39] The combination of these elements favoring the notion of common provenance has propagated, notably in popular assemblies, the theory of Africans as people of Hamitic descent, unquestionably recovering a lost identity by affiliating with Judaism.

The telescoping of racial myths between Blacks and Jews is unlimited if one considers that from the seventeenth century English travelers renewed the accepted stereotypes of racial Otherness, including the belief that Jews were black-skinned.[40] William Brereton noted his impressions of Jews in the synagogue of Amsterdam in 1635 as: the "Jewish men are most Black…and insatiably given unto woman", drawing on contemporary prejudices linking blackness and licentiousness.[41] Around the mid-nineteenth century, Robert Knox shared this analysis and wrote:

> The African character of the Jew, his muzzle-shaped mouth and face, removing him from certain other races…the contour is convex; the eyes long and fine, the outer angles running towards the temples; the brow and nose apt to form a single convex line; the nose comparatively narrow at the base, the eyes consequently approaching each other; lips very full, mouth projecting, chin small, and the whole physiognomy when swarthy, as it often is, has an African look.[42]

The racial proximity of Jews and Africans was supported by the end of the nineteenth century by contradictory theses, such as that of Friedrich

Ratzel and other scientists, going back to the works of Samuel Stanhope Smith (1787), president of the University of Princeton.[43] It came to be adopted as such within twentieth-century anthropology, which declared on occasion that Jews were Black. Nowadays it can be observed that the blurring of racial boundaries has been incorporated by the communities of Black Jews. Rabbi Capers Funnye, the spiritual and intellectual leader of the Agudath Achim-Bikur Cholim synagogue in Chicago, points out: "When we look at the location of the State of Israel and its proximity to Africa, it makes sense to me that those people may not have been fair-skinned".[44]

Concluding Remarks

One can seek through the metaphor of "hybridization" or *bricolage* the religious and cultural process that is at work in Black philo-Semitism, keeping in mind that every analytical scheme is but one among many.[45] Black Jews identify themselves as sharing a common descent with the members of the contemporary Jewish community and manifest a fiery philo-Semitism regardless of any racial consideration. They created original and new responses to the theological impact of biblical texts, illustrating the relationship between innovation and genesis, while proceeding—notably in Africa—to a new structuring of pre-existing religious elements. Dealing with a system of values, norms, and moral codes that provides a sense of identity to its members, Black philo-Semitism can be approached as a phenomenon of culture meaningfully constructed through symbolic resources linked to the religious-historical consciousness of people of Black descent. Black Jews initiated their own religious-sociological process of "Judaization", illustrating the biblical word *hityahadut* that Ben-Gurion asserted was the authentic way of joining the Jewish people when he said, "The Bible only speaks of Judaizers (*mityahadim*)".[46]

African Jews' self-identification with Judaism—both innovative and provocative—claims that they are not encapsulated in racial boundaries and assumes a strong universalist inclination. In its variegated discourses, the identification of people of African origins with biblical Israel assumes symbolical significance while rejecting the negative interpretation of the myth of Ham and ignoring physical characteristics. When identifying as Jews and with other Jews, Jews of African descent deny the existence of distinctive categories in popular concepts of Jews and subvert the racist image of Blacks as a cursed people. In parallel, by its very existence, Black philo-Semitism undermines the image of Jews as a race or as belonging to a single race, rejecting religious purism and conceiving blended worlds. In overcoming the misunderstandings inherent in racial myths and creating their own interpretations, Black Jews maintained an ongoing dynamic process of identification characterized by continual negotiation and contestation about racial stereotypes. In "rediscovering" the true secret of their origin as descendants of Adam through Noah, they challenged the imposed categories of "Black" and "Jewish" and by an arduous process boost paradoxical inversions.[47] The notion of Jewishness implied by Black Judaism is not one of narrow racial-genealogical ethnicity. Black Judaism contributes to the new patterns in which individuals and communities in India, China, and as far as Papua New Guinea decide to join the Jewish people reinforcing the idea of Jewish particularism. These communities and individuals enlarge the diversity of understandings of Jewishness and modes of adopting the Jewish tradition—a change of paradigm that Shalva Weil comments on as follows: "The result of this pattern is a more multicultural view of 'Who is a Jew?' emergent with a reinvention of the essence of the Jewish people."[48]

Works Cited

Aaron, David H. "Early Rabbinic Exegesis on Noah's son of Ham and the So-Called Hamitic Myth." *Journal of the Academy of Religion* 63, no. 4 (Winter 1995): 723.

Adamo, D. T. "Africa and the African in the Old Testament Scheme of Salvation." *Theologia Viatorum* 35, no. 1 (2011): 144.

Alaezi, O. *Ibos: Hebrew Exiles from Israel; Amazing Facts and Revelations*. Aba, Nigeria: Onzy Publications, 1999.

Basso, Rossana. "Myths in contemporary oral transmission: A children's strike." In *The Myths We Live By*, edited by P. R. Thompson, 61. London: Routledge, 1990.

Bennett, Robert. "Africa and the Biblical Period." *Harvard Theological Review* 64, No 1 (1971): 483-500.

Brereton, Sir William. *Travels in Holland, the United Provinces, England, Scotland and Ireland, 1634–1635*, ed. E. Hawkins. London: Chetham Society,1844.

Brotz, Howard M. *The Black Jews of Harlem*. New York, NY: Schocken Books, 1970, 16, excerpt from a conversation with Matthew or another member of the group.

Bruder, Edith. *The Black Jews of Africa: History, Identity, Religion*. New York, NY: Oxford University Press, 2008 and 2012.

Bruder, Edith. "The Proto-History of Igbo Jewish Identity from the Colonial Period to the Biafra War, 1890-1970." In *African Zion: Studies in Black*

Judaism, edited by Edith Bruder and Tudor Parfitt, 31–64. Newcastle upon Tyne: Cambridge Scholars Publishing, 2012.

Bruder, Edith. "Philo-Semitism and Affiliation to Judaism in Africa." *Common Knowledge*, 23:3, (September 2017): 440-467.

Chireau, Yvonne. "Black Culture and Black Zion," in *Black Zion*, edited by Yvonne Chireau and Nathaniel Deutsch. New York, NY: Oxford University Press, 2003. See also Bruder, *Black Jews*, 73–93; Edith Bruder. "Noirs et juifs: Les Black Jews aux Etats Unis." *Diasporas* 9, (2nd semester 2006): 207–21.

Chrétien, Jean-Pierre. "Les deux visages de Cham. Point de vue français du XIXe siècle sur les races africaines d'après l'exemple de l'Afrique Orientale." In *L'idée de race dans la pensée politique française contemporaine*, edited by Pierre Guiral, 171–99. Paris: CNRS, 1977.

Copher, Charles. "Racial Myths and Biblical Scholarship: Some Random notes and Observations." In *Black Biblical Studies*, 121. Chicago, IL, 1993.

Cronon, Edmund. *Black Moses: The Story of Marcus Garvey and the Universal Negro Improvement Association*. Madison, WI: University of Wisconsin Press, 1969. See also Rupert Lewis, *Marcus Garvey: Anti-colonial Champion*. Trenton, NJ: Africa World Press, 1988.

Diner, Hasia R. *In the almost promised land: American Jews and Blacks, 1915-1935*. Westport, CT and London: Greenwood Press, 1977.

Ehrman, Albert. "The Commandment Keepers: A Negro Jewish Cult in America Today." *Judaism* 8, no. 3 (1959): 267.

Fauset, Arthur H. *Black Gods of the Metropolis: Negro Religious Cults of the Urban North*. Philadelphia, PA: University of Pennsylvania Press, 1944.

Fisher, Netanel. "Joining the Jewish State: Israel's Conversion Policies." In *Becoming Jews*, edited by T. Parfitt and N. Fisher, 228. Newcastle upon Tyne: Cambridge Scholars Publishing, 2017.

Goldenberg, David M. *The Curse of Ham: Race and Slavery in Early Judaism, Christianity and Islam*. Princeton, NJ: Princeton University Press, 2005. See also Stephen Pepper quoted in Sander L. Gilman, *Difference and Pathology: Stereotypes of Sexuality, Race, and Madness*. Ithaca, NY and London: Cornell University Press, 1986.

Hervieu-Léger, Danièle. *Le pélerin et le converti*. Paris: Flammarion, 1999.

Holter, Knot. "Old Testament Scholarship in Sub-Saharan Africa North of the Limpopo River." In *The Bible in Africa*, edited by Gerald O. West and Musa W. Dube Shomanah, 57–58.

Howe, Stephen. *Afrocentrism: Mythical Pasts and Imagined Homes*. London: Verso, 1998.

Isaac, Ephraim. "Genesis, Judaism and the Curse of Ham." *Slaves and Slavery in Muslim Africa* 1, (2014): 77–78. Moshe Weinfeld, *The Promise of the Land: The Inheritance of the Land of Canaan by the Israelites*. Berkeley, CA: University of California Press, 1993.

Karp, Jonathan. "Philo-Semitism in African American Culture." In *Philo-Semitism in History*, edited by Jonathan Karp and Adam Sutcliffe, 6. New York, NY: Cambridge University Press, 2011.

Knox, Robert. *Races of Men*. London: H. Renshaw, 1862.

Lehmann, David. "Religion and Globalization." In *Religions in the Modern World: Traditions and Transformations*, edited by Linda Woodhead, Paul Fletcher, Hiroko Kawanami, and David Smith, 346–47. London: Routledge, 2002.

Mbiti, John S. "The Role of the Jewish Bible in African Independent Churches." *International Review of Mission* 93, no. 369 (April 2004): 221.

Melamed, Abraham. *The Image of the Black in Jewish Culture: A History of the Other*, translated by Betty Sigler Rozen, 54. London: Routledge Curzon, 2003.

Mveng, Engelbert. "La Bible et l'Afrique noire." *The Jerusalem Congress on Black Africa and the Bible*, edited by E. Mveng and R. J. Z. Werblowsky, 23–39. Jerusalem: 1972.

Parfitt, Tudor, and N. Fisher, eds. *Becoming Jews*. Newcastle upon Tyne: Cambridge Scholars Publishing, 2017.

Ratzel, Friedrich. *History of Mankind*. London: Macmillan, 1896–1898.

Robertson, Roland. "Globalization and Glocalization." In *Globalization: Critical Concepts in Sociology*, edited by R. Robertson and K. White, 3:31–51. London: Routledge, 2003.

Sala-Mollins, Louis. *Le code noir ou le calvaire de Canaan*. Paris: PUF, 2002.

Sanders, Edith R. "The Hamitic Hypothesis: Its Origin and Functions in Time Perspective." *Journal of African History* 10, no. 4 (1969): 521–32.

Seligman, Charles G. *Races of Africa*. London: Oxford University Press, 1966.

Smith, Samuel S. *An Essay on the Causes of the Variety of Complexion and Figure in the Human Species* Cambridge, MA: Belknap Press, 1965.

Trevisan-Semi, Emanuela. "Universalisme juif et prosélytisme. L'action de Jacques Faitlovitch, le 'père' des Beta Israel (Falashas)." *Revue de l'Histoire des Religions* 216, no. 2 (1999): 193–211.

Weil, Shalva. "The Unification of the Ten Lost Tribes with the Two 'Found' Tribes." In *Becoming Jews*, edited by T. Parfitt and N. Fisher, 26. Newcastle upon Tyne: Cambridge Scholars Publishing, 2017.

Werbner, Pnina, and T. Modood, eds. *Debating Cultural Hybridity*. London: Zed Books, 1997.

Wilson, Bernard J. "African American Jews, Dispelling Myths, Bridging the Divide." In *Black Zion*, edited by Yvonne Chireau and Nathaniel Deutsch, 44. New York, NY: Oxford University Press, 2003.

Notes

[1] Edith Bruder, "Philo-Semitism and Affiliation to Judaism in Africa," *Common Knowledge* 23, no. 3 (September 2017). Some of the material presented in this essay has also been discussed in Edith Bruder, *The Black Jews of Africa: History, Identity, Religion* (New York, NY: Oxford University Press, 2008 and 2012); Edith Bruder, "The Proto-History of Igbo Jewish Identity from the Colonial Period to the Biafra War, 1890-1970," in *African Zion: Studies in Black Judaism*, ed. Edith Bruder and Tudor Parfitt (Newcastle upon Tyne: Cambridge Scholars Publishing, 2012), 31–64.

[2] For an overview on these communities, see Edith Bruder, *The Black Jews of Africa: History, Identity, Religion* (New York, NY: Oxford University Press, 2008 and 2012).

[3] Yvonne Chireau, "Black Culture and Black Zion," in *Black Zion*, eds. Yvonne Chireau and Nathaniel Deutsch (New York, NY: Oxford University Press, 2003). Bruder, *Black Jews*, 73–93; Edith Bruder, "Noirs et juifs: Les Black Jews aux Etats Unis," *Diasporas* 9 (2nd semester 2006), 207–21.

[4] Bruder, "Philo-Semitism", 448–53.

[5] John S. Mbiti, "The Role of the Jewish Bible in African Independent Churches," *International Review of Mission* 93, no. 369 (April 2004): 221.

[6] David Lehmann, "Religion and Globalization," in *Religions in the Modern World: Traditions and Transformations*, eds. Linda Woodhead, Paul Fletcher, Hiroko Kawanami, and David Smith (London: Routledge, 2002): 346–47. See also Roland Robertson, "Globalization and Glocalization," in *Globalization: Critical Concepts in Sociology*, eds. R. Robertson and K. White (London: Routledge, 2003), 3:31–51. Also, P. Beyer, and L. Beaman, *Religion, Globalization, and Culture* (Leiden: Brill, 2007); Jan Nederveen Pieterse, *Globalization and Culture: Global Mélange* (Lanham, MD: Rowman and Littlefield, 2015).

[7] Lehmann, "Religion and Globalization,"426.

[8] Jonathan Karp and Adam Sutcliffe, eds., *Philo-Semitism in History* (New York, NY: Cambridge University Press, 2011), 6.

[9] Karp, "Philo-Semitism in African American Culture," in *Philo-Semitism in History*, 233.

[10] For an overview on the relations between Blacks and Jews see: Hasia R. Diner, *In the almost promised land: American Jews and Blacks,* 1915-1935, (Westport, CT and London: Greenwood Press, 1977); Ethan Goffman, *Imagining each other: Blacks and Jews in contemporary American literature* (Albany, NY: State University of New York Press, 2000); Jonathan Kaufman, *Broken alliance: the turbulent times between Blacks and Jews in America* (New York, NY: C. Scribner's Sons, 1988).

---

[11] Rossana Basso, "Myths in contemporary oral transmission: A children's strike," in *The Myths We Live By*, ed. P. R. Thompson (London: Routledge, 1990), 61.
[12] David M. Goldenberg, *The Curse of Ham: Race and Slavery in Early Judaism, Christianity and Islam* (Princeton, NJ: Princeton University Press, 2005), 101; Stephen Pepper quoted in Sander L. Gilman, *Difference and Pathology: Stereotypes of Sexuality, Race, and Madness* (Ithaca, NY and London: Cornell University Press, 1986), 22.
[13] On the subject in general, see Robert Bennett, "Africa and the Biblical Period," *Harvard Theological Review* 64 (1971), who gives an overview of scriptural references to Africa and the African, with linguistic, historical, and textual questions relevant to determining the place of Africa in the biblical period.
[14] Abraham Melamed, *The Image of the Black in Jewish Culture: A History of the Other*, trans. Betty Sigler Rozen (London: Routledge Curzon, 2003), 54.
[15] Ephraim Isaac, "Genesis, Judaism and the Curse of Ham," in John R. Willis, *Slaves and Slavery in Muslim Africa* 1, (London: Frank Cass, 1985), 77–78; Moshe Weinfeld, *The Promise of the Land: The Inheritance of the Land of Canaan by the Israelites (*Berkeley, CA: University of California Press, 1993).
[16] David M. Goldenberg, *The Curse of Ham: Race and Slavery in Early Judaism, Christianity and Islam* (Princeton, N.J.: Princeton University Press, 2005); Also M. Prior, *The Bible and Colonialism* (Sheffield: Sheffield Academic Press, 1997).
[17] Melamed, *The Image of the Black*, 54–55.
[18] Charles Copher, "Racial Myths and Biblical Scholarship: Some Random notes and Observations," in *Black Biblical Studies* (Chicago, IL, 1993), 121; David Goldenberg, "Review Essay of Abraham Melamed, 'The Image of the Black in Jewish Culture'," *The Jewish Quarterly Review,* XCIII, nos. 3–4 (January-April 2003): 557–58.
[19] Goldenberg, *Curse*, 99–109.
[20] Ibid.
[21] Aaron explains that "paronomasia" can only be appreciated in Hebrew and is commonly used in Aramaic, Greek, and Latin as well. David H. Aaron, "Early Rabbinic Exegesis on Noah's son of Ham and the So-Called Hamitic Myth," *Journal of the Academy of Religion* 63, no. 4 (Winter 1995): 723.
[22] Aaron, "Early Rabbinic Exegesis," 745.
[23] Arthur H. Fauset, *Black Gods of the Metropolis: Negro Religious Cults of the Urban North* (Philadelphia, PA: University of Pennsylvania Press, 1944), 31–40.
[24] Ibid.
[25] Albert Ehrman, "The Commandment Keepers: A Negro Jewish Cult in America Today," *Judaism* 8, no. 3 (1959): 267.
[26] Howard M. Brotz, *The Black Jews of Harlem* (New York, NY: Schocken Books, 1970), 16, excerpt from a conversation with Matthew or another member of the group.
[27] See Emanuela Trevisan-Semi, "Universalisme juif et prosélytisme. L'action de Jacques Faitlovitch, le 'père' des Beta Israel (Falashas)," *Revue de l'Histoire des Religions* 216, no. 2 (1999): 193–211.
[28] Brotz, Black Jews, 49.
[29] Stephen Howe, *Afrocentrism: Mythical Pasts and Imagined Homes* (London:

Verso, 1998), 73–79.
[30] See, e.g., Edmund Cronon, *Black Moses: The Story of Marcus Garvey and the Universal Negro Improvement Association* (Madison, WI: University of Wisconsin Press, 1969); Rupert Lewis, *Marcus Garvey: Anti-colonial Champion* (Trenton, NJ: Africa World Press, 1988).
[31] John Upkong, "Developments in Biblical Interpretation," in eds. Gerald O. West, and Musa W. Dube Shomanah, *The Bible in Africa: Transactions, Trajectories, and Trends* (Leiden: Brill, 2000), 15–16; Knot Holter, "Old Testament Scholarship in Sub-Saharan Africa North of the Limpopo River," in eds. Gerald O. West, and Musa W. Dube Shomanah, *The Bible in Africa*, 57–58.
[32] D. T. Adamo, "Africa and the African in the Old Testament Scheme of Salvation," in *Theologia Viatorum* 35, no. 1 (2011): 144.
[33] Engelbert Mveng, "La Bible et l'Afrique noire," *The Jerusalem Congress on Black Africa and the Bible*, eds. E. Mveng and R. J. Z. Werblowsky (Jerusalem: 1972), 23–39.
[34] Gilman, *Difference and Pathology*, 12.
[35] See Edith R. Sanders, "The Hamitic Hypothesis: Its Origin and Functions in Time Perspective," *Journal of African History* 10, no. 4 (1969): 521–32; Charles G. Seligman, *Races of Africa*, (London: Oxford University Press, 1966), 96. On the theological roots of the Hamitic myth, see Louis Sala-Mollins, *Le code noir ou le calvaire de Canaan* (Paris: PUF, 2002); Rémi Brague, "Le déni d'humanité," *Lignes 12* (1990): 217–32; and, more generally, Jean-Pierre Chrétien, "Les deux visages de Cham. Point de vue français du XIXe siècle sur les races africaines d'après l'exemple de l'Afrique Orientale," in *L'idée de race dans la pensée politique française contemporaine* (Paris: CNRS, 1977), 171–99.
[36] Joseph J. Williams, *Hebrewisms of West Africa* (New York, NY: Biblo and Tannen, 1930), 7–14, 16–43, 51–93.
[37] Bruder *Black Jews*, 51–59.
[38] O. Alaezi, *Ibos: Hebrew Exiles from Israel; Amazing Facts and Revelations* (Aba, Nigeria: Onzy Publications, 1999), 27, 32–36, 113–14, quotation 32.
[39] See Bruder, *Black Jews*.
[40] See, e.g., Edgar Rosenberg, *From Shylock to Svengali: Jewish Stereotypes in English Fiction* (London: Peter Owen, 1961).
[41] Sir William Brereton, *Travels in Holland, the United Provinces, England, Scotland*
and Ireland, 1634 1635, ed. E. Hawkins (1844).
[42] Robert Knox, *Races of Men* (London: H. Renshaw, 1862), 134.
[43] Friedrich Ratzel, *History of Mankind* (London: Macmillan, 1896–1898), 112; Samuel S. Smith, *An Essay on the Causes of the Variety of Complexion and Figure in the Human Species* (Cambridge, MA: Belknap Press, 1965), 42.
[44] Personal communication, Bec'chol Lashon Conference, San Francisco, May 15 2008.
[45] Pnina Werbner, and T. Modood, eds., *Debating Cultural Hybridity* (London: Zed Books, 1997); Danièle Hervieu-Léger, *Le pélerin et le converti* (Paris: Flammarion, 1999).
[46] Netanel Fisher, "Joining the Jewish State: Israel's Conversion Policies," in

Becoming Jews, eds. T. Parfitt and N. Fisher (Newcastle upon Tyne: Cambridge Scholars Publishing, 2017: 228.

[47] Bernard J. Wilson, "African American Jews, Dispelling Myths, Bridging the Divide," in *Black Zion*, eds. Yvonne Chireau and Nathaniel Deutsch (New York, NY: Oxford University Press, 2003), 44.

[48] Shalva Weil, "The Unification of the Ten Lost Tribes with the Two 'Found' Tribes," in *Becoming Jews*, eds. T. Parfitt and N. Fisher, (Newcastle upon Tyne: Cambridge Scholars Publishing, 2017), 26.

CHAPTER TWO

A CRITICAL STUDY FOR THE NEW NORMATIVE: A NEW PARADIGM FOR APPROACHING AFRICAN JUDAISM

SAR AHMADIEL BEN YEHUDA

> I, the savage, reversed the roles; by casting an anthropological gaze upon my own group, I posed a challenge to that belittling glance [of others] by making it my own. Joëlle Bahloul (an Algerian Jew)[1]

> I am invisible, understand, simply because people refuse to see me. Ralph Ellison's *Invisible Man*[2]

> The Black Jews of Africa must contend with invisibility at the socio-religious level, an invisibility which also extends to the academic world. Nduwa Guershon Nduwa[3]

The social sciences were deeply influenced by social Darwinism (a doctrine of White supremacy). A consequence of this was the presumption that the ancient Israelites were White. Essentially unchallenged for more than a century, this skewed worldview has been virtually enshrined in Western social thought. Anthropologists and ethnographers engaged in the investigation of African Hebrew Israelites/Jews/Judeans and their intersections, interactions, and influences, have, by and large, faithfully tracked a Eurocentric course. Neither the exigencies of "political correctness" nor compelling DNA studies have resulted in a change of course. The fundamentally Eurocentric definition of "normative" Judaism rules the day.

Howard Brotz's pivotal 1964 *Black Jews of Harlem* set a standard, however dubious, for scholarship in the arena. In the opening pages of his work on the iconic Black Jewish community, Brotz declared that the African and Jewish worlds were "different and unrelated to each other".[4] As Walter Isaac writes, Brotz's "ideas about the nature of Jewish racial identity played a commanding role in establishing the investigative parameters for studying Black Jewish movements well into the 21st century".[5] Brotz's "investigative parameters" would consign Black Jews, in effect, to invisibility.

Ralph Ellison was scathing in his analysis of the social scientists' gaze upon the African but equally critical of the African's own dependence "upon outsiders—mainly sociologists—to interpret our lives for us. It doesn't seem to occur to us that our interpreters might well be not so much prejudiced as ignorant, insensitive, and arrogant."[6] As racism is difficult to pin down, let's accept Ellison's restrained assessment that ignorance, insensitivity, and arrogance are more likely the problem and grapple here with the first element—ignorance—to provide a new perspective. The obvious place in which to address this "invisibility" is in the academy itself. Not only are African Hebrew Israelites/Jews/Judeans (henceforth designated as "AHI/J") invisible under a Eurocentric gaze, but our voices are also rendered practically mute. They are unwilling, perhaps unable, to see or hear me.

My premise here is simple: When Whiteness is the baseline paradigm for Jews in both the ancient and contemporary settings, the approach to AHI/Js is invariably "How and when did you change/convert?" A surfeit of conjectural apologia arises: cultural diffusion and transmission, adaptation, adoption, conversion, syncretism, missionary influence, psychological association and projection, metaphorical identification, the embracing of outright myth—some form of "Judaization". We are "emerging" and "re-emerging"; our claims are the "unexpected reactions to colonialism",[7] "an erratic way of acquiring a new religion",[8] and even the ploy of economic refugees. (Who in their right mind would consciously embrace such an ontological double jeopardy?) Under such a gaze, we begin and end as anything *but* Jews!

Children of a Lesser God? … Or Lesser Children of the Same God?

"The study of Judaism has long been associated with expertise in scholarly writings," writes Harvey Goldberg.

"Today, anthropologists often begin their analyzes with close attention to the exegesis offered by members of the society with which they are concerned. Phrased differently, anthropology now takes the views that a group of people have of themselves and their traditions seriously."[9] Frankly, that's not been our experience. In rebuffing skeptical interlocutors, Rabson

Wuriga, a Lemba, pleads the 5th (Commandment, not Amendment): "My father told me I am a Jew. To whom am I going to listen? I am going to listen to my father."[10]

Renato Rosaldo's "Lone Ethnographer" epitomizes the old paradigm—the "classic norm"—of anthropological study, in which the observer was "willy-nilly complicit with the imperialist domination of his epoch". Rosaldo warns that "We should not impose our categories on other people's lives because they probably do not apply, at least not without serious revision".[11]

The need for baselines aside, Judaism is a conundrum without peer: Is Jewishness a religious or ethnic identification? As Goldberg posits, "Can one speak of the 'the Jews' in the absence of a centralized authority with the power to determine 'what Judaism is', and when scholars writing about 'Jewish tradition' now recognize that they are dealing with phenomena whose contents and boundaries are fluid?"[12] What, then, *are* those contents and boundaries…and from whence comes the authority to impose such definitions?

A Well-Crafted Narrative?

Narratives present us with a framework in which historical and cultural evidence is assembled, often painstakingly, impartially reviewed and determined to render the hypothesized scenario plausible or implausible; however, predetermined ideas can render the investigator virtually blind to what is before her/him. The erudite Jacob Neusner frames the issue perfectly:

> The logic of connection demonstrated through narrative rather than philosophy is simply stated. It is connection attained and explained by invoking some mode of narrative in which a sequence of events, first this, then that, is understood to yield a proposition, first this, then that *because of this*…. Whether or not the generalization is stated in so many words rarely matters, because the power of well-crafted narrative is to make unnecessary explicit drawing of the moral.[13]

Generalization, according to sociologist Eva Illouz, "is a crucial strategy for thinking and making arguments".[14] Only via an incessant and often painful probing—and the subsequent cleansing of infected tissues (thinking) and organs (practices) in the diseased body (academia)—are we enabled to uncover that most elusive of treasures: Truth.

Neusner employed this strategy of generalization to conclude that the Mishnah was responsible for "starting a new Judaism as a matter of fact",[15] the consequences of which "will require a wide-ranging reconsideration of how we shall describe, analyze, and interpret—and therefore also define what we mean by—"Judaism".[16]

Rabbi Aharon Wexler, quoting Neusner, says in fact that "there is no Judaism per se; what we have are Judaisms, of which 'rabbinic Judaism' is the one that survived".[17] With one qualification—that rabbinic Judaism is not the *only* Judaism to have survived—let me now summarize these scholars' findings: rabbinical Judaism (another creation entirely) emerged to become the default Judaism that now holds sway over all of the older, more obscure—but ostensibly more authentic—Judaisms. These Judaisms were not dead but dormant; rather, because of their African origins, they were rendered invalid…and invisible. We are obliged to seriously consider these new-old pieces of the Judaic puzzle.

Border Scuffles: Egypt and Israel

From whence came the idea that the ancient Israelites were White (a fanciful notion at best)? Count Arthur de Gobineau's *Essay on the Inequality of the Human Races* (1853) asserted that "All civilizations derive from the white race and none can exist without its help".[18] Gobineau, "the master of racial science", enjoyed "an honored place among all writers on anthropology and history".[19] To situate the development of modern Judaic studies outside of the reigning Eurocentric mindset, philosophy, and system would be intellectually dishonest and scurrilously irresponsible.

In fact, the academy often incubated such ideas. Anthropologists organized the sadistic exhibitions of Ota Benga (the Congolese "Pygmy in the Zoo") and Saartjie Baartman (the "Hottentot Venus"). While the prejudices of social scientists of the 1800s are understood in context, the stubborn residual bias cannot be. It is a deeply ingrained bias, as deeply offensive as it is deeply flawed, and it can no longer accompany any serious foray into African Judaism.

The refusal to seriously entertain, let alone accept, another narrative has run its course. Why? Because the existing baseline for the study of African Judaism is rooted in the sordid underpinnings of a White-supremacist politic. Renato Rosaldo speaks of "academic warfare" as a "raging battle" of "competing political and intellectual visions"—strong language to describe the usually pleasant decorum that governs the exchange of ideas. "These are legitimate grounds for conflict," says Rosaldo, "but one wonders at the intensity of debate. What is really at stake?"

> Ancient Egypt is an appropriate reference point for any discussion about the racial/ethnic identity and origin of ancient Israel. Preserving the whiteness of ancient Egypt looms large in Egyptology, and is the source of great consternation. A pathological resistance to define ancient Egypt as a part of what is now called "Black Africa" leaves Egypt situated *outside* of Africa. When the truth was reluctantly acknowledged, it was qualified: "Yes, Egypt is a part of Africa, but they (its ancient inhabitants) weren't Black like that"![20]

In *Black Genesis*, Robert Bauval and Thomas Brophy appealed for the field "to remove their blinders and look at the wider picture".

> There is still much work to do in bringing to the world a new vision of the Black African origins of civilization. Yet if we buttress the theory with solid, current research and exploration, and if we look at the evidence with open minds free of prejudice and bias, progress of this notion of origins is gaining momentum. For many centuries the Black race of the world has either been exploited by its White counterpart or looked upon as inferior. Although many in the Western world have advanced a great deal in curbing such an attitude, the truth is that racial prejudice is still very much rampant.... *Black Genesis* thus becomes not only a scientific thesis but also a testament of respect and admiration of all whose skin happens to be black and who have a direct ancestral line to Black Africa.[21]

A minor broadening of the scope of their work—to include neighboring ancient Israel—will help to reveal its relevance here. Consider this passage, taking note of the four words that I have emboldened and my substitutions:

> This book is a product of a deep and strong desire to use the best of our intellect, knowledge, and abilities to put right an issue that has long beleaguered historians and prehistorians alike: the vexed question of the Black African origins of the ancient **Egyptian [Israelite]** civilization. In spite of many clues that have been in place in the last few decades, which strongly favor a Black African origin for the **pharaohs [the Hebrews]**, many scholars and especially **Egyptologists [biblical historians]** have either ignored them, confused them, or, worst of all, derided or scorned those who entertained them. It is not our business to know whether such an attitude is a form of academic racism or simply the blindered way of looking at evidence to which some modern **Egyptology [Judaica]** has become accustomed, but whatever the cause, this issue has remained largely unresolved.[22]

It will likely continue to remain unresolved because once scholars concede the Blackness of ancient Egypt they will also be required to forfeit the racial identification of ancient Israel. At stake are the foundations of the Western world, the pillar of its mythic "Judeo-Christian tradition" among them.

Inconvenient Truth

Ancient legacies were essentially pilfered, Martin Bernal asserts, and academics are "still working with models set up by men who were crudely positivist and racist", making it "extremely implausible to suppose that the models were not influenced by these ideas". Bernal conveys the "Egyptian problem" as follows:

> If it had been scientifically "proved" that Blacks were biologically incapable of civilization, how could one explain ancient Egypt–which was inconveniently placed on the African continent? There were two, or rather, three solutions. The first was to deny that the Ancient Egyptians were black; the second was to deny that the Ancient Egyptians had created a "true" civilization; the third was to make doubly sure by denying both.[23]

Jerusalem too—the geo-spiritual center of the world—was "inconveniently placed on the African continent". A fourth "solution" also existed: to effectively remove Egypt from Africa altogether, at least mentally, accomplished in two masterstrokes. First, the Suez Canal facilitated much more than Europe's access to the East. It essentially decapitated Africa by rendering the Red Sea as a boundary of the African landmass, despite the fact that the African tectonic plate encompasses all of modern Israel/Palestine and beyond. Second, the imaginative term "Middle East" was applied to the region. The phrase carried some geopolitical (not geographical) plausibility: it *was* the middle of the route to imperial Britain's east.

Such evidence is strangely inadmissible, though, where ancient Israel's ethnicity or racial identity is concerned. A Eurocentric academy appears determined to continue to ignore this while maintaining its claims, however tenuous. In the 1980s and 1990s, as African American theologians began to argue for the identification of biblical figures as Africans, logically included as part of the spoils that "Afrocentrism" had fought for (and won, at least in their own minds) over Egypt, such claims were attacked as "the most absurd distortion".[24] Charges that our current claims are "Afrocentric" (and implicitly lacking sound historical facts and methodology) may be countered by Bauval and Brophy's suggestion that "drawing such a conclusion need not be labeled Afrocentric or anti-Eurocentric—it may be thought of simply as accurate."[25] How novel an idea. The truth would provide scholars with the tools necessary to breach the intellectual dam that currently exists and help to regenerate Judaism with a reconstituted image of its *original* self.

The Existing Paradigm: Wrong! Wrong! Wrong!

Psychiatry is another arena in which the status quo has been challenged. "Psychiatric practice today continues to reflect assumptions that come from the past or permeate into psychiatry from society at large," writes Suman Fernando. "Such cultural arrogance which sees pathology in deviation from (assumed) white nuclear family structures is a reflection of racist ideology within psychiatry and allied social work."[26] Fernando finds an "ethnocentric arrogance amounting to racism…close to the surface" of practitioners in which "experiences of non-Western people are dismissed as 'anomalies' presumably because they are from 'primitive cultures'".

Fernando's deconstruction of psychiatry serves our purposes here: "When a black group is compared to a white group, characteristics of the latter are assumed to be the norm" and will "merely reinforce the racist model which sees black people as requiring a psychiatry that would 'educate' them into white norms".[27] Must AHI/Js be "educated" into the norms of a Eurocentric Judaism? With conversion put forth as a "solution", the answer is apparently "yes".[28]

Surely, the new paradigm presents a monumental challenge. In response, the field might take a cue from our colleagues in astronomy: a review of new evidence challenging Pluto's status as a planet determined that Pluto just didn't measure up, and it was downgraded accordingly. Of course, anthropology is not subject to the same dynamics governing astronomy, but things do need to make sense. For the cultural norm of white turbans and long robes (Ethiopian) to be replaced by shtreimels and knickers (Russian)—and all of its cascading implications—does not make sense. It is, in fact, absurd. To the extent that "anomalies" reveal flaws and demand re-evaluations, longstanding benchmarks across the societal spectrum are called into question, recalibrated, and even discarded daily. Pluto's relegation went scarcely noticed; who knew or cared? This paradigm shift, however, would erode the very foundations of Western civilization, which is daily imploding.

A change is overdue. "The idea of what we mean when we say *anthropology* is probably going to have to change," says John L. Jackson, Jr.[29] "A challenge is being mounted to some of the central assumptions of mainstream social science," warned Clifford Geertz, who saw in 1983 nothing less than "a sea change" coming.[30] Until that change comes, the marginalization will continue.

The narrative crafted from the many AHI/J voices I have heard over the course of many years—my travels, experiences, interviews, research, and "spirit"—informs me that the foundational paradigm for the study of

African Judaism is wrong, completely and absolutely wrong.

In 1985, former Ashkenazi Chief Rabbi Shlomo Goren told his Yom Kippur minyan that "When the first Ashkenazi Jews [followers of the Lithuanian Vilna Gaon] came to the Land of Israel early in the last century, they appealed to the Jews of Ethiopia for spiritual guidance… asking them to send three of their rabbis to Jerusalem to ordain the rabbis of the Land of Israel".[31]

These Ethiopian "rabbis" were from an entirely different Judaic world, from an entirely different historical paradigm. Though clearly acknowledged as being an authentic source from which the now-reigning "mainstream" Judaism sought its early validation, conversion of the Ethiopians was demanded. Are we really expected to endure the old paradigm in the face of such countervailing evidence? Rabbi Goren's candid admission alone would seemingly be sufficient to determine that the old paradigm is invalid. I have much more similar evidentiary material.

"I'm not a *historical* Jew," Rabbi Jo David defensively blurted out at the 2012 International Society for the Study of African Jewry (ISSAJ) conference in South Africa during an aggressive interrogation by an African Israelite observer, "I'm a *rabbinical* Jew".[32] Taken aback by her frankness, I motioned to several Lemba delegates across the room and a visibly irritated Igbo behind me. "Listen!" I said, pulling on my earlobe for effect. This was no mere nuance; her qualification was, as much, a *dis*qualification.

The controversial Shlomo Sand asks—and proceeds to answer—a most pertinent question:

> Is there no chance that a new historiography would invite those ancient Jews, who have been forgotten by their descendants, to reappear in the legitimate sphere of public memory?… For now, it is difficult to predict whether the Israeli politics of identity will permit, in the early twenty-first century, the emergence of fresh paradigms for the investigation of the origins and history of Jewish faith communities.[33]

Experience suggests that no invitations are forthcoming. Is there no chance that "those ancient Jews" have *already* reappeared but have gone unrecognized, by virtue of arrogance or ignorance? They have reappeared in the person of the Bayt Israel and the Lemba, as well as the Igbo and Yoruba of Nigeria, the Ashanti, Ga, and Ewe of Ghana, the Bassa of Cameroon, and the African Hebrews from the West, to name but a few. They have all gone unrecognized, based upon preconceived notions (i.e., prejudices). To suggest that these ancient cultures have "recently discovered Judaism" is an egregious affront, and correlates to perceiving Christopher Columbus as a hero. Contrary to Brotz's assessment that they were "different and unrelated to each other", this new paradigm finds the African and Judean worlds inextricably linked. The tendency incumbent under the old paradigm to render such linkages as "easily dismissible" is easily dismissible.[34]

Rosaldo rails against exclusivist paradigms that claim "a monopoly on truth that excludes other ways of thinking about the world" and that "simply ignore the views of people they never invited to the meeting".[35] Invisible men are never invited to such meetings; we often invite *ourselves*, knowing full well that our presence lends our reluctant hosts an essential legitimacy. But whether such "fresh paradigms" will emerge into the mainstream of our debate is of greater importance than that these "emerging" groups find their way into the "mainstream" of Judaism…or even that they find their way to Israel.

Who is a Jew? "An Increasingly Unsustainable Muddle"

A New York Times columnist warned in 1965 that "there will be an ugly streak of bigotry in Israel as long as the rabbinate can say who is a Jew and who is not".[36] Indeed, his assessment was accurate, as skirmishes in recent years between normative Judaism's various streams—particularly over Jewish identity—have brought Judaism to the brink of a crisis. Jewishness had been rather nebulous prior to the 1969 arrival in Israel of African Hebrew Israelites from America via Liberia. A 1962 Bible dictionary concluded that "perhaps the best that can be said is that *he is a Jew who says he is*".[37] What precipitated the change in Israel's Law of Return in 1970—from "every Jew" to the halakhic definition of those who can provide proof of a Jewish mother or maternal grandmother? The definition of Jewishness now excluded us, along with a substantial segment of "normative" Jews, who, in the eyes of Israel's gatekeepers, are today deemed "not Jewish enough". Are they "collateral damage" in the campaign to keep AHI/Js at bay? (The new law also ran diametrically opposite the Hebraic/biblical cultural norm of patriarchal lineage.) That the rabbinate doesn't recognize us is fine: we don't recognize them either!

According to Alfred Bodenheimer, in an op-ed supportive of Igbo, "the definition of Jewish affiliation is increasingly escaping the control of those authorities that declare themselves responsible for it"; he finds it "symptomatic of how, in both ethnic and religious contexts, the concept of Jewishness is beginning to break down and to be deconstructed". It is all, in his words, "an increasingly unsustainable muddle".[38] In 1958, Israeli Prime Minister David Ben-Gurion asked the *hachmei Israel* (wise men of Israel) for their "statements of opinion" on the "Who is a Jew?" matter.[39] One respondent saw problems looming on the horizon should biological markers be applied to the question of Jewish identity: "The aberration of racism exists sometimes among certain Jews," wrote Henri Baruk in a footnote, "as if the fact of being Jewish were especially a fact of blood, or race. This attitude, not unlike the Hitlerian racism of blood, is the very negation of the principles of Judaism".[40] Baruk capitulated: "The problem of the identity of the Jews in Israel cannot be solved at the moment; it necessitates new studies".[41]

What have studies shown us? In contrast to the genetic testing of the Lemba (which lends credibility to their migration saga), another study weighs heavily in the argument against the old paradigm:

> Most Ashkenazi Jews are descendants of European women who converted to Judaism, possibly around the time of the early Roman Empire, concludes a new genetic study that casts doubt on many prevailing theories about the origins of Ashkenazim.... The finding flies in the face of previous research and the commonly accepted wisdom that European Ashkenazim are descended from ancestral mothers of Jews who left Israel and the Middle East some 2,000 years ago, or in later migrations. The study suggests instead that large numbers of European women converted to Judaism and points to the European women and the Jewish community of the early Roman Empire as the possible sources of the Ashkenazi ancestors.[42]

Consider, alongside the above, the findings of rabbi and Judaic scholar Burton Visotzky:

> When I refer to Judaism, I am referring to "rabbinic Judaism." This form of Judaism, so overwhelmingly prevalent today, did not become the normative flavor of Judaism until a mere eight hundred years or so ago.... In short, what is now called "Judaism" was invented in the matrix of Roman culture. Even as some rabbinic texts depicted Rome as the enemy, there is overwhelming evidence that Judaism took root in Roman soil, imbibed its nourishment, and grafted the good and pruned the bad from the Roman Empire, until a vibrant new religion—Judaism—arose from the wreckage of Israelite religion and the Temple cult, nurtured by the very empire that had destroyed it.[43]

Are such important, albeit controversial, artifacts to be ignored, or are they to be placed on the table for serious consideration? Even the most cursory probe into this field will conclude that "rabbinical" Judaism has strayed from the "original intent" of Moses and the Hebrew prophets. Rabbinical Judaism hardly qualifies as the measuring rod for approaching the study of African adherents to Hebraic identity.

What, then, makes rabbinical Judaism superior to the Judaisms of Guershon Nduwa or Rabson Wuriga? Of those "ancient Jews" that Sand referred to? Of those "historical Jews" that Rabbi Jo David so quickly dissociated herself from? What authority, save that of a sacrosanct sense of Eurocentric privilege, makes *halakha* the legitimating norm for ontological Jewishness? Five hundred years of European global hegemony? I think not! Can normative Judaism, in true survival-of-the-fittest form, proclaim victory even as it continues to excise its African roots?

The "well-crafted narrative" requires no real "crafting", merely an honest appraisal. Ancient Israel's shattered narrative may require a bit more painstaking effort and sensitivity, but where there is the intent to deceive narratives take on an ever-more confusing storyline, which eventually requires a CSI forensics team. Lies inevitably necessitate additional layers of deception and soon become unwieldy fictions, as their discordant and contradictory threads unravel. "Liars should have good memories," as the Arab proverb attests.

Lies, Outliers and Outright Lies

Social Darwinism is enshrined in Western social thought, and it comprises the core of Eurocentrism. "From the very first encounter, the Europeans established as a principle their superiority over the Black race," wrote Basil Davidson.

"They affirmed it by a profound contempt for the inferior race."[44] Like a trailer in tow, anthropologists and ethnographers investigating AHI/J and their intersections, interactions, and influences, have faithfully followed the trajectory of the lead vehicle. Noam Chomsky claims that intellectuals are inherently "servants of power" whose biases and interests often overshadow honest inquiry. While not accusing Euro-American scholarship of overt bigotry, stealthiness is the very hallmark of contemporary "dog-whistle" racism. Its olfactory nature belies its presence.

One scholar articulated the Judaic universe as a set of "concentric circles",[45] with (you guessed it!) a Eurocentric "normative Judaism" at the center. Alas, however creative, it is a rigidly defensive (if ultimately indefensible) position, more akin to a circling of the wagons. Roland Littlewood and Maurice Lipsedge provide a perfect rejoinder:

> Every society has its own characteristic pattern of normative behavior and beliefs. It has therefore to solve the threat not only of antagonists external to the group but also of those inside who may be deviant.... However, we conceive of our group, whether a class, a nation, or a race, we define it by those we exclude from it.... We forget that the outsiders are part of the

definition of ourselves. To confirm our own identity, we push the outsiders even further away.[46]

These circles are then, to quote Fernando, just "another way of marginalising the experience of Black people and relegating it to an inferior position".[47] Those on center stage in the "surge" of interest in African Hebraic identity—AHI/Js themselves—take serious umbrage to being ignored and/or marginalized. After all, what means our "re-emergence" if not that we are no longer invisible? No matter how numerous or asthetically arranged these circles might be, normative Judaism remains at the center. It is no more accommodating than Israel's rabbinate. Africans are simply left on the outside. The current paradigm forever relegates AHI/Js—indeed all Jews of color—to being the subaltern outliers of Judaism.

Failure to adjust the paradigm will only perpetuate and prolong the reigning power dynamic with all of its inherent flaws and unpleasant outcomes. Isaac framed the challenge succinctly: "If scholars and researchers can reveal their prejudices more honestly and accurately, then the value of their work can improve. But such improvement will stand at a nadir if scholars continue to impose categories onto human subjects of study without admitting and addressing a variety of biases and prejudices that inform the social worlds attendant to any scholarly enterprise."[48] Sadly, the colonial mindset (deemed prematurely dead) would doom studies of AHI/Js to being "premised on ignoring what [they] said about themselves"[49]—hardly a prudent ethnographic approach.

Truth or Consequences: Will the *Real* Judaism Please Come Forth?

Again, what *is* really at stake? For those in the field of African Judaism, it is nothing less than your scholarly integrity, your institutional legacies, the legitimacy of Judaism's gatekeepers, Jewish identity itself—perhaps even the very existence of the Jewish state. To the global Jewish community, we say this, in humility, but without flinching: Africa is knocking at the door, which may be left unanswered only at your own peril.

The dehumanizing cycle has ended, if only because the "savage" has "reversed the roles." Our new view is empowering, as Kurt Vonnegut Jr.'s words convey: "I want to stand as close to the edge as I can without going over. Out on the edge you see all kinds of things you can't see from the center. Big, undreamed-of things—the people on the edge see them first."[50]

"The head-in-the-sand anthropologist of yesteryear," says Jackson, was "a fiction created, among other reasons, to justify the discipline to itself".

Included among the "other reasons" is the need to buttress the fictional superiority of that discipline's fundamental paradigms. As when the tools and instruments required for building walls evolve and are abandoned, obsolete paradigms give way as well. Perhaps a retooling is underway. Jackson articulates a new focus for the anthropological gaze, in which ethnographers are:

> required to look up, out, and beyond what easy borders they are quick to create, beyond the arbitrary boundaries of the locations they translate into and onto anthropological field sites. They open up the ethnographic view to include international connections that link places through the flow of never-ending, mobile capital and hard-journeying peoples. Anthropologists ask for ethnographic engagement with people and cultures that take mass media gatekeeping and stereotyping seriously as obstructions to any ethnographic understanding.[51]

No better examples of "arbitrary boundaries" exist than those which have marginalized AHI/Js. Moreover, juxtaposed against a global diaspora, transnational slavery, and subsequent centuries of oppression, there can be no better example of "international connections", "mobile capital", and "hard-journeying peoples" than those associated with AHI/Js. As diligently and efficiently as they were utilized to rearrange landscapes and erect walls, perhaps now those tools may be applied in the building of bridges to a mentality in which the discredited social constructs of race and racial superiority have no place.

Centuries have passed since Europe's first encounters with the Outsider, and we need not revisit its vile nature or violent outcome. Little has changed, save for the refined language of its observers. The celebrated Charles Dickens, an earlier observer, was unrestrained in his opinion of whom he facetiously called "The Noble Savage": "I call him a savage.... a howling, whistling, clucking, stamping, jumping, tearing savage.... (H)e is a savage—cruel, false, thievish, murderous".[52]

Like Dickens' "Noble Savage", "a prodigious nuisance", "an enormous superstition", and "a *something* highly desirable to be civilized off the face of the earth"[53]—AHI/Js are survivors. We may indeed be a nuisance, but we are no superstition. For wherever one looks upon the earth, we are there...watching, and with some choice commentary of our own. For like Bahloul's "savage", we have turned the tables to become the observer. What will we see? More importantly, what will you hear?

Works Cited

Aderet, Ofer. "Study traces Ashkenazim to European women who converted." *Haaretz*, October 11, 2013.

Atkinson, Brooks. "Critic at Large." *New York Times*, January 19, 1965.

Bahloul, Joëlle. *Le culte de la table dressée: Rites et traditions de la table juive algérienne*. Translated in *Judaism Viewed from Within and Without*, edited by Harvey E. Goldberg. Albany, NY: State University of New York Press, 1987.

Baruk, Henri. "Response." In *Jewish Identity: Modern Responsa and Opinions on The Registration of Children of Mixed Marriages* (David Ben-Gurion's Query to Leaders of World Jewry), compiled by Baruch Litvin. Jerusalem: Feldheim Publishers, 1965, 169-205.

Bauval, Robert, and Thomas Brophy. *Black Genesis: The Prehistoric Origins of Ancient Egypt*. Rochester, NY: Bear & Company, 2011.

Ben-Gurion, David. "The Prime Minister's Letter." In *Jewish Identity: Modern Responsa and Opinions on The Registration of Children of Mixed Marriages* (David Ben-Gurion's Query to Leaders of World Jewry), compiled by Baruch Litvin. Jerusalem: Feldheim Publishers, 1965, 11-15.

Bernal, Martin. *Black Athena: The Afro-Asiatic Roots of Classical Civilization, Vol. 1: The Fabrication of Ancient Greece, 1785-1985*. New Brunswick, NJ: Rutgers University Press, 1987.

Bodenheimer, Alfred. "In favor of politicizing Jewish identity." *Haaretz*, December 30, 2011.

Brotz, Howard. *The Black Jews of Harlem: Negro Nationalism and the Dilemmas of Negro Leadership*. New York, NY: Schocken Books, 1964.

Bruder, Edith. *The Black Jews of Africa: History, Religion, Identity*. New York, NY: Oxford University Press, 2008 and 2012.

David, Rabbi Jo. "A Vision for the Development of a Strong Africa-Wide Jewish Community." ISSAJ Conference, Pietermaritzburg, South Africa, June 20–21, 2012.

Davidson, Basil. *The Story of Africa*. London: Mitchell Beazley, 1960.

Dickens, Charles. "The Noble Savage." *Household Words*, June 11, 1853.

Fernando, Suman. *Race and Culture in Psychiatry*. London: Croom Helm, 1988.

Ellison, Ralph. *Invisible Man*. New York, NY: Random House, 1952.

Ellison, Ralph. *Going to the Territory*. New York, NY: Random House, 1986.

Geertz, Clifford. "Blurred Genres: The Refiguration of Social Thought." In Geertz, Clifford, *Local Knowledge: Further Essays in Interpretive*

Anthropology. New York, NY: Basic Books, 1983, 19-35.
Goldberg, Harvey E. *Jewish Passages: Cycles of Jewish Life*. Berkeley, CA: University of California Press, 2003.
Illouz, Eva. "Apology as an act of moral strength." *Haaretz*, July 10, 2015.
Isaac, Walter R. "Beyond Ontological Jewishness: A Philosophic Reflection on the Study of African American Jews and the Social Problems of the Jewish and Human Sciences." Unpublished dissertation for Temple University, January 2011.
Jackson, John L., Jr. *Harlem World: Doing Race and Class in Contemporary Black America*. Chicago, IL: University of Chicago Press, 2001.
Jerusalem Post. "Ashkenazim Once Sought Help of Ethiopian Jews." September 27, 1985.
Jerusalem Post. "Double Standards." Editorial, October 25, 1991.
Kestenbaum, Sam. "Can This Rabbinic Revolutionary Make Hebrew Israelites Mainstream?" *The Forward*, July 7, 2015.
Layman, Charles. *Interpreter's Dictionary of the Bible*. Nashville, TN: Abingdon Press, 1962.
Littlewood, Roland, and Maurice Lipsedge. *Aliens and Alienists: Ethnic Minorities and Psychiatry*. Hove: Psychology Press, 1997.
Miles, William. "Concentric Circles of Historicized Jewish Identity in Africa." ISSAJ Conference, Paris, November 10–11, 2015.
Nduwa, Guershon. "The Association of Black Jews: Why in Africa?" Federation Internationale des Juifs Noirs, August 23, 2014. http://www.feujn.org/spip.php?article101.
Neusner, Jacob. *Judaism as Philosophy: The Method and Message of the Mishnah*. Baltimore, MD: John Hopkins University Press, 1991.
Petrilla, Molly. "John L. Jackson, Jr., Ethnography, and the Hebrew Israelites." *The Pennsylvania Gazette*, March-April 2014.
Rosaldo, Renato. *Culture and Truth: The Remaking of Social Analysis*. Boston, MA: Beacon Press, 1993.
Sand, Shlomo. *The Invention of the Jewish People*. London: Verso, 2010.
Snyder, Louis L. *Race: A History of Modern Ethnic Theories*. New York, NY: Longmans, Green & Co, 1939.
Visotzky, Burton L. *Aphrodite and the Rabbis: How the Jews Adapted Roman Culture to Create Judaism as We Know It*. New York, NY: St. Martin's Press, 2016.
Vonnegut, Kurt, Jr. *Player Piano*. New York: Dial Press, 1999.
Wexler, Aharon. "On the emergence of Judaism." *The Jerusalem Post*, July 31, 2015.

Notes

[1] Joëlle Bahloul, *Le culte de la table dressée: Rites et traditions de la table juive algérienne*, translated in Harvey E. Goldberg, *Judaism Viewed from Within and Without* (Albany, NY: State University of New York Press, 1987).
[2] Ralph Ellison, *Invisible Man* (New York, NY: Random House, 1952).
[3] Guershon Nduwa. "The Association of Black Jews: Why in Africa?" Federation Internationale des Juifs Noirs, August 23, 2014.
http://www.feujn.org/spip.php?article101.
[4] Howard Brotz, *The Black Jews of Harlem: Negro Nationalism and the Dilemmas of Negro Leadership* (New York, NY: Schocken Books, 1964), v.
[5] Walter R. Isaac, "Beyond Ontological Jewishness: A Philosophic Reflection on the Study of African American Jews and the Social Problems of the Jewish and Human Sciences," (unpublished dissertation for Temple University, January 2011), 72.
[6] Ralph Ellison, *Going to the Territory* (New York, NY: Random House, 1986), 276.
[7] Edith Bruder, *The Black Jews of Africa: History, Religion, Identity* (New York, NY: Oxford University Press, 2008), 133–34.
[8] Brotz, 49.
[9] Harvey E. Goldberg, *Jewish Passages: Cycles of Jewish Life* (Berkeley, CA: University of California Press, 2003), 6.
[10] http://bechollashon.org/population/africa/africa_jews.php
[11] Renato Rosaldo, *Culture and Truth: The Remaking of Social Analysis* (Boston, MA: Beacon Press, 1993), 26, 30.
[12] Goldberg, 11.
[13] Jacob Neusner, *Judaism as Philosophy: The Method and Message of the Mishnah* (Baltimore, MD: John Hopkins University Press, 1991), 290.
[14] Eva Illouz, "Apology as an act of moral strength," *Haaretz*, July 10, 2015.
[15] Neusner, 273.
[16] Neusner, 8 fn.
[17] Aharon Wexler, "On the emergence of Judaism," *The Jerusalem Post*, July 31, 2015.
[18] Louis L. Snyder, *Race: A History of Modern Ethnic Theories* (New York, NY: Longmans, Green & Co, 1939), 121.
[19] Snyder, 106.
[20] Rosaldo, 218, 219.
[21] Robert Bauval and Thomas Brophy, *Black Genesis: The Prehistoric Origins of Ancient Egypt* (Rochester, NY: Bear & Company, 2011), 3–4.
[22] Bauval and Brophy, 1.
[23] Martin Bernal, *Black Athena: The Afro-Asiatic Roots of Classical Civilization, Vol. 1: The Fabrication of Ancient Greece, 1785-1985* (New Brunswick, NJ: Rutgers University Press, 1987), 9, 241; [emphasis: original].
[24] Editorial, "Double Standards," *The Jerusalem Post*, October 25, 1991.
[25] Bauval and Brophy, 163.
[26] Suman Fernando, *Race and Culture in Psychiatry* (London: Croom Helm, 1988), 56–57.
[27] Fernando, 54, 55.

[28] Fernando, 53.
[29] Molly Petrilla, "John L. Jackson, Jr., Ethnography, and the Hebrew Israelites," *The Pennsylvania Gazette*, March-April 2014.
[30] Clifford Geertz, "Blurred Genres: The Refiguration of Social Thought," in *Local Knowledge: Further Essays in Interpretive Anthropology* (New York, NY: Basic Books, 1983), 34.
[31] "Ashkenazim Once Sought Help of Ethiopian Jews," *The Jerusalem Post*, September 27, 1985.
[32] Rabbi Jo David, "A Vision for the Development of a Strong Africa-Wide Jewish Community," ISSAJ Conference, Pietermaritzburg, South Africa, June 20–21, 2012.
[33] Shlomo Sand, *The Invention of the Jewish People* (London: Verso, 2010), 248–49.
[34] Sam Kestenbaum, "Can This Rabbinic Revolutionary Make Hebrew Israelites Mainstream?" *The Forward*, July 7, 2015.
[35] Rosaldo, 220, 221.
[36] Brooks Atkinson, "Critic at Large," *New York Times*, January 19, 1965.
[37] Charles Layman, *The Interpreter's Dictionary of the Bible*, Vol. 2 (Nashville, TN: Abingdon Press, 1962), 898; [emphasis: author].
[38] Alfred Bodenheimer, "In favor of politicizing Jewish identity," *Haaretz*, December 30, 2011.
[39] David Ben-Gurion, "The Prime Minister's Letter," in *Jewish Identity: Modern Responsa and Opinions on The Registration of Children of Mixed Marriages* (David Ben-Gurion's Query to Leaders of World Jewry), comp. Baruch Litvin (Jerusalem: Feldheim Publishers, 1965), 11.
[40] Henri Baruk, "Response," in *Jewish Identity: Modern Responsa and Opinions on The Registration of Children of Mixed Marriages* (David Ben-Gurion's Query to Leaders of World Jewry), comp. Baruch Litvin (Jerusalem: Feldheim Publishers, 1965), 201.Baruk, 201.
[41] Baruk, 204 fn.
[42] Ofer Aderet, "Study traces Ashkenazim to European women who converted," *Haaretz*, October 11, 2013.
[43] Burton L. Visotzky, *Aphrodite and the Rabbis: How the Jews Adapted Roman Culture to Create Judaism as We Know It* (New York, NY: St. Martin's Press, 2016), 8, 12.
[44] Basil Davidson, *The Story of Africa* (London: Mitchell Beazley, 1960), [pagination forthcoming].
[45] William Miles, "Concentric Circles of Historicized Jewish Identity in Africa," ISSAJ Conference, Paris, November 10–11, 2015.
[46] Roland Littlewood and Maurice Lipsedge, *Aliens and Alienists: Ethnic Minorities and Psychiatry*. (Hove: Psychology Press, 1997), 27.
[47] Fernando, 55.
[48] Isaac, 113.
[49] Isaac, 382.
[50] Kurt Vonnegut, Jr. *Player Piano*. (New York; Dial Press, 1999).
[51] John L. Jackson, Jr., *Harlem World: Doing Race and Class in Contemporary Black America* (Chicago, IL: University of Chicago Press, 2001), 209–10.

[52] Charles Dickens, "The Noble Savage," *Household Words*, June 11, 1853.
[53] Ibid.

CHAPTER THREE

THE LONG WAY HOME: LIVING AS AN AFRICAN AMERICAN JEW IN A TIME OF TURMOIL

CAROL CONAWAY

Introduction[1]

The Black Civil Rights Movement in the United States from 1954 to 1968 made significant strides in procuring Constitutional rights and the protection of federal law for African Americans. Northern whites—including many European-heritage Jews—worked side-by-side with African Americans in pursuit of justice. As a young African American who had been committed to converting to Judaism since the age of thirteen, I saw Jewish involvement in the Civil Rights Movement as just another example of the ethical and spiritual values that drew me to Judaism (Conaway 2004). When I became a Jew by choice in my early twenties, however, I found myself shunned by white Jews in the northern city of Philadelphia and my idealistic vision shattered. In the 1970s and 1980s, there were racial and class conflicts between urban white Jews and urban African Americans. I believe those conflicts greatly influenced the way many white Jewish individuals and institutions perceived me in the 1970s and 1980s.

The following excerpt from my memoir-in-progress is a critical example of how racial, class, and gender bias, as well as homophobia, contributed to my being suspected of anti-Semitism. I was a poor, young, Black woman living in an urban area where conflict between African Americans and white Jews had been extensive and intense. I was also an easily identifiable, "out" lesbian. Taken together, these factors made it highly unlikely for many white Jews to believe, or even want to accept, that my commitment to Judaism was sincere, although a Conservative rabbinic court of three European-heritage white rabbis had declared me a "righteous proselyte". Many white Jews never accepted that declaration as valid.

Knowing and Nurturing the Jew in Me

The renowned scholar and author Benedict Anderson first published his *Imagined Communities* in 1983. I was drawn to Anderson's book because I was about to begin work at MIT on my doctoral dissertation in political theory. My dissertation questioned how the Jews had remained a people with an attachment to the specific Land of Israel for thousands of years, despite the widespread Jewish diaspora, which followed the Roman conquest in 44 CE. Although Anderson's work in this volume dealt with the subject of nationalism, he made a statement that both intrigued and liberated me because, as a Jew by choice, I had sought validation and credibility as a genuine member of the Jewish people since my conversion in 1971. According to Anderson:

> In fact, all communities larger than primordial villages of face-to-face contact (and perhaps even these) are imagined. Communities are to be distinguished, not by their falsity/genuineness, but by their style in which they are imagined. (2006 edition, 6)

Did this mean that, in my early teens, I had become a Jew because I imagined myself to be a Jew? If the Jews were another "imagined" community, and I was ready to accept the style of what I knew at the time was the worldwide Jewish community and had imagined as my own, did that mean that I would no longer be viewed with suspicion or as "other" than those born and raised as "us"? I finally felt vindicated. I truly was a member of *my* chosen people!

Although Anderson's book focused on the birth of nation-states in the nineteenth century, and not specifically on Jews living thousands of years earlier, I took heart from his words about communities and their members. I believed more than ever that I had found myself in my chosen people—that I belonged here no matter what some in the Jewish community believed or refused to believe. I was a Jew by choice. I knew that my soul was Jewish, no matter what the color of my skin or the size of my Afro, and regardless of the men's jeans and blue work shirts that I wore on evenings and weekends when I did not have to wear my "workday drag". I thought, "I do not have to look like you! It does not matter that my ancestors did not immigrate to this country from Eastern or Western Europe or shtetls in Russia. No, my family was not herded off in trains to Auschwitz, Treblinka, or Dachau; however, I am willing to accept this heritage as my own. My fate is the fate of Jews everywhere throughout history and in the future".

It was a very daring challenge that proved largely unsuccessful. I had no idea how major a factor race would be in preventing me from being accepted by white Jews of European heritage. These were people whose families had suffered centuries of discrimination, torture, and death because of their beliefs and culture. Surely, I had thought, they would accept me—a convert to Judaism who chose to be part of the Jewish people for the rest of her life—no matter what our fate. Not so.

As my family of birth was engaged in its own quest to become "whiter", if not altogether white, US American Jews of European heritage also struggled to be accepted as "white" by white nativists. Anthropologist Karen Brodkin (1998) argues that European-heritage or white US American Jews came to be seen as "white" only after World War II.[2] Given this racial repositioning in the 1970s and 1980s, I, an African American, was not uniformly welcomed in most Jewish congregations. No matter how hard I tried, I could not transform myself into a young white woman. My educational background, my developing professional credentials, and my burgeoning upward mobility did not matter. I was not white.

The class status of many white Jews had changed for the better in the US in the post-war years. Many "newly" white Jews entered the middle class and began to assimilate into white US American culture. They began to be part of the country's dominant white power structure. This development did not escape the attention of Blacks. Many Black people—especially intellectuals and radical organizations—accused Jews of participating in the system that had oppressed them since the nineteenth century. I was very naïve about the history of Black and Jewish relations and never considered that race would be a factor in my life as a Jew. However, to my adopted people, race was a critical issue at this historical moment. Race was becoming such a central issue primarily because Black anti-Semitism was rearing its ugly head among some radical political groups, such as the Black Power movement and the Nation of Islam, two prominent groups in the United States that gained media attention from the early 1970s onward. Growing Black anti-Semitism attracted the attention of a radical, violent group of white Jews of European heritage known as the Jewish Defense League (JDL). Through their publicity, anti-Black anxieties were heightened in the US Jewish community. The JDL was founded in the late 1960s by Rabbi Meir Kahane to protect Jews against anti-Semitism, particularly in the Soviet Union; however, the JDL was also racist. The JDL specifically targeted Blacks who called for, or committed, violence against Jews.

My Unlikely Journey to Judaism

As an African American born into an African Methodist Episcopal (AME) family, I grew up religiously observant in a Christian denomination whose members were predominantly Black. My maternal grandfather was a highly-regarded minister who had become a Presiding Elder of the denomination. The kindliest human being one could ever hope to meet, he stood more than six feet tall, quite slender, his skin color a beautiful chocolate reddish shade that was always shiny because his clerical garb and collar made him perspire profusely. Whenever he gave one of his rousing sermons or listened to a choir sing, he constantly wiped his brow with a huge white handkerchief. He and my late maternal grandmother raised a family of seven children on a shoestring salary. He was a strict parent but an extraordinarily lenient grandfather. We grandchildren adored him, and he us. He always had a kind word for each of us and a huge, gentle smile. When he laughed at our antics, he grabbed his belly and shook up and down as if the most comical event in the world had just happened. The only negative thing I remember about him was that he always reeked of chewing tobacco—a substance that stained his teeth a deep shade of yellow. To my mother's dismay, he kept his green and white china spittoon right beside his tall, straight, high-backed chair in the living room, so he could conveniently aim his used tobacco wad into the bowl of spittle.

My grandfather was a devout Christian who never doubted the divinity of Jesus and the truth of every word in the Bible, especially the teachings of the New Testament. He believed that Jesus was with him and guided his every move and thought each second of the day. To attest to that, he always wore a large silver cross on a black ribbon around his neck. Neither I nor anyone else doubted how strongly he felt the presence of his Lord and Savior at all times. Because of his extraordinary humanity, he noticed when I was twelve or thirteen that I had very few friends. I was shy and quite lonely. In response, he decided to take me under his broad wing and invited me to read theology with him. Perhaps I had expressed some doubt about the divinity of Jesus or the idea of the Holy Ghost that made him think that he needed to probe my questions and help me find much-needed answers.

Nevertheless, it was my grandfather the minister who introduced me to the people called the Jews and who inspired my curiosity about them. Although my parents and extended family were anti-Semites, my grandfather spoke highly of Jews and introduced me to philosopher and theologian Martin Buber's work *I and Thou*. I became fascinated with Jewish thought. During one of my discussions with my grandfather, I told him that I thought I was a Jew and that I wanted to become one officially. There was a hugely pregnant pause in our conversation. Finally, he looked at me, wiped his face with his handkerchief, and said: "You must follow your heart". My heart was Jewish.

The more I learned, the more I came to believe that the Jews were my people and that I was a Jew. Overall, my Jewish friends did not know what to make of me. Generally, the only other Black people with whom their families had come into contact were the women who cleaned their homes or who were otherwise employed by them. Still, these Jewish friends in my junior high school classes helped me begin to learn Hebrew, invited me to their bar and bat mitzvah ceremonies, and took me into their homes so I could celebrate Shabbat and various Jewish holidays. Even with the racial and Jewish-non-Jewish divides, in the end, these Jewish friends generally took an avid interest in this curious Black girl who believed that she was a Jew.

When the 1960s came about—the time of the African American Civil Rights Movement—radical changes occurred in US American society. There was an unleashing of hatred, vile acts, physical and verbal attacks, and other abuse by many whites who railed against Blacks who were marching, boycotting, "freedom riding", registering voters, and engaging in other forms of non-violent protest for justice and equality. Led primarily by the Reverend Dr. Martin Luther King, Jr., a young Baptist minister from Atlanta, hundreds of northern and southern African Americans heeded the call for courage and commitment, even to the point of sacrificing their lives. They were joined by hundreds of whites—from the North; students, teachers, and religious leaders from many faiths joined their African American counterparts and suffered similar abuse, intolerance, and, in some cases, death at the hands of white Ku Klux Klan members and other hostile groups. There was a huge influx of white European-heritage Jews, primarily from northern states, who participated in every aspect of the movement for social justice. Many Jewish women were at the fore here (Schultz 2001). Rabbis and other clergy risked their lives to support the movement. Prominent rabbis such as Dr. Abraham Joshua Heschel joined Dr. King, the Southern Christian Leadership Conference, and others in the pursuit of racial equality. It is likely that many white Jews joined this movement because, like African Americans, Jews had suffered terrible prejudice and persecution throughout history just because they were different. Despite the anti-Semitic conversations I had witnessed in my family, I was impressed by Jewish devotion to Black civil rights.

All of the Jews I knew or knew of at this time were white. I knew of no other African or African American Jews except for the renowned US American entertainer, Sammy Davis, Jr. Still, it never occurred to me that our embrace of Judaism would be questioned or disparaged because of our race. I never entertained the notion that, among the people who marched and died for civil rights, some might also become racists when they felt threatened by the changing relationship between some African Americans and some white Jews in various urban areas in the United States, or when the hard-won improved status of European-heritage Jews was threatened.

My First Experience with Jewish Racism

I became a Jew by choice formally in my early twenties. The sincerity and fervor with which I had considered myself a Jew from my early teens had persisted into my adulthood. I anticipated joining a Conservative synagogue in Philadelphia and settling into life as a Jew; however, I made the mistake of not keeping up with the news about the deteriorating relationship between certain African American and white Jewish groups and individuals in many of the major urban areas of the country. My lack of awareness about this news exposed me to a rude awakening as I tried to follow my plans to assimilate into the US Jewish community.

In the early 1970s when I converted, the relationship between African Americans and white Jews was beginning to fray in some of the large urban areas of the northern United States. Radical Black groups, such as the Nation of Islam (a.k.a. the Black Muslims), members of the Black Power movement, and certain prominent Black intellectuals were alleging that white Jews were racists; they directed this accusation particularly towards Jewish landlords and merchants taking advantage of low-income Blacks in urban ghetto areas. During these confrontations, bitterness often led to violence in many cities across the US. Another point of contention was the charge that Jews had stepped up on the backs of poor Blacks to become economically and socially more secure, while Blacks had been left behind, once again prevented from attaining "the American dream".

I was naïve about the extent of this chilling conflict until I became a Jew. Soon after my conversion, a white rabbi pointed to me during his *dvar* and, in front of his congregation, accused me of being representative of Blacks who murdered Jews—the very people who had helped them to gain civil rights. I was shocked by his accusations and his humiliating me. Not one congregant disputed his words; not one voice spoke on my behalf. In a diatribe of just a few minutes, the rabbi had labeled me part of "them" rather than "us". Suddenly, I was identified mistakenly as a member of a group victimizing Jews, rather than being recognized as a potential victim and ally because I was both Jewish and Black. The friend with whom I had come to services recognized my shock, grabbed my arm, and told me that we were leaving immediately.

I reported this incident to the Jewish family who had befriended me when I was fourteen years old. Outraged at how I had been treated by this rabbi, they immediately called a rabbi whom they respected. His Reconstructionist congregation in my neighborhood warmly welcomed me, and on Rosh Hashanah gave me an Aliyah and the honor of carrying one of the Torah scrolls around the synagogue so that all of the congregants could touch or kiss it. This was a totally new and wonderful experience for them and for me. I was so deeply moved that I joined the congregation and remained a member until I moved to Boston in 1973. From this experience, I learned that as a Black lesbian, I might not be welcome in all Jewish environments. I would have to be highly selective to find a welcoming synagogue or organization. I made several mistakes while trying to learn which places might be forthcoming. My friends had taken me to services at their Conservative synagogue for at least five years, so I had "grown up" in the Conservative Jewish tradition. I was always in their protective care, however. I intended to seek a Conservative synagogue with which to affiliate. Perhaps in the 1970s that was not the best choice. Perhaps affiliating with the Reform or Reconstructionist movements might have netted better results; however, I continued to seek what I knew best suited my deepest self, no matter the consequences. Just as my mother had made a crucial decision to leave the AME church and become Episcopalian in a white church, I sought just the right group of Conservative Jews and remained confident that if I found it I would be accepted in their all-white synagogue as a "righteous proselyte". My search might take years, but I was determined to succeed.

As the antagonism between African Americans and white Jews in urban areas continued for the following twenty or more years, other complications developed. During this period, bitter questions arose about Jewish participation in the American slave trade and about the ongoing Israeli/Palestinian conflict. The accusation that significant numbers of white Jews had been involved in slavery was disproven fairly quickly. The Israeli/Palestinian conflict predated Israel's declaration of independence in 1948, however, and some people, both Jews and non-Jews, began accusing Israel of maintaining a system of apartheid rather than the democracy it proclaimed.

At a time of such bitter division, I sometimes suffered ostracism on an individual level. Most Black Christians and Muslims could not understand the idea that I had "gone over to the other side". Similarly, many white Jews refused to accept the notion that an African American woman who is a lesbian of modest means, well-educated and politically radical, would willingly and seriously take on an identity as a Jew. In some congregations I was shunned and treated as an alien rather than a Jew. There were Jewish gatherings where I was not asked to participate. I used to dread the High

Holidays because they meant another occasion with the potential for humiliation.

I attributed my lack of acceptance by European-heritage white Jews primarily to my being both Black and a lesbian. This was a very painful realization because I could change neither my race nor my sexual orientation. I felt bitter and deeply hurt for many years. Considering all of the pain, discrimination, and suffering that white Jews had endured for thousands of years, I could not understand how they could inflict pain, discrimination, and suffering on one who had cast her lot with them. I had renounced my family, my culture, and my former religion to become a woman whose soul was Jewish. I shed many tears because I found myself a pariah among Blacks and Jews alike. Yet, as my maternal grandfather had told me to do, I followed my heart, despite the cost.

This situation did not improve until the early 1990s, when I became friends with a white Jewish couple who lived just outside of Boston. They had recently returned from living in Israel in an Orthodox Jewish collective and joined a synagogue that considered itself to be "Traditional" rather than Orthodox, Conservative, Reform, or Reconstructionist. Instead, while its tendencies aligned more closely with the Conservative movement than with any of the other Jewish movements, it also followed certain Reform and Reconstructionist practices. It was, for example, an egalitarian congregation in which women and men participated equally in Torah readings and most other traditions. Women and men sat together during services and all other functions. The synagogue accepted non-Jewish spouses as members if the family so chose. This predominantly white and Ashkenazi congregation welcomed Jews of any race, ethnicity, or background. Many members were "1960s people" with a very mellow attitude about membership; yet, religious intensity felt apparent everywhere.

In the mid-1970s, I had also been one of the founders of a lesbian, gay, bisexual, and transgender congregation in Boston. This was a group in which I was not only accepted but welcomed, but its practices were more Reform than Conservative. I found myself longing for services in Hebrew, observance of most holidays for two days instead of one, Torah readings, daylight services rather than evening gatherings, and other Conservative traditions. I wanted "real" services—ones like those that I had attended for years when I was younger. This LGBT congregation, however, addressed my loneliness and removed me from pariah status. It was a gentle salve for the pain I had suffered for the years following my conversion. This congregation, Am Tikva (People of Hope), accepted me as I was—a Black lesbian Jew by choice.

Despite this acceptance, the synagogue that my formerly Orthodox friends described to me in 1991 sounded appealing. I was at first afraid to attend services there by myself, fearing humiliation by congregation members. The grief from my previous experiences remained almost unbearable and the pain still seared. As a result, I had promised myself to continue attending services only at Am Tikva (where I always felt welcome and loved) or with friends whom I knew would protect me at another synagogue. I was tired of being “the only one” or “the first”. I had played that role for far too long. I no longer wanted to be “the pioneer”. I wanted to fit in and feel at home, just like everyone else. When my new friends took me to their shul, that is exactly what occurred. No one stared at me. People were warm and welcoming. At this time, at a synagogue other than Am Tikva, I was able to pray and socialize in peace. I had found a synagogue whose members included other Jews of color as well as LGBT Jews. There was no need to shed more tears.

In my experience by the 1990s, synagogues were finally becoming more welcoming. One major event that I believe contributed to the changes that I witnessed was the Israeli airlift of Ethiopian Jews to Israel. Until the airlift, many European-heritage white Jews in the United States had very little, if any, familiarity with Jews of color; however, a massive influx of Jews with Black skin and a long history of Jewish observance, portrayed in the media as dating back to the Queen of Sheba, made it impossible to deny the multicultural, multiethnic face of Judaism. This multiplicity was not actually a new phenomenon. Long before the exile from the Land of Israel in 44 CE and the ensuing worldwide diaspora, many Jews settled in regions across the globe; however, European-heritage white Jews were the group whose practice of Judaism, adherence to the Babylonian Talmud, and generations of sages and scholars became emblematic of Jewry in modernity. They generally did not recognize other Jewish practices and rituals as valid. Unfortunately, this situation sometimes continues; when the Ethiopian Jews arrived in Israel, European-heritage white Jews would not accept them as authentically Jewish until they made various changes to their rituals and way of life. The white rabbinate prevailed, despite protests from the Ethiopians. Racism from white Jews has continued to plague newcomers to Israel with dark skin and persists to this day. This phenomenon is heartbreaking.

Also, in the past thirty or more years in the United States particularly, tens of thousands of African American Jews have stepped forward to be counted as members of the worldwide Jewish community. We are Jews due to a variety of circumstances; what matters is that we are a part of the covenant and the people Israel. Still, much needs to be done to expose white

Jewish racism when it occurs, and this should not lead anyone to label those calling out racism either traitors or self-hating Jews. Non-Orthodox white communities have achieved acceptance of non-white Jews far more easily than those that are Orthodox. While the situation varies, in my experience, Reform, Conservative, Reconstructionist, and other denominations are more open to inclusiveness than are Orthodox Jews. Many Jews of color have their own congregations, while others are members of white congregations. There are organizations such as the Jewish Multiracial Network founded on the premise that we Jews are one people regardless of our skin color or ethnicity.

While I am infuriated that the growing Jewish phenomenon in sub-Saharan Africa appears to remain unacceptable to most Ashkenazi Jews, I am not surprised, based upon my personal experience as a Jew by choice. It is clear that many white Jews worldwide refuse to recognize First World/Third World dichotomies and biases when they involve Jewish communities that are different from what we commonly identify as post-Babylonian, rabbinic Jewry. I urge Jews to read and support the work of such scholars as Dr. Edith Bruder (2008) and Dr. Marla Brettschneider (2015), and I urge these scholars to continue their work. Thanks to their academic work, our understanding of sub-Saharan Jewry will continue to increase substantially over the coming years. As we learn about observance and rituals among African Jews, other Jews may become open to new understandings of who we are as a people.

I was largely ignorant of the existence of Jews throughout the African diaspora until I was invited to present a paper about ten years ago at the annual meeting of the Caribbean Philosophical Association. The director of the organization is Lewis Gordon, a scholar of great repute. He is also a Black Jew. He took me aside after my panel finished and said, "Carol, look around you. More than ninety-five percent of the people around you—our fellow members—are Black Jews from all over the world". I was stunned. Moments later, it occurred to me that I was surrounded by my Jewish sisters and brothers, a community of Black Jewish intellectuals that I had never imagined existed or could include me.

My increasing awareness of African Jews and African-diaspora Jews has helped me to heal my wounds from the past. This knowledge has been a great salve for me and has given me contentment while at the same time increasing my commitment to the worldwide Jewish community. I no longer suffer the slings and arrows of rejection, for I truly believe that I have found my spiritual family among others like me—African American Jews and other Jews of color.

Conclusion

Benedict Anderson was correct in postulating that our ties to various communities, geographic and mental "homelands", constitute the connections binding all of us to our "social and cultural identity".[3] The community into which I was born and the spiritual and cultural community with which I chose to align myself have, over time, coalesced for me more and more. I embrace myself as an African American Jewish woman who is a lesbian, an intellectual, and a feminist. I have learned that identity is not a one-way street. I am shaped by the intersection of two major spiritual and cultural communities, as well as by my gender, sexual orientation, and class. As a result of my affiliations, I have learned a great deal about how human beings seek to differentiate themselves from others; however, African and African American Jews, other Jews of color, and Jews of all ethnicities and racial groups—particularly those not always deemed "true Jews" in the past—comprise the hope of the Jewish people. We are one worldwide community with one future for all of us, including those of European heritage and those of other ethnicities, those whose acceptance as Jews has been fraught and those accepted more readily, including Mizrachi Jews and Jews of Africa and the African diaspora.

Works Cited

Anderson, Benedict. *Imagined Communities: Reflections on the Origin and Spread of Nationalism.* London: Verso, 1983.

Brettschneider, Marla. *The Family Flamboyant: Race, Politics, Queer Families, Jewish Lives.* Albany, NY: SUNY Press, 2006.

Brettschneider, Marla. *The Jewish Phenomenon in Sub-Saharan Africa: The Politics of Conflicting Discourses.* Lewiston, NY: Edward Mellen Press, 2015.

Brodkin, Karen. *How Jews Became White Folks and What That Says About Race in America.* Piscataway, NJ: Boston University Press, 1998.

Bruder, Edith. *The Black Jews of Africa. History, Identity, Religion.* New York, NY: Oxford University Press, 2008.

Conaway, Carol. "Journey to the Promised Land: How I Became an African-American Jew Rather Than a Jewish African American." *Nashim: A Journal of Jewish Women's Studies & Gender Issues* 8, no. 1 (2004): 115–28.

Kaye/Kantrowitz, Melanie. *The Colors of Jews: Racial Politics and Radical Diasporas.* Bloomington, IN: University of Indiana Press, 2007.

Schultz, Debra L. *Going South: Jewish Women in the Civil Rights Movement*. New York, NY: New York University Press, 2001.

Notes

[1] This article was originally prepared as a paper for delivery at the International Society of the Study of African Jewry Conference, November 2015, Paris, France.
[2] (See also Brettschneider 2006 and Kaye/Kantrowitz 2007).
[3] Anderson, Benedict. *Imagined Communities: Reflections on the Origin and Spread of Nationalism.* (London: Verso, 1983).

CHAPTER FOUR

MISREPRESENTATION OF JEWISH SOCIAL ORGANIZATION IN KERALA, INDIA THROUGH MODELS OF RACE, CASTE, AND SLAVERY

BARBARA C. JOHNSON

This critical and self-critical evaluation of scholarship on the Jews of Kerala in southwest India—formerly known as the "Cochin" Jews[1]—focuses on the role of Western scholars in misrepresenting and exoticizing just one element of their social organization: a division into competing factions. Drawing on insights from almost forty years of archival and ethnographic research about the community and personal relationship with many of its members, I criticize Western scholars of Kerala Jewish history and culture, myself included, for both misinterpreting and over-emphasizing their historical social divisions. I also note the negative impact of some of our work on Kerala Jews themselves. My critique is focused on the scholarly use of paradigms of race, caste, and slavery.

We do have evidence that for at least a few centuries there were internal divisions among the Jews of southwest India—Jews who were labeled "White" and "Black", who did not marry each other, and who competed for social status. There were also Kerala Jews within both the so-called "White" and "Black" factions who were denied social and ritual equality by more prominent members of their own congregations. I am certain that we can think of many places around the world where Jewish communities or congregations manifest social divisions and inequalities, but somehow the particular separations and inequalities found in Kerala Jewish history were seen by scholars from outside Kerala (most of whom were themselves Jewish) as uniquely fascinating, exotic, and contrary to their understanding of Jewish values. To quote the British scholar J. B. Segal:

> This division, however, is peculiar to India.... In no other country has hereditary antagonism between sections of a Jewish community, otherwise

> united in the minutiae of ritual observance, been rigidly maintained for centuries. Discrimination by White Jews against Black Jews... became... a permanent cancer on the body of the community.[2]

First, a brief historical background.[3] There is ample evidence that a well-established community of Jews lived in peace with their Hindu, Muslim, and Christian neighbors on the Malabar Coast of southwest India for at least one thousand years—probably much longer. Since the fourteenth century, many, but not all of them, lived in what was once the Hindu-ruled Kingdom of Kochi, now part of the modern Indian state of Kerala. In the 1950s, most of these Jews migrated to Israel, where there are now more than five thousand Kerala Jews identified ethnically as "Kochinim".

At least since Roman times, seaports along the Malabar Coast were a center of international trade, attracting merchants and settlements of Christians and Muslims as well as Jews. Medieval travelers who reported meeting Jews in southwest India did not mention internal divisions among them. During the period of Portuguese colonial rule in the sixteenth and early seventeenth centuries, significant numbers of Sephardic and Mizrachi Jews moved to Kerala, some perhaps fleeing directly from persecution and expulsion in Spain or Portugal, and they were joined by other Jews coming by way of North Africa and the Middle East. It seems likely that, at first, the new immigrants worshipped together with the long-established Jewish communities in the area. José Alberto Tavim's research in Portuguese records reveals participation by Sephardic Jews and *Conversos* (forced converts from Judaism to Christianity or their descendants) in the construction of a new synagogue in the port city of Kochi, begun in 1544 presumably to handle the overflow from the Kochindagi synagogue that had been built two centuries earlier.[4] By 1568, the Sephardic and other Jewish newcomers had become numerous enough to build a separate synagogue of their own in Kochi. This synagogue was called the "Paradesi *Palli*" or "the synagogue of the foreigners".

Even when they had their own synagogue, however, these Paradesis did not remain "foreign" to southern India in their way of life. They adopted the Malayalam language of Kerala and the customs of the much older Jewish community there. Evidence of their conflict with, or at least antipathy towards, the older Jewish community is not documented until more than a century later, when a delegation of four Sephardic Jews from Amsterdam visited Cochin in 1685, not long after the establishment of Dutch colonial rule. Mosseh Pereyra de Paiva, the leader of this delegation, reported back to Amsterdam that the congregation of Jews who had hosted them did not marry the Jews of the nine other area congregations, whom their hosts called "*Malabarees*", alleging that they were "the slaves of slaves" and were mixed with non-Jews.[5] Pereyra de Paiva labeled some but not all of the host congregation "White" without calling the other Kerala Jews "Black", but the White/Black labels were used early in the next century by Dutch chaplain Jacob Visscher in describing the Jews of the Malabar Coast.[6]

Jonathan Schorsch's ground-breaking work on fifteenth- to seventeenth-century Jewish history[7] includes a long-overdue analysis of the Pereyra DePaiva report and of the situation of the Jewish community on the Malabar Coast at that time. Rather than viewing the emerging "Black" versus "White" social division among Kerala Jews as unique to India, Schorsch situates it in the broad historical context of pre-modern colonialism. Explaining what he calls the "invention of Jewish whiteness", he argues that it became increasingly important for the Portuguese, then the Dutch and other Europeans involved in colonial trade and administration to distance themselves from the darker-skinned natives of the lands they were ruling. For Sephardic Jews living in colonized India, like those in the Atlantic colonies, their claim to "Whiteness" positioned them as closer to, if not part of, the ruling European elite as opposed to "Black" Jews in Kerala and elsewhere who were among the colonized.

The Black/White color divide among Jews—in India and elsewhere—was then to become part of growing Western discourse about physical differences among human populations, developed into a paradigmatic system of distinct human "races", partially based on a conceived divide in skin color.

Race

To examine more closely the problems with Western scholarly work on social divisions within the Indian Jewish community, let us first look at the outdated paradigm of race—now replaced in at least some scholarly discourse by the less rigid concept of "gene pools". By the end of the nineteenth century, outsiders reporting on the Kerala Jews were using the terminology of race in accord with scientific and popular ideas of the day. Race was a central category of analysis in official ethnographic surveys ordered and carried out by the British colonial government during this period. These surveys have been criticized by post-colonial scholars as an instrument for reifying South Asian social hierarchies in the process of making colonial rule more efficient. Along with an emphasis on the categories of "caste" and "tribe", British colonial surveys applied the concept of "racial purity" and "mixed races" to the analysis of hundreds of social groups in South India alone. Survey researchers valued the new science of "anthropometry", using a technique of comparative anthropometric measurement of skulls and noses.[8]

By the 1930s, scientific methods for investigating "racial" differences had turned to analysis of blood types. In 1936, Eileen MacFarlane, an American physical anthropologist, carried out a comparative blood-type analysis of Kerala Jews, which she called "a serological attack on the race problem". She took blood samples from "White" Jews, from "Black" Jews, and from miscellaneous "low-caste" Hindu patients in a Kerala hospital. She then compared the blood types she found in these samples with earlier data, collected by other researchers, on blood types of Jews from different parts of Europe and from Syria. My quick tabulation of her published data shows that the greatest similarity of these blood-type distributions was in fact between the miscellaneous "low-caste" Kerala Hindus and the Jews of Europe and Syria. MacFarlane herself, however, did not note this statistical similarity. She concluded that "the Black Jews are the descendants of mixed Semitic and native Malayali ancestors".[9] In 1939, cultural anthropologist David Mandelbaum exaggerated MacFarlane's results in citing her report as "factual" evidence and summarizing: "In physical type the Black Jews are indubitably aligned with the Hindu natives".[10] He also referred to her study in a 1975 article,[11] but by this time the analytical paradigm of caste was replacing that of race for most anthropologists.

Before discussing the paradigm of caste, let us note similarities between the "scientific" concept of "racial purity" and a traditional rabbinic concern with "purity" of descent or *yichus*—a Hebrew term indicating verifiable Jewish lineage. An early sixteenth-century question was sent from India to the Talmudic authority Rabbi David ibn Zimra (known as RaDBaZ), in Cairo.[12] Though it is not known who sent the question, it was most likely a Jewish traveler or a Sephardic newcomer. Questions were asked about the status of Jews in Cochin whom the inquirer called "*enam myuchasim*", people without *yichus*, in contrast to *myuchasim* who could prove their Jewish descent. Some of the Jews without *yichus* were identified as slaves or manumitted slaves who had converted to Judaism; others were non-slave converts. RaDBaZ replied that the non-*myuchasim* should be allowed to enter the congregation of the Israelites after undergoing a *tevilah*, or immersion required of converts, in case they couldn't prove they had already done so, and after this ritual they should not be called slaves.

Caste

The English word "caste" comes from *casta,* a Portuguese translation of the Sanskrit-based term *jati*—an endogamous South Asian social group that maintains external boundaries and orderly marriage patterns. Although colonial officials and scholars had referred to the entire group of Kerala Jews as a caste, anthropologist David G. Mandelbaum was the first to apply the term to internal divisions among them. As a young Jewish post-doctoral researcher, his first trip to India was in 1937 to investigate the Kota, a remote "tribal" group living in the inland Nilgiri Hills of Kerala. Taking a break for the Jewish holidays, he traveled down to the port city of Kochi and spent three weeks there, celebrating the holidays from Rosh Hashanah to Simchat Torah with fellow Jews and taking copious fieldwork notes. He then wrote an ethnographic article about them for the very first volume of the journal *Jewish Social Studies.*

In this article, Mandelbaum stated that the Jews of Kerala were divided into three castes, who did not intermarry or interdine. He labeled these castes the White Jews (Paradesis), the Black Jews (Malabaris), and the Brown Jews—his label for the faction who were called *mshuchrarim* ("freed slaves"), associated with the Paradesi congregation and numbering only about thirty people. He stated: "This caste structure is as inviolate now as it ever has been. Despite the shoulder-to-shoulder proximity of the three classes in Jews' Street, there is almost no social intercourse among them".[13] His caste analysis was problematic on a number of ethnographic grounds. Having examined his 1937 fieldwork notes,[14] I am impressed by how much he learned in his short stay but also by how much he missed and how much he observed but left out of his analysis. To give just one example, in contradiction to the passage quoted above, his field notes and photographs contain specific examples of close everyday personal interactions—including interdining—between Jews he labeled as "White" and "Brown".

This short 1937 visit to Kochi comprised Mandelbaum's only field research on the Kerala Jews, though he published two more articles about them in the 1970s—by which time the vast majority of them were living in Israel, and ritual and social equality had been established among those who still remained in Kerala. His comprehensive 1975 article focused specifically on their social stratification.[15] It updated his 1939 analysis of Jewish life in Kochi only with information from a 1952 book by a South African rabbi who had visited Kerala for just three days,[16] and it included a section on the Kerala Jews in Israel based on ethnographic studies by other scholars. Unfortunately, this article (along with several others) had a negative impact on some Kochinim when it was translated into Hebrew a decade later as part of a commemorative volume celebrating the thirtieth anniversary of their *aliyah*, stirring up resentments about conflicts that had been left behind in India.[17]

In terms of Mandelbaum's scholarly impact, it is important to recognize his lasting influence on an academic paradigm—that the Indian caste system is central to understanding the Jews of Kerala. He became a recognized expert on Indian culture, a professor of anthropology at the University of California in Berkeley, and author of the two-volume textbook *Society in India.*[18] His work was cited by the noted French structuralist anthropologist Louis Dumont as the basis for Dumont's discussion of three "quasi-castes" of Cochin Jews; Mandelbaum was also cited in the work of J. B. Segal and Nathan Katz, whose influential books on the Kerala Jews likewise emphasized their internal division into three castes (Segal) or subcastes (Katz).[19]

Mandelbaum died in 1987 without engaging the emerging field of post-colonial South Asian anthropology, which called into question much of earlier anthropological theory on caste. This new approach criticized earlier scholars, epitomized by Dumont, who had seen ritually based hierarchy as the overwhelming principle governing Hindu society, as opposed to the individualism and equality that he took to be inherent in his own modern Western culture. In contrast, post-colonial theorists have stressed the flexibility and variety in Indian social organization and the importance of listening to indigenous self-descriptions rather than relying on theoretical models.

My first period of research on the Kerala Jews in the early 1970s was primarily historical, and I had no reason to question Mandelbaum's authority as an anthropologist.[20] During 1981–82, however—my first full year of ethnographic research in both India and Israel—I noticed that Kerala Jews themselves did not speak of their internal social factions as separate castes or *jatis.* I heard them referring to all Kerala Jews as the "Jewish *jati*" or caste, in contrast to "other *jati* people", such as Hindus and Christians in Kerala and Arabs in Israel. Some even referred to foreign Jews as "our caste people". The one time I directly asked a group of Paradesi friends if they considered Jews from other congregations in Kerala to belong to a different caste, they expressed shock at the question, answering that of course not, even if they are from a different community "they are Jews, and we are all part of the Jewish *jati*".

My anthropology dissertation[21] focused on Paradesi identity in India and Israel as grounded in their Kochi-synagogue-based *community*—a term they used constantly. Of course, I was a cultural anthropologist in training, so the theoretical section of my dissertation included plenty of pondering about the concept of *jati*, informed by the scholarship of the time. By then I was critical of Mandelbaum's analysis, but I did continue to draw on his research and that of Israeli scholar Naftali Bar-Giora.[22]

For various reasons, I'm relieved that I didn't publish my dissertation, but still I must acknowledge its influence on ensuing analysis by some other scholars. Both directly and indirectly it also affected the lives of Kerala Jews. Several of those who read the copies I sent to them expressed criticism, whether about what I wrote or what I left out.

Slavery

Let me now address two main points regarding slavery in this context. First, there is documentary evidence that Kerala Jews in the distant past had slaves. It is dangerous, however, for scholars to assume we know what this meant in concrete terms. There has been insufficient scholarly investigation into the nature of the slavery with which Kerala Jews were involved. Rather than assuming a model of slavery based on recent Western history or solely on Jewish custom and law, a thorough study would require examination of the various forms of servitude—both agrestic (land-based) and personal—that were practiced in South India. This would include research on ancient and medieval practices and on forms of slavery that were brought to South India by Arab traders, Portuguese merchants, and colonial settlers and bureaucrats.

Second, to understand slavery in relation to the Kerala Jews, it is important to recall the ruling by RaDBaZ and again in the nineteenth century by the Rishon LeZion of Jerusalem that—once properly converted and manumitted—"they should not be called slaves". In defiance of these rabbinic authorities the term and the category "freed slaves" prevailed as a signifier of discrimination among Kerala Jews down to the middle of the twentieth century, a hundred years after slavery had been outlawed in India. It was used as a catch-all term to include the descendants of not only slaves but also *yelide bayit* (children of Jewish men and servant women) and some, but not all, Indian converts to Judaism.

In my own experience with Kerala Jews over the past forty years, I learned that former practices of ritual and social discrimination had ended and that the term *mshuchrar* is not just impolite but demeaning. I can remember only once hearing a Paradesi use the epithet to refer to another Kerala Jewish person, and I could feel the edge in his remark. A Malabari friend told me that she was taught as a child not to "point the finger", meaning not to identify by name a person or family suspected to be of slave or convert ancestry. Despite this, foreigners continue to use the term in print to refer to particular individuals and families today. I did it myself in my 1985 dissertation, putting the term in quotation marks prefixed with the qualifier "so-called", as if that might make it less insulting. But it didn't. As one of my friends protested to me when he was publically labeled *mshuchrar* by an American scholar: "Do Americans call Martin Luther

King Jr. a freed slave?"

Dramatic nineteenth- and twentieth-century stories about the struggles for equality within the Paradesi community have been repeated in print by outsiders, over and again, with considerable inherent finger-pointing. Hebrew-language travelers' accounts in the 1860s and 1870s reported how a leader of the subordinate Paradesi group was thwarted in his attempt to form a separate Jewish congregation. In the 1930s his grandson, a prominent lawyer in the community, staged a series of non-violent protests to achieve ritual equality in the synagogue. In 1952, Rabinowitz repeated these stories—with the label "freed slaves" and with names of individuals who suffered that label long after slavery had been outlawed. Details from his account of the protests then entered the mainstream of Jewish Studies scholarship when they were cited extensively by Mandelbaum in his 1975 article, this time using the names of people he had not mentioned by name in his earlier publications.

I first read these stories of protest in the 1970s, influenced by my own experiences as a young white American woman during the US Civil Rights Movement and by my four years of residence in South India during the 1960s. I found the stories so compelling, so inspiring of resistance to oppression! Then, during dissertation fieldwork in India and Israel I became personally acquainted with relatives of A. B. Salem, the lawyer who had held the non-violent protests, and they talked freely to me about their own past experience of discrimination within the Paradesi community. I repeated the stories with further personal details in my dissertation, having carefully secured permission from people I was quoting.

Another relative I met was the late Ruby Daniel (1912–2002), who descended directly from a sister of A. B. Salem's grandfather. The female-centered account of the family history that she gave me was significantly different from that of the Salem family, so I incorporated her version along with others in the section of my dissertation that stressed the processes of social change that by this time had effectively ended the old Paradesi divisions. I intended this section to be positive. The following year Ruby Daniel informed me that she was going to write about the controversy herself. "For your information," she wrote in a letter, "a few months ago some of us sat down together…and decided that all that you wrote was bullshit. I am sorry for telling you the truth. But don't be discouraged. Get on."

She and I did get on together, producing her memoir *Ruby of Cochin: An Indian Jewish Woman Remembers*, published in 1995. She initiated this project, and it was written in her own words, which I arranged and edited through a collaborative process.[23] Among many other matters, Ruby

Daniel's book addressed the issue of discrimination against her ancestors, and she summarized decisively her own family's perspective: "We were never slaves, so we should not be called freed slaves." After the book was published, I encountered negative responses by some other friends in the Paradesi community, who resented my attention to these past conflicts. I was not eager to continue scholarly exploration in that area. In fact, I was relieved when Ruby Daniel suggested that we continue working together by concentrating on the Malayalam-language Jewish women's songs—shared by all communities of Kerala Jews—which have been the center of my research ever since.

My writing, teaching, and research are now explicitly based on the model that the internal social structure of the Jews in Kerala as a whole featured eight separate self-governing communities, traditionally called *yogams.* As with Jews elsewhere, social relations within each community and between different yogams have involved both rivalries and cooperation, but for the past half century the identities formerly labeled "Black", "White", and "*mshuchrar*" have had little or no practical social significance for the few Jews remaining in India or for the more than five thousand Kochinim living in Israel. Older Kochinim still preserve an attachment to their former local communities in Kerala and express pride in the positive heritage of their Indian ancestors. They are justifiably tired of outsiders reminding them over and over about past conflicts, and many feel misrepresented by this negative attention on just one aspect of their past.

I have tried a few times to directly confront—in academic presentations or articles—this misrepresentation and over-emphasis by Western scholars.[24] Recently some scholars have adjusted the "caste" or "subcaste" label to discuss "quasi-castes" or "caste-like divisions", though continuing to dwell on past social differences among the Kerala Jews, and in some cases continuing to apply derogatory labels to specific individuals.[25] Unfortunately such writings reach beyond the academic world to influence popular journalistic books, articles and online reports.[26]

In general, I have been content to turn my scholarly attention to the less-fraught yet rich and fascinating topic of the vernacular songs of Kerala Jewish women. So why, for the 2011 AJS conference paper on which this article is based, did I return to the issue of scholarship on historical social divisions among the Kerala Jews? My goal was not to berate myself or my fellow scholars for the unintended damage associated with our research; however, my own sense of mortality, along with increased self-determination as a scholar (which I suspect often comes with retirement), inspired by the influence of Marla Brettschneider, pushed me to acknowledge a responsibility to make my current analysis and critique available to newer and younger scholars wrestling with similar issues as they learn and write about Jewish communities in Africa and Asia. With that in mind, I appreciate the invitation to revise the conference paper for inclusion in this volume.

Works Cited

Ananthakrishna Iyer, L. K. *The Cochin Tribes and Castes,* Vol. 2. Madras: Higginbotham, 1912.

Dirks, Nicolas B. *Castes of Mind: Colonialism and the Making of Modern India*. Princeton, NJ: Princeton University Press, 2001; especially Chapter 9 ("The Body of Caste").

Bar-Giora, Naftali. "Source Materials for the History of Relations between the White Jews and the Black Jews of Cochin." *Sefunot*: *Annual for Research on the Jewish Communities of the East* 1 (1957): 243–78. Hebrew.

Daniel, Ruby, and Barbara C. Johnson. *Ruby of Cochin: An Indian Jewish Woman Remembers*. Philadelphia, PA: Jewish Publication Society, 1985.

Johnson, Barbara C. (Barbara Johnson Hudson), "Shingli or Jewish Cranganore in the Traditions of the Cochin Jews of India, with an appendix on The Cochin Jewish Chronicles" (master's thesis, Department of Religion, Smith College, 1975).

Johnson, Barbara C. "'Our Community' in Two Worlds: The Cochin Paradesi Jews in India and Israel" (PhD diss., University of Massachusetts, 1985).

Johnson, Barbara C. "The Cochin Jews of Kerala." In *The Jews of India: A Story of Three Communities,* edited by Orpa Slapak, 26–35. Jerusalem: The Israel Museum, 1995.

Johnson, Barbara C. "Jews of Kerala." In *Islam, Judaism, and Zoroastrianism. Encyclopedia of Indian Religions,* edited by Zayn R. Kassam, Yudit K. Greenberg , and Jehan Bagli. Dordrecht: Springer, 2018.

MacFarlane, Eileen W. E. "The Racial Affinities of the Jews of Cochin." *Journal of the Royal Asiatic Society of Bengal* 3, no. 1 (1937): 1–23.

Mandelbaum, David G. "The Jewish Way of Life in Cochin." *Jewish Social Studies* 1, no. 1 (1939): 423–60.

Mandelbaum, David G. "Social Stratification among the Jews of Cochin in India and Israel." *The Jewish Journal of Sociology* 17, no. 2 (1975): 165–210.

Mandelbaum, David G. Papers, BANC MSS 89/129 cz, The Bancroft

Library, University of California, Berkeley. Series 8, folder 36, 9/37-10/37.

Paiva, Mosseh Pereyra de. *Noticias Dos Judeos De Cochim*. Amsterdam: House of Vry Levy, 1687. Translated by F. Fegueiredo as "Saga of the Jews of Cochin." In *Cochin Synagogue Quatercentenary Celebrations Souvenir*, edited by S. S. Koder, 31–50. Ernakulam: Thilakam Press, 1968.

Parfitt, Tudor. "'Descended from Jewish Seed': Genetics and Jewish History in India: The Bene Israel and the Black Jews of Cochin." *Journal of Indo-Judaic Studies* 6 (2003): 11–18.

Rabinowitz, Louis. *Far East Mission*. Johannesburg: Eagle Press, 1952.

Schorsch, Jonathan. *Jews and Blacks in the Early Modern World*. New York, NY: Cambridge University Press, 2004; especially 204–13.

Segal, J. B. *A History of the Jews of Cochin*. London: Vallentine Mitchell, 1993.

Silva Tavim, José Alberto Rodrigues da. "Une présence portugaise autour de la 'nouvelle synagogue' de Cochin." In *Les Juifs Portugais: Exil Héritage Perspectives 1496-1996*, edited by Aldina da Silva, André Myre, and Tereza Pinto, 67-81. Montréal, QC: Médiaspaul, 1996. French.

Visscher, Jacob C. cited in Walter Fischel, "Exploration of the Jewish Antiquities of Cochin on the Malabar Coast," *Journal of the American Oriental Society* 87, no. 3 (1967): 235.

Weil, Shalva, ed. *Mikotzin l'eretz Israel* (From Cochin to the Land of Israel). Jerusalem: *Kumu B'rinah*, 1984. Hebrew.

Notes

[1] A note on confusing place names and spellings: "Kerala" is the name of a state in modern India, created in 1956 by combining the Malayalam-speaking regions on the southwest coast, primarily the kingdoms formerly called "Cochin" and "Travancore". In 1996 the English spelling of Cochin was officially changed to Kochi. For centuries the Jews of the region were called "Cochin Jews" because most of them lived in the kingdom of Cochin (Kochi), and when they arrived in Israel during the 1950s, they were called "Kochinim" in Hebrew—an ethnic label that they now use themselves. "Kochi", however, is the name of an important city as well as the former kingdom, and because only three of the eight Jewish communities lived in that city many find the term "Kerala Jews" to be more inclusive.

[2] J. B. Segal, *A History of the Jews of Cochin* (London: Vallentine Mitchell, 1993), 21–22.

[3] For a more detailed overview see: Barbara C. Johnson, "Jews of Kerala." In *Islam, Judaism, and Zoroastrianism. Encyclopedia of Indian Religions,* edited by Zayn R.

Kassam, Yudit K. Greenberg, and Jehan Bagli. Dordrecht: Springer, 2018. Also see Barbara C. Johnson, "The Cochin Jews of Kerala," in *The Jews of India: A Story of Three Communities,* ed. Orpa Slapak (Jerusalem: The Israel Museum, 1995), 26–35.
[4] José Alberto Rodrigues da Silva Tavim, "Une présence portugaise autour de la 'nouvelle synagogue' de Cochin," in *Les Juifs Portugais: Exil Héritage Perspectives 1496-1996*, eds. Aldina da Silva et al. (Montréal: Médiaspaul, 1996), 67–81, French. This "New Synagogue" was the Kadavumbhagam-Kochi Palli, the wooden interior of which can now be viewed in the Israel Museum in Jerusalem.
[5] Mosseh Pereyra de Paiva, *Noticias Dos Judeos De Cochim* (Amsterdam: House of Vry Levy, 1687) trans. F. Fegueiredo, ed. S. S. Koder, "Saga of the Jews of Cochin." In *Cochin Synagogue Quatercentenary Celebrations Souvenir* (Ernakulam: Thilakam Press, 1968), 31–50.
[6] Jacob C. Visscher, *Letters from Malabar* (1723) cited in Walter Fischel, "Exploration of the Jewish Antiquities of Cochin on the Malabar Coast," *Journal of the American Oriental Society* 87, no. 3 (1967): 235.
[7] Jonathan Schorsch, *Jews and Blacks in the Early Modern World* (New York, NY: Cambridge University Press, 2004), especially 204–13.
[8] See Nicolas B. Dirks, *Castes of Mind: Colonialism and the Making of Modern India* (Princeton, NJ: Princeton University Press, 2001), especially Chapter 9 ("The Body of Caste"). For anthropometric measurements of Jews in Kerala see L. K. Ananthakrishna Iyer, *The Cochin Tribes and Castes,* Vol. 2 (Madras: Higginbotham, 1912), 431.
[9] Eileen W. E. MacFarlane, "The Racial Affinities of the Jews of Cochin," *Journal of the Royal Asiatic Society of Bengal* 3, no. 1 (1937): 1–23.
[10] David G. Mandelbaum, "The Jewish Way of Life in Cochin," *Jewish Social Studies* 1, no. 1 (1939): 423–60.
[11] David G. Mandelbaum, "Social Stratification among the Jews of Cochin in India and Israel," *The Jewish Journal of Sociology,* 17, no. 2 (1975): 165–210.
[12] Alexander Marx, "Contribution à l'histoire des Juifs de Cochin," *Revue des Études Juives* 89 (1930): 299, French. An English translation of the Hebrew *responsum* is found in Segal, *Jews of Cochin*, 24–25.
[13] Mandelbaum, "The Jewish Way," 447.
[14] David Goodman Mandelbaum papers, BANC MSS 89/129 cz, The Bancroft Library, University of California, Berkeley. Series 8, folder 36, 9/37-10/37.
[15] Mandelbaum, "Social Stratification," 19.
[16] Louis Rabinowitz, *Far East Mission* (Johannesburg: Eagle Press, 1952).
[17] Shalva Weil, ed., *Mikotzin l'eretz Israel* (From Cochin to the Land of Israel) (Jerusalem: *Kumu B'rinah*, 1984), 60–91, Hebrew.
[18] David G. Mandelbaum, *Society in India* (Berkeley, CA: University of California Press, 1970).
[19] Louis Dumont, *Homo Hierarchicus* (Chicago: University of Chicago, 1970), 328. Segal, *Jews of Cochin.* Nathan Katz and Ellen S. Goldberg, *The Last Jews of Cochin: Jewish Identity in Hindu India* (Columbia, SC: University of South Carolina Press: 1993). Katz, *Who Are the Jews of India?* (Berkeley, CA: University of California Press, 2000), 59–69.
[20] Barbara C. Johnson (Barbara Johnson Hudson), "Shingli or Jewish Cranganore in

the Traditions of the Cochin Jews of India, with an appendix on The Cochin Jewish Chronicles" (master's thesis, Department of Religion, Smith College, 1975).

[21] Barbara C. Johnson. "'Our Community' in Two Worlds: The Cochin Paradesi Jews in India and Israel" (PhD diss., University of Massachusetts, 1985).

[22] Naftali Bar-Giora, "Source Materials for the History of Relations between the White Jews and the Black Jews of Cochin," *Sefunot*: *Annual for Research on the Jewish Communities of the East* 1 (1957): 243–78, Hebrew.

[23] Ruby Daniel and Barbara C. Johnson, *Ruby of Cochin: An Indian Jewish Woman Remembers* (Philadelphia, PA: Jewish Publication Society, 1985).

[24] Barbara C. Johnson, "Caste in the Ethnohistory of the Cochin Jews: A Reconsideration," paper presented at the 11th World Congress of Jewish Studies, Jerusalem, 1993. More recently, Barbara C. Johnson, "New Research, Discoveries and Paradigms: A Report on the Current Study of Kerala Jews," in *Indo-Judaic Studies in the Twenty-first Century: A View from the Margin,* eds. Nathan Katz et al. (New York, NY: Palgrave Macmillan, 2007), 129–46.

[25] To give one example, Tudor Parfitt devoted half of a short article about genetic testing of Indian Jews to a discussion of what he called the "obscure" history of "the mysterious Black Jewish community of Cochin", reiterating misinformation from outdated literature by Mandelbaum, Segal, and Bar Giora about "the stratification of Cochin Jewry" into three distinct and unequal groups—also stating incorrectly that "the old divisions between White, Black and meshuhararim" are still maintained in Israel today. Parfitt, "'Descended from Jewish Seed': Genetics and Jewish History in India: The Bene Israel and the Black Jews of Cochin," *Journal of Indo-Judaic Studies* 6 (2003): 11–18.

[26] See, for example, this current *Encyclopedia Britannica* article online (s.v. "Cochin Jews"): https://www.britannica.com/topic/Cochin-Jews.

PART TWO:

ISLANDS AND "INSULARITY"

CHAPTER FIVE

ANTI-COLONIALISM AND JEWISH WOMEN IN MADAGASCAR

MARLA BRETTSCHNEIDER

> "The soul is the effect and instrument of a political anatomy; the soul is the prison of the body."
> —Michel Foucault, *Discipline and Punish: The Birth of the Prison*

Introduction[1]

A number of academics have posited that the Jewish phenomenon sweeping across sub-Saharan Africa today is part of a long process of throwing off the yoke of colonialism. Yet, often when I have questioned male leaders of communities on the ground these men have not agreed and they have been rather offended at this apparently "imposed" Global Northern, academic analysis. Many men in these communities with whom I have worked have also shied away from discussing the history of European Christian missionizing in their regions in political terms and as part of the trajectory of their Jewish development. At the same time, almost no Global Northern academics have worked with groups of women in sub-Saharan Jewish and Jewish-related communities.[2] In Antananarivo, Madagascar, the women with whom I met in 2016 in three communities began our conversations by grounding their experience in a history of colonialism and continued to discuss their circumstances specifically within this context. Additionally, Malagasy Jewish women's politically radical perspective instantiates Michel Foucault's important insight that the soul is the prison of the body.

A common conceptualization from Christianity is the bifurcation of human existence into body and soul.[3] Historically, Christian theology rendered the soul eternal and imprisoned within the decaying body. This view grew from and enabled relations of power that particularly targeted certain groups as inferior, associated with the despised body, and subjugated. Women, Jews, those differently abled, and Africans (including those of African descent following the Atlantic slave trade, and those in multiple abject categories) have been primary targets in such systems of power. In this chapter, I discuss the origins of Malagasy Jewish life as described by groups of women in the capital city Antananarivo. I will analyze these women's accounts of their experiences and connect them to concrete statistics of life in Madagascar in terms of politics, economics, and gendered power dynamics.

Malagasy Jewish women's continued assertion that Christian missionizing was an oppressive tool of European colonialism will make sense in this gendered, political, and economic rendering. Interestingly, Malagasy Jewish women's self-conceptualizations and analysis of their positionality in global power dynamics, particularly in relation to processes of European Christian colonizing and missionizing, echoes Foucault's conceptualization that in the modern Christian West the soul is the prison of the body—and not the reverse, as is commonly asserted. I realize that the following discussion is open to criticism. It is legitimate to critique my making sense of Malagasy Jewish women's anti-colonialism via a discussion of the work of a white French man raised in an upper-middle-class Christian family.[4] At the same time, Foucault's anti-foundationalist politics have helped Western academics, such as myself, think against the grain of Western modernism and its Christian roots and provides an opening for Western scholars to productively engage with Malagasy Jewish women.

Malagasy Jewish History

During the twentieth century, Christianity and Islam spread rampantly throughout the sub-Saharan region. From 1900 to 2010, the number of Christians in sub-Saharan Africa rose by a remarkable 48%, making Christianity the dominant religion in the region. This surge was due to a history of European Christian missionizing that was part of colonizing processes and a central mechanism of the Atlantic slave trade. Notably, as formal European colonization drew to a close around the 1950s, Christian missionizing as a regime of control in the region increased. In large part as a response to this mid-century development, Islam also grew to incorporate 29% of the population in 2010.[5]

At the same time, Madagascar is one of the few countries in sub-Saharan African that already had a substantial Christian following by the turn of the twentieth century. Traditional non-Christian African religions, which Global Northern academics call "ethnoreligions", were still dominant at that time, but tremendous Christian missionary efforts dating from the end of formal French colonial rule changed this landscape profoundly. Today, over

60% of the Malagasy population practices Christianity, while only 36% practices an ethnoreligion.[6]

Due to tremendous European imperialist pressure, Malagasy leaders allowed missionaries into the country in the early 1800s. Malagasy leaders were navigating power relations with England and France, and one of their compromises was to lessen their resistance to missionizing. Throughout the century, the tousle of growing and violent European control with local attempts to resist such incursions and protect Malagasy traditions led different rulers to either endorse or renounce Christianity.[7] This was the case long before formal French colonization. Also of note is the fact that the Christian Bible was the first printed text in the Malagasy language, as technology and missionizing were used as multiple prongs of systems engaging locals in networks of control in colonial history. This account of the growing presence of Christianity, however, does not describe the complexity of the picture according to Malagasies. Many Malagasies also describe themselves as Israelite or Jewish.

Mamy members of the 2016 newly converted Jewish communities tell the following story: There were different waves of migration from ancient Israel to Madagascar. One group journeyed through Asia and came from Beit Yehuda. The royal line in Madagascar has often claimed its descendants from this migration. This is the most ancient wave, coming with the Israelites who were forced into diaspora when Nebuchadnezzar took over Judea and Jerusalem. Thus, descendants of the royal line often refer to themselves in contemporary language as Jews (from the tribe of Judah).[8] Another migration went through Africa. The story of this migration is rooted in the story of the offspring from the union of the biblical King Solomon and the Queen of Sheba. The third major wave of Jews came from Medina after fleeing in connection with the rise of Islam.[9]

Many in Madagascar claim their heritage hails from these migrations from ancient Israel, while most would say that now they are Christians, and occasionally some of them identify as Muslim. Others report that their families joined a church for public reasons of safety; at home they still practiced their traditional ways, which they understand as rooted in ancient Israel. Finally, there are those who explain that their families never gave in to European forcible conversion campaigns. Additionally, some regions in Madagascar are known to have been less impacted by Christian missionizing work. Many from these regions relate that they are Jewish, or Israelites, as they have been from ancient days. Given this multi-faceted origin story, there are many Malagasy people who say that they are Jewish and do not need any formal "return" or conversion ceremony, especially if such rituals are run by people from the Global North, long aligned with colonizers.[10]

Gender and Life Status Issues in Madagascar

Life in Madagascar is very difficult for most people. This affects all those involved in Jewish developments. In the capital city, Antananarivo, the streets are congested and public transportation is not easily accessible. Because of this, it takes a long time to travel even short distances. This is a challenge for the members of all the communities involved in the 2016 conversions.

Numerous broader economic and political difficulties further complicate Jewish communal participation in Madagascar; for example, comparatively, GDP (gross domestic product) growth is slow and the GNI (gross national income) low. A staggering estimated 70.7% of the country's population is living below the poverty line.[11] Given such extreme poverty levels, many Jewish community members cannot easily contribute financially to the growth and needs of their community or to their individual Jewish aspirations. Similarly, a violent history of colonialism and the ongoing struggle of the country to emerge as actually independent in a post-colonial global climate continue to hamper the basic rights and civil liberties of Madagascar's citizens. The political situation and barriers to civil liberties make it challenging for new communities to emerge and thrive.[12]

The situation for women in Madagascar is even more difficult. Women are actively involved in Jewish life in Madagascar. They are engaged learners and take responsibility for numerous significant communal tasks, such as providing food for gatherings and taking care of children. However, men are the formal leaders in the communities that recently converted. The gender situation in these new communities is familiar to their members. Jewish women in Madagascar are both empowered and constrained in many ways that relate directly to the situation of women in the country more broadly.

Regional gender comparisons show some areas in which Madagascar fares relatively well. Madagascar became formally independent from French colonial power in 1960. As of 1959, women gained the right to vote in Madagascar,[13] and there are comparative advantages for Malagasy women in terms of literacy,[14] life expectancy at birth,[15] and contraception availability.[16]

As well as these advantages, Malagasy women also face significant challenges with gender differentials. Comparatively, they have low representation rates in politics,[17] tend to marry early,[18] are disadvantaged in inheritance laws,[19] are at risk for human trafficking, [20] face significant obstacles in reproductive justice,[21] and have higher levels of rape, abuse, and HIV/AIDS-related deaths.[22] This level of gender disparity both mirrors and contributes to other aspects of gender-based inequality in the country and forms the contours of the Jewish women's agency.

The financial challenges faced by most Malagasies hurt women disproportionately. In Madagascar, where there is much poverty overall, gender income equality within professional and technical fields is relatively high compared to that in other countries surveyed globally. However, Madagascar fares worse on other indicators of gender income equality.[23] The often extreme poverty, inequality, and obstacles to agency and bodily integrity that Malagasy Jewish women face is best understood in a political context as part of the long-term impact of a history of European colonialism. The women with whom I interacted in May 2016 spoke concretely of the role of Christian missionizing activity as part of this history of oppression.

Malagasy Jewish Women's Anti-Colonialism

From my first meeting with small groups of Malagasy Jewish women in 2016, my interlocutors spoke of their lives in the context of the history of colonialism. During the course of conversations over several days, different women delved deeper into analyzing their circumstances. Keenly concerned with their history of oppression, the groups of women with whom I spoke pointed directly to violent processes of colonialism. Christian missionizing was prime among the colonial processes they noted.

The groups of Malagasy Jewish women with whom I spoke discussed European Christian missionizing as a concrete set of practices wielded deliberately to squelch the power and independence of Malagasies during and following formal colonization. These women understood colonization as continuing in less formal modes after the changes that marked its official end. They discussed their interest in becoming Jews, or in embracing their existent Jewishness more formally, as part of the long history of their people's resistance to global oppression. In their varied Jewish studies and practices, they are disrupting the continued repetition of their oppression through interruption of the repetition of Christian practices.

These women also spoke eloquently of their understanding of the role of religious resistance to the materiality of European colonial Christian oppression. They described European Christian spirituality as working on their material bodies within complex systems of oppression. In (re-)claiming their Jewishness, they saw themselves as jettisoning these nuanced aspects of European Christian colonization of their bodies. Throughout, Malagasy Jewish women expressed their anti-colonialism with an incisive analysis of the dynamics of colonial oppression. These women were clear on the radical transformative potential of their movement (back) to Judaism. As much as this move towards Jewishness was part of their anti-colonial journey, cracks in the apparently seamless logic of Jesus as savior and Christianity as salvation also contributed to their decision. Simultaneously, however, their anti-colonial politics nourished their daily efforts to live Jewish lives.

Concrete practices of rejecting the Christian New Testament and a Sunday Sabbath are part of these women's active anti-colonialism. As practiced, Christianity in Madagascar often merges with various historical non-Christian traditions; this merging became common throughout sub-Saharan Africa in the wake of Christian missionizing. In expressly exploring Jewish frames and inspiration in their spiritual quests, Madagascar's Jewish women take another step away from the legacy of colonial persecution, which imposed Christian frameworks. In their public and private embrace of Judaism, Jewish women in Madagascar seek to free themselves, bodies and souls, and their communities, from a history of violent abuse.

In an interesting way, Malagasy Jewish women's critical political analysis and plans to fulfill their spiritual desires on individual and communal levels seem a concrete example of Michel Foucault's theory on the power regimes of body and soul in European Christian history. The Malagasy Jewish women with whom I spoke never mentioned Foucault or his ideas. Few women or men in these communities have had a university education or opportunities for advanced secular study. There is a poignant irony in their connection to the theory of this white French male philosopher who sought to dismantle patriarchal European Christian power regimes through his academic work.

Malagasy Jewish Women's Anti-Colonialism: Foucault and the Break from Christianity's Prison-Soul Dynamic

The notion of a "soul" is central to most Christian theology, which often juxtaposes this creation, "the soul", to "the body" as a parallel and constitutive creation. For much of history, Christians have understood the mortal vessel of the body as imprisoning the immortal soul. This worldview regards temptations of the flesh as obstacles to the purity of the soul. The soaring, free soul must transcend its despised, quotidian, material cage. All people need to eschew their bodily prison in pursuit of the potential glory of an untainted soul. This idea, key to much of Christian theology, has oppressed and justified the oppression of many groups and individuals, particularly those understood by elites as more tightly bound to the body, or more susceptible to bodily soiling, than others: those differently abled so that their bodies are imagined as their destiny, women conceptualized in binary opposition to a group called men, Jews and non-Christians as opposed to Christians, Africans and other non-white skinned peoples compared to lighter skinned Christian Europeans, and combinations of these groupings.

In a significant turn, French philosopher Michel Foucault re-signified this relationship between a so-called body and a so-called soul. Foucault writes: "But let there be no misunderstanding: it is not that a real man, the object of knowledge, philosophical reflection or technological intervention, has been substituted for the soul, the illusion of theologians". Founcault continues: "The man described for us, whom we are invited to free, is already in himself the effect of a subjection more profound than himself. A 'soul' inhabits him and brings him to existence, which is itself a factor in the mastery that power exercises over the body. The soul is the effect and instrument of a political anatomy; the soul is the prison of the body".[24]

Judith Butler (1989) analyzes the ways in which Foucault argues that the body is constituted by power regimes. Foucault determines that the individual emerges as a result of strategies and practices of individualization to which the person is subjected. From such individuation emerges the soul (Montag 1995). Malagasy Jewish women's critical rendering of the Christian theology of a soul, over and against a body, similarly de-stabilizes these relations of power. A violent, required Christianity creates the body as abject and simultaneously inscribes these power regimes on the body in its materiality. The power regimes of European colonization master, discipline, and punish the colonized. This colonization relies on Christian missionizing.

Malagasy Jewish women seek to live beyond the confines of the disciplining, co-constructed regimes of European colonization and Christianity. They desire to free themselves of these violent power regimes. Jewishness presents a significant opportunity for freedom. The popular Israelite origin stories of Madagascar make Jewishness a recognizable status. It also has the benefit of being nearly unintelligible in contemporary Christian-dominant Madagascar. Butler[25] writes that Foucault "seems to find the seeds of transformation in the life of a passion that lives and thrives at the borders of recognizability, which still has the limited freedom of not yet being false or true, which establishes a critical distance on the terms that decide our being".

With these insights, we can further appreciate the radically transformative power of Malagasy Jewish women's intense and critical Jewish anti-colonialism. The groups of women engaged in building the Jewish communities of Madagascar today are practicing a deep and insistent anti-colonialism. Their Jewishness is steeped in the collective self-understanding of Madagascar as part of ancient Israelite history. At the same time, the current forms of the Jewish communities of Antananarivo mark a new phase in the passionate spiritual and communal quest of these women. These women's spiritual and communal quest has taken new turns in the Jewish communities of Antananarivo. Over time, we will see in what ways these women's brilliant resistance to the continued legacy of European colonialism determines the contours of their freedom as they break the chain of colonial Christian formations as well as re-claim and create Jewish forms.

Works Cited

Belser, Julia Watts. "Returning to Flesh: A Jewish Reflection on Feminist Disability Theology." *Journal of Feminist Studies in Religion* 26, no. 2 (2010): 127–32.

Berkowitz, Adam Eliyahu. "100 Members of 'Lost' Jewish Community of Madagascar Enter Covenant of Abraham." *Breaking Israel News*, May 30, 2016. Accessed December 16, 2016. https://www.breakingisraelnews.com/68765/100-members-of-lost-jewish-community-of-madagascar-enter-covenant-of-abraham-05-16/#1AXjdPJRorby8ifj.97.

Bruder, Edith. *The Black Jews of Africa: History, Religion, Identity*. New York, NY: Oxford University Press, 2008.

Butler, Judith. 1989. "Foucault and the Paradox of Bodily Inscriptions." *The Journal of Philosophy* 86, no. 11 (November 1989): 601–7. http://www.jstor.org/stable/2027036.

Butler, Judith. "Bodies and Power Revisited." In *Feminism and the Final Foucault*, edited by Dianna Taylor and Karen Vintges, 183–94. Urbana and Chicago, IL: University of Illinois Press, 2004.

Devir, Nathan. "Origins and Motivations of Madagascar's Normative Jewish Movement." In *Becoming Jewish: New Jews and Emerging Jewish Communities in a Globalized World*, edited by Netanel Fisher and Tudor Parfitt, 49–63. Newcastle upon Tyne: Cambridge Scholars Publishing, 2016.

Devir, Nathan. "Propagating Modern Jewish Identity in Madagascar: A Contextual Analysis of One Community's Discursive Strategies." In *Connected Jews: Expressions of Community in Analogue and Digital*

Culture, edited by Caspar Battegay, Simon J. Bronner, and Andrea Lieber. Oxford: The Littman Library of Jewish Civilization, forthcoming 2018.

Foucault, Michael. *Discipline & Punish: The Birth of the Prison*. Translated by by Alan Sheridan. New York, NY: Vintage Books, 1995.

Freedom House. *Freedom in the World 2015: Discarding Democracy: Return to the Iron Fist*. Washington, DC: Freedom House, 2015. https://freedomhouse.org/sites/default/files/01152015_FIW_2015_final.pdf.

Grenn-Scott, Deborah. "For She Is a Tree of Life: Shared Roots Connecting Women to Deity—An Organic Theological Inquiry into Identities, Beliefs and Practices Among South African Lemba and European American Jewish Women." Doctoral dissertation, California Institute of Integral Studies, 2003.

Inter-Parliamentary Union. *Women in Parliament: 20 Years in Review*. Geneva, Switzerland: Inter-Parliamentary Union, 2015. http://www.ipu.org/pdf/publications/WIP20Y-en.pdf.

Josefson, Deborah. "In remote Madagascar, a new community chooses to be Jewish." *The Times of Israel*, June 6, 2016. Accessed December 16, 2016. http://www.timesofisrael.com/in-remote-madagascar-a-new-community-chooses-to-be-jewish/.

King, Angela. "The Prisoner of Gender: Foucault and the Disciplining of the Female Body." *Journal of International Women's Studies* 5, no. 2 (2004): 29–39.

Miles, William F. S. "The Secrets of the Malagasy Jews of Madagascar." *The Jerusalem Post*, September 26, 2015. Accessed December 16, 2016. http://www.jpost.com/Jerusalem-Report/The-Malagasy-secret-415164.

Montag, Warren. "'The Soul Is the Prison of the Body': Althusser and Foucault, 1970-1975." *Yale French Studies*, no. 88 (1995): 53–77.

Parfitt, Tudor. *Black Jews in Africa and the Americas*. Cambridge, MA: Harvard University Press, 2012.

Pew Research Center. "Tolerance and Tension: Islam and Christianity in Sub-Saharan Africa." *Pew Research Center*, April 15, 2010. Accessed July 24, 2017. http://www.pewforum.org/2010/04/15/executive-summary-islam-and-christianity-in-sub-saharan-africa/.

Terry, Peter (Yakov Zamir). "Gan Eden Rediscovered." Kulanu, 2014. Accessed December 16, 2016. http://kulanu.org/communities/madagascar/gan-eden-rediscovered/.

UNdata. "Contraceptive prevalence, any methods (% of women ages 15-49)." United Nations Statistics Division, 2016. Accessed October 1, 2016.

http://data.un.org/Data.aspx?d=WDI&f=Indicator_Code%3ASP.DYN.CONU.ZS.

United Nations. *World Abortion Policies 2013*. New York, NY: Department of Economic and Social Affairs, Population Division, 2013. http://www.un.org/en/development/desa/population/publications/pdf/policy/WorldAbortionPolicies2013/WorldAbortionPolicies2013_WallChart.pdf.

US State Department. *Trafficking in Persons Report July 2015*. Washington, DC: US State Department, 2015. Accessed July 26, 2017. https://www.state.gov/documents/organization/245365.pdf.

US State Department. *2010 Human Rights Report: Madagascar*. Washington, DC: Bureau of Democracy, Human Rights and Labor, 2010. Accessed July 26, 2017. https://www.state.gov/documents/organization/160130.pdf.

Women Suffrage and Beyond. 2015. "Africa." Accessed June 28, 2016. http://womensuffrage.org/?page_id=203#.

World Bank (a). "GNI per capita, Atlas method (current US$): Madagascar." n.d. Accessed July 26, 2017. http://data.worldbank.org/indicator/NY.GNP.PCAP.CD?locations=MG.

World Bank (b). "GNI per capita, Atlas method (current US$): Sub-Saharan Africa, Excluding high income." n.d. Accessed July 26, 2017. http://data.worldbank.org/indicator/NY.GNP.PCAP.CD?locations=ZF.

World Bank (c). "Literacy rate, adult female (% of females ages 15 and above): Madagascar." n.d. Accessed July 26, 2017. http://data.worldbank.org/indicator/SE.ADT.LITR.FE.ZS?locations=MG.

World Bank (d). "Literacy rate, adult female (% of females ages 15 and above): Sub-Saharan Africa, excluding high income." n.d. Accessed July 26, 2017. http://data.worldbank.org/indicator/SE.ADT.LITR.FE.ZS?locations=ZF.

World Bank (e). "Life expectancy at birth, female (years): All countries and economies." n.d. Accessed July 26, 2017. http://data.worldbank.org/indicator/SP.DYN.LE00.FE.IN?view=chart.

World Economic Forum. *The Global Gender Gap Report 2014*. Geneva, Switzerland: World Economic Forum, 2014. Accessed July 26, 2017. http://www3.weforum.org/docs/GGGR14/GGGR_CompleteReport_2014.pdf.

World Economic Forum. *The Global Gender Gap Report 2015*. Geneva, Switzerland: World Economic Forum, 2015. Accessed June 28, 2016. http://www3.weforum.org/docs/GGGR2015/cover.pdf.

World Factbook. "Madagascar: Economy: Population Below Poverty Line." Washington, DC: Central Intelligence Agency, 2017. Accessed

July 26, 2017. https://www.cia.gov/library/publications/the-world-factbook/geos/ma.html.

Johnson, Todd M., and Brian J. Grim, eds. *World Religion Database: International religious demographic statistics and sources*. n.d. Accessed October 1, 2016. http://www.worldreligiondatabase.org.libproxy.unh.edu/wrd_default.asp.

Notes

[1] I would like to thank particularly Elysha Netsarh and Ahava/Randrianaivoson Lazanirainy of the Malagasy Jewish community. Rabbi Bonita Nathan Sussman made these visits possible. Nathan Sussman organized through a US-based Jewish organization, Kulanu, an option for formal conversion to Judaism within this community. Gratitude to Elisabeth Lohmueller for research assistance. Appreciations to Walter Isaac for the opportunity to present a version of this work in progress at the Afro-Jewish Studies Association Conference in Manhattan 2017 and to Nathan Devir for the same opportunity at the Association for the Study of the Middle East and Africa 2017.

[2] Grenn-Scott 2003 is a helpful exception.

[3] See Belser 2010 for a helpful Jewish analysis.

[4] Also, see a gender-based feminist critique of Foucault relevant here: King 2004.

[5] According to the Pew Research Center (2010), the sub-Saharan region generally was 9% Christian in 1900. By 1950, the number of Christians represented roughly 26% of the population, and by 1970 this population had grown to 49% of the region. By 2010, 57% of the sub-Saharan population, or approximately 470 million people, were practicing Christianity. Islam has also risen in sub-Saharan Africa, though to a lesser extent. In the last century, the number of Muslims has grown twenty-fold, reaching 234 million and comprising 29% of the total population in 2010.

[6] The percentage of Christians in Madagascar has risen from 39% in 1900 to 58% in 2015. The percentage of Muslims in Madagascar has risen slightly from less than 1% in 1900 to 2.1% in 2015. Conversely, the percentage of those practicing what are referred to in this database as "ethnoreligions" has decreased from 60% in 1900 to 39% in 2015 (World Religion Database).

[7] This was the case even in the rule of one significant Malagasy Queen: Ranavalona Ist, (1828–1861). She allowed missionaries into Madagascar but later reversed her position and became an important example of Malagasy (and Malagasy women's) anti-colonialism. Thank you to Elysha Netsarh for our exchange on this matter. Randrianaivoson/Ahava Lazanirainy also noted this Malagasy queen, as well as Gisele Rabesahala, as a significant inspiration for Malagasy women's anti-colonialism; the latter was a freedom leader during Madascar's movement for independence in the 1950s.

[8] For example, a popular news feature (Josefson 2016) reported: "Prince Ndexriana Rabarioelina, a descendant of the Merina monarchy of Madagascar, proudly asserts

Jewish ancestry. He told JTA that up to 80% of Malagasies can claim Jewish roots. He asserts that portions of the tablets, Moses's rod and a copy of the Book of Daniel are safeguarded by descendants of Levites in the Vatamasina-Vohipeno region of Madagascar."

[9] The story that I heard many times from members of the three communities that gathered in May 2016 is most closely represented in this accounting in Peter Terry's (Yakov Zamir) (2014) "Gan Eden Rediscovered". Berkowitz (2016) and Miles (2015) offer various other accountings. See also Parfitt (2012), Bruder (2008), and the resources at http://www.kulanu.org/madagascar/index.php. Nathan Devir (2016; 2018) has done much research, in addition to his contribution to this volume (which suggests there may be something unique in Madagascar's anti-colonialism). Malagasies often place biblical texts alongside understandings of waves of immigration to the island as a proof of this historical understanding.

[10] In addition to the ancient narrative, any Jewish exploration of Madagascar should also note a twentieth-century feature that came to be known as the Madagascar Plan. During World War II, Franz Rademacher, head of the Jewish Department of the German Ministry of Foreign Affairs in 1940, proposed relocating European Jews to Madagascar as one of the territorial solutions to what was considered "the Jewish question". At that time, Madagascar was a French colony. As part of France's surrender agreement with Germany, Madagascar was to be transferred to German rule. Hitler approved the plan, and in August of 1940 Adolf Eichmann issued a memorandum declaring a resettlement of 1 million European Jews per year to Madagascar for the following four years. Madagascar would be run as a police state governed by the SS (the Schutzstaffel or Protection Squadron, a key paramilitary group of the Nazi regime). Nazis believed that European Jews would not survive the local conditions in Madagascar, and thus the Madagascar territorial plan was part of a broader developing Nazi genocidal program against Jews. The plan was not actualized. It was eventually thwarted by a British naval blockade in September of 1940. By 1942, the Nazis had lost control of Madagascar and abandoned the plan in favor of alternative initiatives for their genocide of European Jewry.

[11] The GDP growth of Madagascar was forecast as at a slower rate than the sub-Saharan Africa region generally, and the GNI per capita was significantly lower than the regional average (World Bank n.d.-a and b).

[12] Freedom House rates Madagascar, along with eighteen other countries in sub-Saharan Africa, as "Partly Free"; twenty-one countries in the region are designated as "Not Free," and ten countries are "Free" (Freedom House 2015, 24).

[13] Women Suffrage and Beyond 2015.

[14] The adult literacy rate for women in Madagascar is slightly higher than that for other developing countries in the sub-Saharan African region; the rate for females aged 15 and older was 61.6% in 2009 (World Bank n.d.-c). In 2010 it was 53% for the sub-Saharan Africa region (developing countries only) (World Bank n.d.-d).

[15] The life expectancy of females at birth is as follows for the year 2014: 84.1 years of age in Israel, 81.4 in the United States, and 66.6 in Madagascar, although it was 59.9 in other developing countries in the sub-Saharan African region and 59.3 in South Africa (World Bank n.d.-e).

[16] According to the United Nations Statistics Division, the contraception prevalence

rate among women ages 15–49 for Madagascar was 39.8% in 2009, while sub-Saharan Africa more broadly had a rate of 23.6% in 2011 (UNdata 2016).

[17] Women make up only a small percentage of the members of both the lower and upper houses of parliament (Inter-Parliamentary Union 2015, 16), and in this respect Madagascar is ranked 73 out of 145 countries and has a score of .26 out of 1.00, with a sample average as .27 out of 1.00 (World Economic Forum 2015, 63). Regarding gender equality at the legislative, senior official, and managerial level, Madagascar is ranked 86 out of 145 countries; it has a score of .33 out of 1.00, while the average for the sample is .27 (World Economic Forum 2015, 55).

[18] (World Economic Forum 2015, 243).

[19] Widows with children can inherit half of the marital property, although the husband's surviving kin take priority over a widow without children (US State Department 2010, 21).

[20] Madagascar is on Tier 2 for sex/human trafficking, according to the US State Department (US State Department 2015, 47 and 54). A Tier 2 designation means that the number of victims of severe forms of trafficking is significant or is increasing significantly and the country has not provided evidence that it has ramped up its efforts to combat the problem in the past year. Examples of other countries in sub-Saharan Africa which are on Tier 2 are: Cameroon, South Africa, Gabon, and Côte D'Ivoire (US State Department 2015, 54). According to the US State Department, "Most child sex trafficking occurs with the involvement of family members, but friends, transport operators, tour guides, and hotel workers also facilitate the trafficking of children" (US State Department 2015, 230).

[21] Most countries in sub-Saharan Africa have legislation that permits abortion services under specific circumstances. A total of 71% of sub-Saharan countries legally permit abortions to preserve the woman's physical health; 68% to preserve the woman's mental health; 39% due to fetal impairment; and 36% in cases of rape or incest. An abortion performed due to any of these circumstances is still illegal and subject to prosecution in Madagascar. Both providers and women face imprisonment and heavy fines if abortion is performed. Also, while contraception is used, economic hardships and relative lack of legislative power leave women little autonomy over their own reproductive matters (United Nations Department of Economic and Social Affairs Population Division—World Abortion Policies 2013).

[22] According to the World Economic Forum (2014, 251), the HIV/AIDS "age-standardized deaths per 100,000" people in Madagascar is 28.8 for females and 38.1 for males. According to the US State Department (2010, 19), rape is illegal in Malagasy law, but the law does not specify whether spousal rape is included. Rapes are noted as underreported, and not all of those reported are investigated. Other forms of abuse of girls and women within families, including intimate partner violence, are prevalent and largely go unprosecuted. Women and girls have little protection from predatory males in Madagascar, as in most of the world.

[23] For example, Madagascar ranks somewhat lower than the global average for wage equality for similar work and estimated earned income, and significantly lower for the percent of women participating in the labor force. Madagascar's rank on gender income equality within professional and technical careers is relatively high at 92 out of 145 with a score of .77 out of 1.00 (which would signal complete equality), with

a sample average being .64 (World Economic Forum 2015, 56). For estimated earned income (purchasing power parity US$), Madagascar is ranked 37th out of 145 countries and scores .77 out of 1.00, and the sample average for the countries rated is .54 (World Economic Forum 2015, 54). For the percentage of labor force participation, Madagascar is .97 out of 1.00 but is ranked 7th out of 145 countries (World Economic Forum 2015, 52).

[24] Michel Foucault, *Discipline & Punish: The Birth of the Prison*, trans. Alan Sheridan (New York, NY: Vintage Books, 1995), 30.

[25] Judith Butler, "Bodies and Power Revisited," in *Feminism and the Final Foucault*, eds. Dianna Taylor and Karen Vintges (Urbana and Chicago: University of Illinois Press, 2004), 183–94.

CHAPTER SIX

POPULAR PERCEPTIONS OF ISRAELITE GENEALOGY IN MADAGASCAR: DISSOCIATING BIO-RACIAL SIGNIFIERS FROM MAINSTREAM JEWISH PRACTICE

NATHAN P. DEVIR

In many countries on the African continent, the emergence of so-called "self-defining", "neo-Jewish", or "Judaising" groups whose members possess neither known historical nor discursive ties with Jews elsewhere is becoming increasingly common.[1] One neglected geographic focus of contemporary inquiry in this domain is the island of Madagascar, where the prevalence of the belief in Israelite provenance among many inhabitants of the island is so commonplace that, to some, referencing the Israelite identity model seems almost pedestrian.[2] To date, only Bruder has composed substantial scholarship on that subject, while shorter articles by Brettschneider (see her essay in this volume) and Devir focus on the aspects of recent organized religious life among one specific Judaising community in that country.[3] What is currently missing from the aforementioned Jewish-oriented discussion is an analysis of the individuals, communities, and religious movements in Madagascar that have publicly proclaimed an Israelite identity while expressly dissociating themselves from the normative religious practices of established Jewish communities overseas.

In order to remedy the deficit of understanding regarding such current proponents of the Israelite identity model, this study provides new information on, and an analysis of, the widespread perceptions surrounding the supposed Israelite origins of Madagascar's indigenous inhabitants. Based on ethnographic fieldwork conducted on the island in 2013, this essay provides an overview of several key individuals, communities, and religious associations in Madagascar whose perceptions surrounding Israelite identity have become an integral part of the continuously-evolving discourse about

Jewish identity on the island.[4]

Contextualizing the milieu: A brief ethno-political history of Madagascar

The first inhabitants of Madagascar were Malayo-Indonesians who likely originated from Borneo, and who arrived on the island between 550 BCE and 250 BCE.[5] Approximately fourteen hundred years later, Bantu peoples from East Africa arrived. Muslim Arab merchants traded regularly with the island's inhabitants between the seventh and ninth centuries, and their presence is corroborated in the writings of the Mutazilite Arab explorer Abul Hasan Ali Ibn Husain Ibn Ali Al-Masu'di.

Europeans first encountered the island of Madagascar around the year 1500. For almost two hundred years, the Portuguese, British, French, and Dutch competed to dominate European trade on the island. At the end of the 1600s, the French were the first to successfully establish permanent trading posts, which were placed on the eastern side of the island. By the mid-1800s, France had thoroughly displaced the spectre of British influence on the island. In 1897, the French took all the territory previously held by the Imerina (i.e., of the Merina ethnicity) Kingdom, thus cementing the rule they maintained until Madagascar's eventual independence in 1960. The popular anecdotal parallels between the lineages of Malagasies and Hebrews/Israelites/Jews date back to at least the seventeenth century.[6]

European testimonies on these supposed parallels provide a lens through which we may see the times when Jewishness as a perceived hereditary trope among Malagasies might have come to the fore. Early European scholars writing about Madagascar were convinced that its inhabitants were of Hebraic ancestry. One well-known claim was articulated in a volume by Augustus Henry Keane, titled *The Gold of Ophir: Whence Brought and by Whom?* (1901).[7] In this work, Keane suggests that "the fleets of Hiram and Solomon [who supposedly had brought gold for Solomon's Temple from modern-day Zimbabwe to Israel, via Madagascar] must have been partly manned by Jews". Keane based his suppositions about Malagasy Jewish origins on earlier claims by writers such as Étienne de Flacourt, the French governor of Madagascar, who held office on the island between 1648 and 1655. In his *Histoire de la grande isle Madagascar* (History of the Great Island of Madagascar) (1658). Flacourt posited a Jewish origin of the natives based on practices such as circumcision and food taboos.[8] Alfred Grandidier, a French contemporary of Keane's who drew on Flacourt's narratives as well, wrote much about this particular ceremonial rite in his multivolume *Histoire physique, naturelle, et politique de Madagascar*

(Physical, Natural, and Political History of Madagascar) (1901–1904).[9]

The most famous location of supposed Jewish sightings in the premodern period occurred on the Island of St. Marie, or *Nosy Boraha* in Malagasy. Many explorers thought that the isle's inhabitants, a clan originally called *Zafi Ibrahim* (literally, "the Seed of Abraham", using the Arabic name for the patriarch), were of Jewish extraction. For instance, according to popular lore, the Dutch explorer Cornelis de Houtman, who visited in 1595, assumed that the "White" people on the island (i.e., those clearly not of Bantu stock) must be Hamites, Jews, or descendants of Ishmael.[10] In 1870, the Reverend James Sibree, who served between 1863 and 1916 in Madagascar with the London Missionary Society, also claimed to have met "Jews" at the same site.[11]

Another ethnicity with which Israelite origins have commonly been associated is that of the highland Merina people. Traditional Merina practices such as menstrual seclusion, animal sacrifice, food taboos concerning the consumption of eel or pork, and the *Alahamady* (New Year's) custom of painting one's doorposts with the blood from a recently-slaughtered sheep (a supposed parallel with the feast of Passover), are often cited as proof of this connection. In the same vein, the Antemoro people of the southeastern coastal areas, the Sakalava, and the pastoralist Antandroy all profess similar ties with ancient Israel.[12]

Sagas of migration and incorporation

According to one popular legend, Malagasies are descended from one or more of the Ten Lost Tribes of Israel. Again, the details on this provenance are unclear. No one among the hundreds of people whom I interviewed agreed on which specific tribe would be the one from which Malagasies descended, although responses tended generally to favor Gad, Issachar, Dan, and Asher. I could find no discernable reason as to why these particular tribes were the most frequently cited. The popular public Facebook group "MERINA: Jews or Malayu?" is one forum in which this particular migration claim frequently appears. Before discussing its treatment of the claim as a microcosm for other widespread perceptions of Israelite origins, a few words about the group are in order.

The overwhelming majority of posts to the group's page support the theory of Israelite provenance, while very few deal at all with attributes common to modern normative Jewry. Those which point to a Malayo-Indonesian origin of the island's inhabitants are often attacked, deleted, or both. In response to one user who provided a link to genetic studies of the Malagasy population that support an origin thesis from Borneo, an anonymous member posted the following comment: "Que les malgaches soient fiers de leur origine hébraïque!" (Malagasies should be proud of their Hebraic origin!). The person then reiterated the claim that, "Nos lointains ancêtres faisaient partie des tribus du nord d'Israël qui avaient été déportées par les Assyriens" (Our distant ancestors were part of the northern Tribes of Israel, which were deported by the Assyrians). Immediately, several dozen people liked the post. One person, however, wrote, "Fuck you Jews!" in English in the section allocated for comments. The responses to the obscenity, written mostly in Malagasy, universally reputed the user.

In addition to presenting an example of the pervasiveness of the Assyrian exile version of the migration story, this online exchange is instructive in that it scratches below the surface of language choice, idiom, register, and politesse to expose the latent ideological content of the postings on each side of the debate. The exchange begins with a posting in French, the official language of instruction, which seeks to refute the popular story about exiled Israelites to Assyria eventually finding their way to Madagascar. A rebuttal follows, evoking ethnic pride and appealing to the readers' emotional dispositions. It then repeats the already-understood origin claim, as if repeating it (in the language of the privileged literati) somehow provides a logical counter to the genetic study asserting the contrary. The appearance of a new user, who introduces an element of globalized persuasion into the mix by interjecting a vulgarity in English, the universal lingua franca, showcases a view that ostensibly appeals to a postmodern and postnational (not to mention potentially anti-Semitic) crowd outside of the "Malagasy pride" narrative. The swift expressions of condemnation cause the exchange to revert to Malagasy, the offline language of the home, and likely the users' most visceral medium of speech. Once removed, the absence of the comment effectively ends the debate.

Another migration story, which is also the most popular, has been cited earlier in the discussion of Keane's work on the supposed emissaries sent by King Solomon to collect gold from the biblical Ophir. According to this version of the migration saga, Madagascar was the offshore port through which gold from Ophir (supposedly in present-day Zimbabwe) was processed and transported back to the Temple in Jerusalem. Since this legend appears in many different heritage narratives among the island's numerous ethnic groups, let us focus on one group (and its associated clans) for which this version of the story has been particularly meaningful: the Merina.

Although the migration story highlighting an origin from those exiled to Assyria is, as the Facebook group demonstrates, a widely-accepted one, belief in the veracity of another Israelite migration to Madagascar is also considered permissible. Among the Merina elite of the "Royal House of Madagascar" association (the title is usually given in English), one proponent of such a stance is His Royal Highness the Prince and Reverend Dr. Ndriana Rabarioelina, whose official title is "Direct Descendant of the Eldest Branch of the Royal House in Madagascar and Head of the Council of Kings and Princes in Madagascar". An Anglican priest and esteemed figure in the Malagasy political scene, Rabarioelina also claims to be a descendant of Aaron, evoking the Levite assertion of many of the island's inhabitants.

For Rabarioelina and his close circle of coreligionists—a cohort of practising Christians frequently active on social media sites such as Twitter, the *Royal House of Madagascar* and *Diary & Tora-po* blogs, and the "Madagascar for Israel", "GassYehoudim", and "Firenena Merina" Facebook pages—ancient Israel and Madagascar were linked more closely than many realize. In fact, Rabarioelina conjectures that there may have been many more migrations than the ones already referred to here. Acknowledging that genetic tests of the population have proven that most Malagasies are of Malayo-Indonesian descent, he surmises that exiles from ancient Israel may have gone by way of China down through Indonesia, and from there proceeded to Madagascar.

According to Rabarioelina, the Merina Royalty "have close links to the First Temple of Jerusalem", especially through their contribution to the construction of Solomon's Temple project.[13] Rabarioelina claims that he and other noble descendants from the Royal House of Madagascar cohort "have safeguarded the old Jewish identity, old Jewish customs and culture during more than 3,000 years, and have safeguarded many treasures from the First Temple of Jerusalem", including those of King David and King Solomon.[14] By way of their Facebook page, Rabarioelina and others in the Royal House of Madagascar cohort often publish announcements about the return to the political scene of this royal lineage. According to them, Madagascar is on its way to becoming *Fanjakan'i Madagasikara* (the Kingdom of Madagascar), a "modern monarchy" with members of the Royal Merina Household at its head. Notably absent in this and other communiqués is any indication that those of this noble line might wish to end their formal practice of Christianity.

The same claim of Solomonic descent *sans* modern Jewish predilections is held by the Betsileo, a highland people related to the Merina, who inhabit the south-central part of the island. In particular, the Betsileo site of Alakamisy-Ambohimaha, a rocky plateau overlooking rice fields near the Haute Matsiatra regional capital of Fianarantsoa, has long been rumoured to be a place in which King Solomon's emissaries found gold for his

Temple. According to local legend, two Betsileo ancestors, Antos and Cathy, were sent by Solomon to Madagascar to prospect for gold and other precious stones. During their mission, they married locals of the tribe of Zafindrandoto and eventually decided to settle in the region.[15] Although details of the oral account concerning Solomon end here, the atmosphere of Israelite sanctity surrounding the site of Alakamisy-Ambohimaha has remained a constant in the Betsileo imagination.

Other groups on the island are also beginning to express an interest in this Solomonic legend and the physical places connected to it, apparently without any connection to overseas Jewish movements. One reporter for a national online magazine who recently visited Alakamisy-Ambohimaha, for instance, notes that, in addition to the Solomonic legend connected to the plateau, certain "Jewish" supernatural happenings are said to occur there. Chief among these involves the stream whose water supposedly changes color daily, an occurrence that may be connected to the post-exilic trope about the *Sambation*, the so-called "Sabbath river" beyond which remnants of the Lost Tribes are said to dwell.[16] The reporter points out that the only apparent commonality between the customs of the locals and those of modern-day Jews has to do with the prohibition against eating pork. Interestingly, though, this proscription only applies to locals who set foot on the embankment leading up to the rocky plateau, where the consumption of mutton is also forbidden.

Often referred to in French simply as "le rocher qui parle" (the boulder that speaks), or "le rocher sacré" (the sacred boulder), the plateau of Alakamisy-Ambohimaha first came into the larger public consciousness as a marker of Israelite identity in 1953. In February of that year, a local stonemason named Edouard Randrianasolo discovered mysterious writings on one of the rocks. Unsure of their meaning, he made an etching and took it to Jacques Auber, the provisional French governor of the region. Knowing about the legends connected to the site, Auber suspected that the writings might be from the Solomonic period, and he therefore decided to consult with clergy at a local Catholic seminary, who, in turn, suggested sending a geologist from the *Institut de Recherche Scientifique de Madagascar* (Scientific Institute of Research of Madagascar) to examine the writings. A professor from a university in the capital city of Antananarivo, who was involved in a team of later excavations at the site and who wishes to remain anonymous, told me during a conversation on this topic that the government had quietly shut down their excavations and prevented the publication of the provisionary proceedings. According to the professor, state officials were afraid that showcasing the material evidence of Israelite origin would highlight the chosen lineage of the Malagasies, which the colonial powers "had taken pains to hide, in order to dominate us more easily". This act of (as he put it) "sticking our finger in France's eye" by demonstrating the extent of the prestigious, pre-colonial past would only serve to disrupt the country's relations with the Catholic Church, which was the primary source of aid and educational opportunities for the country's impoverished masses after the withdrawal of the French colonial powers. The government therefore ordered the excavations cancelled and the researchers recalled.

What to make of "the boulder that speaks"? We unfortunately do not possess enough information at this time to offer any empirically-based postulations; however, the conceptual categories of the Betsileo migration sagas examined here are thematically and symbolically instructive in that they dovetail very closely with other categories of widespread belief in Israelite ancestry on the island. All rely on a combination of colonially-inspired notions of provenance as well as a healthy dose of indigenous ethnocentrism. Divorcing the discourses of colonialism from indigenous claims to Israelite identity may be impossible, since such claims depend on those discourses both as an object of revolt as well as potentially authoritative points of reference; and this is true whether or not the claimant is aware of the possibility of this mimetic transaction. In any event, the veneration and possible restoration of perceived ancestral codes related to ancient Israel represents a counter-movement that, for many Betsileo, is a logical progression in the struggle against perceived neocolonial cultural hegemony.

Organized efforts towards ancestral recognition

Despite the common enthusiasm for resurrecting the lost Malagasy heritage and the shared opinions regarding the colonial drive to suppress Madagascar's "true" history, many dissenters have their reasons for not wanting to formally join the normative Jewish religious community. In my conversations with them, the most prevalent reason given is that they wish to remain faithful Christians. Unlike the individuals who publicly espouse Israelite heritage narratives in both online and offline fora but who do not belong to organisations involved in constructing policy, however, the second category of proponents of the Israelite identity model showcased below has, in fact, endeavored to do just that by forming official, like-minded constituencies where perspectives surrounding Israelite identity can be formally discussed, encouraged, and propagated both at the state and "soft" levels. Two such constituencies are Israel-centered enthusiasts and Merina traditionalists.

The most viable example of the constituency of Israel-centered enthusiasts is the Club Shalom Madagascar. An active and publicly-visible association dedicated to celebrating Israelite lineage through the promotion of alliances with the modern geopolitical state of Israel, the practising Christian members of the club also maintain close ties with the American Jewish Committee and the African Jewish Congress. The club is currently led by its founder, former parliamentarian Raherimasoandro Andriamamonjy, a member of the royal family and at present a senior official in the Ministry of Commerce.

Andriamamonjy's dedication to the state of Israel as a way of honoring his own perceived roots was kindled during two visits to Israel that he made at the invitation of *Mashav* (Israel's Agency for International Development Cooperation) and the *Histadrut* (Israel's Organization of Trade Unions).

During his first sojourn in Israel, Andriamamonjy tried both officially and unofficially to improve diplomatic relations between the two countries, which had soured after an initially promising series of collaborations following Madagascar's independence. Upon his return to Madagascar in 1992, Andriamamonjy founded the Club Shalom Madagascar, whose objective is to liaise between Madagascar and Israel in the areas of diplomacy and commerce, as well as to "favor the cultural ties with the Malagasy people and the Israeli people".[17] Initially, all of the members were, like Andriamamonjy, governmental employees who had previously spent time in Israel. Later, those who simply wanted to explore their lost lineage joined. Frequent topics of the lecture series and discussion groups organized by the club, as well as the content of the club's monthly magazine, include Jewish life around the world, Malagasy heritage and traditional religion, the dangers of Islamic fundamentalism, examples of security and agricultural innovation pioneered by Israel, the lessons of the Holocaust, Israel's diplomatic activities in Africa, and the normative Jewish resurgence in Madagascar.

The formation of the religious Jewish Community of Madagascar did not have anything to do with the activities of the club, although they share similar interests. Members of the club who are actively involved in Christian churches see no contradiction between their religious lives as Christians and their sense of affiliation with the move towards resuscitating lost knowledge about the Israelite identity of Madagascar's inhabitants. As one member of Club Shalom told me: "I am a Hebrew by blood, and that is the irrefutable proof that I belong to the Jewish people. I should not have to change my religion to make this fact any truer than it already is".

The second category of non-normative, organized constituencies worthy of mention is made up of Merina traditionalists who have recently discovered, or have been discovered by, the organized Jewish Community of Madagascar. Often claiming to possess the secrets long held by the descendants of the Aaronite line, these traditionalists have, for the most part, embraced the commonalities they share with the organized Jewish community. Just like the members of Club Shalom Madagascar, they do not see the need to "update" their practices in order to align themselves with the ways in which the Israelite religion has morphed into contemporary Judaism. They remain content to "maintain traditional practices".

One such group of traditionalists particularly relevant to the topic at hand calls itself the Church (or Temple, depending on whom you ask) of *Loharanom-Pitahiana* (the Source of the Blessing), located in the farming commune of Ambohimiadana, near the village of Mananjara, about three hours southeast of Antananarivo. One of the leaders of this organization with whom I have been in frequent contact insists upon using the terms "Hebraic religion", "Israelite religion", or "Aaronism" to describe their religion in place of "Judaism," which is, in his view, a later and somewhat corrupted version of their ancestors' creed. To date, they have politely declined invitations to become part of the Jewish Community of Madagascar.

When asked which customs the Aaronites share with normative Jews, informants mention circumcision, menstrual seclusion, monotheism, and the prohibitions on consuming unclean animals and mixing milk with meat. Also included in their "shared morals" are the imperatives to "respect truth and justice, live with humility, and not cause harm to others". When I inquired as to which particular customs of the Levites they follow—customs that differ from those expected of "ordinary Jews"—the leaders confirmed that, as descendants of Aaron, they do everything according to the duties outlined in Numbers 18 for "Priests and Levites".

The narrative account of this group's origins, which, in many ways, resembles the series of other heritage narratives mentioned earlier, was related to me as follows:

> Before the Babylonian invasion that destroyed the Temple of Solomon, our priestly and Levite ancestors had received prophetic messages that foresaw this devastation. They were instructed to leave Jerusalem and to take with them the sacred objects held in the Holy of Holies […] They left Jerusalem before the disaster and arrived on the eastern coast of Madagascar in 1305, having passed by India, Vietnam, Indonesia [Java], and the Indian Ocean [a sea voyage guided by the winds and the tides].

Note that this description of the migration story incorporates other popular versions of the tale: an Aaronite lineage, the Babylonian exile, and the preservation of material remnants of that era. Much like the thesis of

Ndriana Rabarioelina's cohort, it cedes a place to current scientific research, acknowledging the documented Malagasy point of origin as Indonesia. It also puts the time of the arrival around the historical period in which scholars agree that maritime migration to, and trade around, the island notably spiked.

According to the local priests, the community would welcome assistance from Hebrews, Israelites, Jews, and "others who share the same chosen lineage" provided that there was no pressure put on the Aaronites to "accept other religious ways of being".

Conclusion

This essay has provided an analysis of several case studies of the individuals, communities, and religious associations in Madagascar that claim an Israelite identity based on perceptions of shared origins without having adopted normative religious Jewish practices. It has shown that the religious backgrounds of all of the proponents of an Israelite identity are decidedly and professedly Christian, save the Aaronites of Ambohimiadana, who claim to never have been "corrupted" by Christianity. It has also shown how pre-colonial customs and taboos with which the mission churches were often at odds happen to correspond with many of the Hebraic or Israelite customs found in the Hebrew scriptures. As noted, this parallelism exhibits a kind of symbolic struggle against the (perceived) continued neocolonial hegemony of the European (especially Catholic) churches, whose leaders have discouraged traditional religious practices deemed to be primitive and out-of-step with the trappings of modernity. Finally, the individuals, organisations, and communities profiled in this article see their concerted efforts to dignify long-held notions about Malagasy provenance as part of an ethno-religious identity movement that is firmly dissociated from normative-style Judaism.

Works Cited

Brettschneider, Marla. *The Jewish Phenomenon in Sub-Saharan Africa: The Politics of Contradictory Discourses*. Lewiston, NY: Edwin Mellen Press, 2015.

Bruder, Edith. *The Black Jews of Africa: History, Religion, Identity*. New York, NY: Oxford University Press, 2008.

Bruder, Edith. "The Descendants of David in Madagascar: Crypto-Judaism in Twentieth-Century Africa." In *Race, Color, Identity: Rethinking Discourses about "Jews" in the Twenty-First Century*, edited by E.

Sicher. New York, NY: Berghahn Books, 2013, 196–216.
Devir, N. P. "Origins and Motivations of Madagascar's Normative Jewish Movement." In *Becoming Jewish: New Jews and Emerging Jewish Communities in a Globalized World*, edited by N. Fisher and T. Parfitt, 49–63. Newcastle upon Tyne: Cambridge Scholars Publishing, 2016.
Flacourt, E. de. *Histoire de la grande isle Madagascar*. Paris: G. Clouzier, 1661.
Grandidier, A. *Histoire physique, naturelle et politique de Madagascar*, Vol. 4. Paris: Imprimerie nationale, 1908.
Jaovelo-Dzao, R. *Anthropologie religieuse sakalava: Essai sur l'inculturation du christianisme à Madagascar*. Antsiranana: Institut supérieur de théologie et de philosophie de Madagascar, 1987.
Keane, A. H. *The Gold of Ophir: Whence Brought and by Whom?* London: Edward Stanford, 1901.
Le Roux, Magdel. *The Lemba: A Lost Tribe of Israel in Southern Africa?* Pretoria: Unisa Press, 2003.
Lis, Daniel. *Jewish Identity among the Igbo of Nigeria: Israel's "Lost Tribe" and the Question of Belonging in the Jewish State*. Trenton, NJ: Africa World Press, 2015.
Miles, William F. S. *Jews of Nigeria: An Afro-Judaic Odyssey*. Princeton, NJ: Markus Wiener, 2012.
Miles, William F. S. *Afro-Jewish Encounters: From Timbuktu to the Indian Ocean and Beyond*. Princeton, NJ: Markus Wiener, 2013.
Parfitt, Tudor. *Operation Moses: The Untold Story of the Secret Exodus of the Falasha Jews from Ethiopia*. New York, NY: Stein and Day, 1985.
Parfitt, Tudor. *The Thirteenth Gate: Travels among the Lost Tribes of Israel*. Bethesda, MD: Adler and Adler, 1987.
Parfitt, Tudor. *Journey to the Vanished City: The Search for a Lost Tribe of Israel*. New York, NY: St. Martin's Press, 1993.
Parfitt, Tudor. *The Lost Tribes of Israel: The History of a Myth*. London: Weidenfeld and Nicolson, 2002.
Parfitt, Tudor. *The Lost Ark of the Covenant: The Remarkable Quest for the Legendary Ark*. New York, NY: HarperCollins, 2008.
Perez, Y. "Sambation." In *Encyclopedia of Jewish Folklore and Traditions*, edited by H. Bar-Itzhak and R. Patai, 467–68. London: Routledge, 2013.
Rabarioelina, N. "History of the Royal House of Madagascar." Royal House of Madagascar. December 4, 2012. http://www.royal-house-of-madagascar.blogspot.com/2012/12/history-of-royal-house-in-madagascar.html.
Rajaonarimanana, N. *Saviors Arabico-Malgaches: La tradition manuscrite des devins Antemoro Anakara*. Antananarivo: Institut national des

langues et civilisations orientales, 1990.
Sibree, J. *Madagascar and Its People: Notes of a Four Years' Residence. With a Sketch of the History, Position, and Prospects of Mission Work the Malagasy*. London: Religious Tract Society, 1870.
Weisfeld, C. "Madagascar Group Seeks Closer Jewish Ties," Kulanu, 2007. https://kulanu.org/communities/madagascar/madagascar-groups-seek-closer-jewish-ties/.

Notes

[1] M. Brettschneider, *The Jewish Phenomenon in Sub-Saharan Africa: The Politics of Contradictory Discourses* (Lewiston, NY: Edwin Mellen Press, 2015); E. Bruder, *The Black Jews of Africa: History, Religion, Identity* (New York, NY: Oxford University Press, 2008); E. Bruder, "The Descendants of David in Madagascar: Crypto-Judaism in Twentieth-Century Africa," in *Race, Color, Identity: Rethinking Discourses about "Jews" in the Twenty-First Century*, ed. E. Sicher (New York, NY: Berghahn Books, 2013), 196–216; M. le Roux, *The Lemba: A Lost Tribe of Israel in Southern Africa?* (Pretoria: Unisa Press, 2003); D. Lis, *Jewish Identity among the Igbo of Nigeria: Israel's "Lost Tribe" and the Question of Belonging in the Jewish State* (Trenton, NJ: Africa World Press, 2015); W. F. S. Miles, *Jews of Nigeria: An Afro-Judaic Odyssey* (Princeton, NJ: Markus Wiener, 2012); W. F. S. Miles, *Afro-Jewish Encounters: From Timbuktu to the Indian Ocean and Beyond* (Princeton, NJ: Markus Wiener, 2013); T. Parfitt, *Operation Moses: The Untold Story of the Secret Exodus of the Falasha Jews from Ethiopia* (New York, NY: Stein and Day, 1985); T. Parfitt, *The Thirteenth Gate: Travels among the Lost Tribes of Israel* (Bethesda, MD: Adler and Adler, 1987); T. Parfitt, *Journey to the Vanished City: The Search for a Lost Tribe of Israel* (New York, NY: St. Martin's Press, 1993); T. Parfitt, *The Lost Tribes of Israel: The History of a Myth* (London: Weidenfeld and Nicolson, 2002); T. Parfitt, *The Lost Ark of the Covenant: The Remarkable Quest for the Legendary Ark* (New York, NY: HarperCollins, 2008).
[2] Bruder has labeled this propensity the "Malagasy secret" (*Black Jews of Africa*, 178). In further acknowledgments of Bruder's work on Madagascar, I will refer to her 2008 study *The Black Jews of Africa* (an expanded version of which appears in her 2013 essay "The Descendants of David in Madagascar").
[3] Bruder, *Black Jews of Africa*; Bruder, "Descendants of David"; N. P. Devir, "Origins and Motivations of Madagascar's Normative Jewish Movement," in *Becoming Jewish: New Jews and Emerging Jewish Communities in a Globalized World*, ed. N. Fisher and T. Parfitt (Newcastle upon Tyne: Cambridge Scholars Publishing, 2016), 49–63. I would like to acknowledge here my debt to Bruder's groundbreaking scholarship in this realm, which is evidenced all throughout the historical background components of this essay. For her explanations on the influence of these Malagasy ethno-historical narratives, see Bruder, *Black Jews of Africa*, 178–85.
[4] Data collection methods used for the fieldwork (May–June 2013) in this study

include those relevant to the domain of quotidian ethnography.

[5] Diagram Group, "Madagascan People," in *Encyclopedia of African Peoples* (New York, NY: Facts on File, 2000), 138.

[6] For the definitive summary on these parallels, see Bruder, *Black Jews of Africa*, 124–32.

[7] A. H. Keane, *The Gold of Ophir: Whence Brought and by Whom?* (London: Edward Stanford, 1901).

[8] É. de Flacourt, *Histoire de la grande isle Madagascar* (Paris: G. Clouzier, 1661), 308. On this point, see Bruder, *Black Jews of Africa*, 124. I have consulted the later edition of Flacourt's work for this citation.

[9] A. Grandidier, *Histoire physique, naturelle et politique de Madagascar*, Vol. 4 (Paris: Imprimerie nationale, 1908), 74. See Bruder, *Black Jews of Africa*, 124–26, 129.

[10] Legends about Ishmael being the progenitor of other tribes on the island are widespread. The tribe most often tied to this assertion is the Zafiramnia of the south. On this point, see Bruder, *Black Jews of Africa*, 127–28, and N. Rajaonarimanana, *Saviors Arabico-Malgaches: La tradition manuscrite des devins Antemoro Anakara* (Antananarivo: Institut national des langues et civilisations orientales, 1990), 170.

[11] J. Sibree, *Madagascar and Its People: Notes of a Four Years' Residence. With a Sketch of the History, Position, and Prospects of Mission Work amongst the Malagasy* (London: Religious Tract Society, 1870), 169.

[12] R. Jaovelo-Dzao, *Anthropologie religieuse sakalava: Essai sur l'inculturation du christianisme à Madagascar* (Antsiranana: Institut supérieur de théologie et de philosophie de Madagascar, 1987), 18.

[13] N. Rabarioelina, "History of the Royal House of Madagascar," Royal House of Madagascar, December 4, 2012, http://www.royal-house-of-madagascar.blogspot.com/2012/12/history-of-royal-house-in-madagascar.html.

[14] N. Rabarioelina, e-mail message to author, May 26, 2013.

[15] "L'histoire de notre commune," Alakamisy-Ambohimaha district website, n.d., accessed June 9, 2014, https://alakamisyambohimahafr.wordpress.com/communaute/general/.

[16] "Le 'rocher qui parle' à Alakamisy-Ambohimaha Fianarantsoa, MADAGASCAR," *Mystères et conspirations*, May 12, 2010, accessed September 7, 2018, http://maitso.over-blog.com/article-le-rocher-qui-parle-a-alakamisy-ambohimaha-fianarantsoa-madagascar-50291238.html. For more on the legendary Sabbath River, see Y. Perez, "Sambation," in *Encyclopedia of Jewish Folklore and Traditions*, eds. H. Bar-Itzhak and R. Patai (London: Routledge, 2013), 467–68.

[17] C. Weisfeld, "Madagascar Group Seeks Closer Jewish Ties," Kulanu, 2007, http://kulanu.org/communities/madagascar/madagascar-groups-seek-closer-jewish-ties/.

CHAPTER SEVEN

RECAPTURING JEWISH ROOTS IN CABO VERDE: CHANGING DIASPORIC IDENTITIES

ALMA GOTTLIEB

The diasporic history of the Jewish people famously includes journeys by generations of Sephardis departing from the Iberian Peninsula and moving west to the Americas and east across Europe and into Asia; but even those extensive travels do not exhaust the seas crossed by this early—and frequently globe-trotting—people. The Cabo Verde islands, located some 350 miles off the coast of Senegal, offer a uniquely riveting space from which to explore Jewish histories. How, when, and why did Jews find themselves on these islands in the north Atlantic?

The journey that begins a few decades before Columbus' seafaring voyages would compel cartographers to redraw maps of the known world. In 1456, European navigators landed on the archipelago they would misname "Cape Verde". If most of the islands were anything but green (and, indeed, largely devoid of vegetation), they were entirely empty of *human* habitation. Strong winds and sea currents alone, however, did not bring emboldened sailors here. A variety of historical forces converged to propel Europeans to explore new spaces, open up new markets, endeavor to convert new "heathens", and find new sources of inexpensive labor to cultivate new crops in those new lands.[1]

As it happened, although ecologically inhospitable to both humans and other animals (due, especially, to unpredictable rains and frequent droughts, among other natural conditions) the Cabo Verde islands proved ideally situated, economically, for Europeans—although not for Africans—for two opposing reasons. Located between Africa, Europe, and South America, the islands quickly attracted European merchants lured by the rapidly developing trans-Atlantic trade in goods—and, increasingly, in humans. Geographically, Cabo Verde proved a convenient stopping-off point while awaiting favorable winds to propel sailing ships. Economically, sailors took advantage of this layover space to stock up on necessary provisions (and, later, crew members) for the long water crossing. The islands quickly became the most active *entrepôt* for kidnapped Africans before being sent off on the infamous Middle Passage.[2] With all these arrivals of people from many ports of call, the archipelago became populated by a blend of people from Catholic, Jewish, and indigenous African religious traditions. Indeed, it was, arguably, here that the world's first systematically "creolized" population was created. As such, as the historian Toby Green suggests, Cabo Verde may be the place where we humans became modern—disturbingly, as part of the expansion of that most inhumane of activities, the trade in humans-as-commodities.

At the same time that the recently-uninhabited islands quickly became an unlikely maritime crossroads, they nevertheless retained an aura of exotic safety for adventurous Europeans—existing, as they did, far from any mainland. As a result, their very remoteness also made the islands attractive to those wishing to hide from any people, institutions, or states looking to do them harm. Prime among such fugitives were Jews fleeing growing anti-Semitism in Iberia.

Just as the Cabo Verde islands began to be populated in the 1460s, anti-Semitic tendencies were intensifying in Spain and Portugal, culminating in catastrophe for Jews. The very year that King Ferdinand and Queen Isabella sponsored Columbus' voyage across the Atlantic in search of a western sea route to India, the same royal couple also issued an edict expelling all Jews from their country. Of course, opening up new sea routes would result in communicating with many new people in lands previously unknown to Spaniards. It seems perplexing—and bitterly ironic—that this expansion of social worlds on one (international) register was counterbalanced by a drastic constriction of social worlds on another (domestic) register. Did the Spanish-Catholic soul somehow lack the cognitive or emotional ability to maintain "others" in the domestic space, if they were to embrace (or, at least, have relations with) multiple new "others" abroad? Such conjectures must await further discussion elsewhere. Here, it will suffice to note the uncanny coordination of dates in what became a momentous year for Christian Spaniards. At once, 1492 saw Spain making enormous (and enormously expensive) efforts to contact "others" across the seas and, at the very same time, enormous (and enormously violent) efforts to evict "others" in their midst.

Four years later, a complicated political relationship uneasily linking Iberia's two nations impelled Spain to pressure Portugal to enact the same policy targeting Jews. While Portuguese navigators were famously starting to circumnavigate the globe and initiate new trade relations everywhere, the Portuguese crown was pressured by their Spanish neighbors (on threat of invasion) to produce its own Edict of Expulsion against all Jews who opted to remain Jewish.[3] In other words, the simultaneous, and contradictory, addition *and* subtraction of social ties with "others" claimed Christian Portugal as well.

In both countries, any Jews who rejected exile and chose to remain were required by the state to convert to Christianity;[4] however, that status proved problematic in the extreme, as these converts were dubbed with the stigmatizing title of "New Christians". This newly-created category immediately made its bearers suspect, potentially accused of not being fully-dedicated Christians. Accusations of secretly observed Jewish practices encompassed the gamut of traditional Judaism, whether circumcising male infants, lighting candles on Friday nights, avoiding eating pork, observing Jewish holidays such as Passover, or any other ritual practice. Anyone suspected of any such activities was subject to arrest—and, often, torture, sometimes followed by execution by being publicly burnt alive at the notorious (and appallingly named) *autos-da-fé* ("acts of faith"). The joint church/state-sponsored institution that implemented this systematic persecution became known as the Inquisition; it lasted legally from 1478–1834 in Spain and from 1536–1821 in Portugal.[5] Alongside this draconian legal and military apparatus arose a veritable culture of mistrust, contributing to some three centuries of horror for anyone accused of being Jewish ("Judaizing").[6]

In such a grim environment, tens of thousands of Jews fled both nations.[7] Their travels in one direction across Europe to Turkey and beyond, and in the other direction to the Americas, are well known.[8] A small number, however, chose to relocate not to Amsterdam, Thessaloniki, or Curaçao but, rather, to one of nine small islands off the coast of West Africa.

Admittedly, the proportion of Iberian Jews heading for Cabo Verde, rather than to other destinations more commonly sought at the time, was low. The converse, however, was also true: the first generations of Europeans who settled on the previously uninhabited archipelago of Cabo Verde included a very high proportion of Jews.[9] As the Inquisition raged in Portugal, former Jews, whom the church/state alliance had forced to convert to Catholicism (with varying levels of sincerity), continued to live in terror of being denounced. This condition of abject fear encompassed both those who continued to secretly practice Judaism and those who had genuinely renounced their former religion but whose Jewish ancestors were known to neighbors. Accordingly, both secret Jews and descendants of former Jews continued to flee Portugal for Cabo Verde (among other destinations) for the first two hundred years of the islands' settlement. Those Jews who selected Cabo Verde as their destination, rather than one of the welcoming cities of Eurasia (especially Amsterdam and Istanbul), or the exciting allure of the Americas still being explored by European "discoverers", must have had a certain kind of temperament. The historian Tobias Green conjectures that these Jewish refugees must have been especially adventurous. He also suggests that they may have been especially inclined towards participating in the developing trans-Atlantic trade opportunities and/or perhaps less spiritually devout than their co-religionists who fled to other cities where active Jewish communities existed.[10]

The numbers of "New Christians" fleeing Portugal no doubt slowed as the Inquisition itself became less virulent; yet, while the Inquisition was weakening in the terror it produced, other forces operating elsewhere were pressing down on Jews in ways with which Jews were, unfortunately, all too familiar from other historical eras. From the early nineteenth century, and lasting for nearly a hundred years, Jews living in Morocco ended up as scapegoats for growing internal political troubles. As their ancestors had done before from the Iberian Peninsula (and from Israel, long before that), Jews fled persecution in Morocco for any other safe space available to them. Popular destinations included Gibraltar, the UK, Portugal, and the Americas; but once again, for about a century (lasting from the early nineteenth century to the early twentieth century), Cabo Verde drew a small proportion of these refugees. Although no practicing Jewish community existed on the archipelago (for reasons to be explained below), it is possible that the islands may have been known by these Moroccan Jews from oral history and family records. That is, one "pull" factor may be that they might have been aware of former Jewish families who had earlier fled Iberia for Cabo Verde.

Today, many Cabo Verdeans both on and off the islands are (re)discovering the Jewish history of their nation, their families, or both. What might we learn about expanding understandings of self, as Cabo Verdeans (re)discover new components of personal identity, family traditions, and national history? What might this singular Sephardic historical engagement instruct us about other Sephardic experiences elsewhere in Africa?

Oppression, Assimilation, and Memories of Origins

Knowledge of the Jewish history of Cabo Verde varies tremendously, both among individuals living on the islands and those in the diaspora. We begin with the case of Cabo Verdeans who have no knowledge that Jews ever lived on the archipelago. This unfamiliarity is at once bizarre *and* understandable.

It is bizarre because, as already mentioned, the early population of the archipelago likely included a very large proportion of Jews. Today, any Cabo Verdean with roots in that early era may well have some Jewish ancestors; however, few descendants of these early Jews know of their Sephardic ancestors. Several factors account for this knowledge gap. At the technical level, archival records are scattered, fragmentary, and multilingual from this early era. To date, only one trained scholar has comprehensively engaged with these globally situated archives to reconstruct a sociological portrait of the first two centuries of Jewish residents of Cabo Verde.[11]

A second reason concerns the early religious constitution of the archipelago. From the beginning, the new island society replicated the very anti-Semitism of the mainland home that its Jewish refugees sought to flee. Tragically, beginning in 1551, the Inquisition legally followed Jews from Iberia to the islands, where some "New Christians" (*cristãos novos*) were accused by Catholic neighbors of continuing to practice Jewish rituals ("Judaizing"). Of those accused, some were denounced to spies, sent back to Lisbon, and tried in the Inquisition's brutal courts.[12] The dream of the islands as a "safe haven" for Jews quickly dissolved, and those who had hoped they might securely practice their religion would soon have discovered their misjudgment. In response, some signed onto Catholicism (the state religion), at least in name, to become "crypto-Jews"; others converted to Catholicism with varying degrees of sincerity, although they and their descendants were long classified by their suspicious neighbors as "New Christians." Either way, the islands' Jewish history became officially erased very soon after Jews arrived. Memories of crypto-Jewish practices survived indirectly, through some quotidian customs—and, more directly (if clandestinely), through some families' whispered oral histories; however, this history became discursively submerged, never to be taught in school curricula nor celebrated via public holidays.

Oral histories suggest that many of these formerly Jewish families frequently intermarried with one another, while others married "old Christians". In both scenarios, though, the children of virtually all marriages were nearly always baptized in the Catholic church.[13] Through such habits, many Jewish customs were forced to go underground and, ultimately, disappeared. Still, other Jewish practices remained, as misunderstood remnants of former traditions no longer recognized as such.

And so, we arrive at the bizarre situation we find today. It is well summarized in the words of the nation's most illustrious living writer, Germano Almeida:

> Well, all the Jews in Cabo Verde have died. But many, many Jews came to the islands and married Cabo Verdeans and had children with Cabo Verdeans. So, although they've all died, they mixed with us, and they are part of us. (Personal communication, April 4, 2007)

Almeida's comment applies aptly to the descendants of these early Jewish settlers; however, it applies less fittingly to the later group of Jewish migrants: those who arrived from Morocco, fleeing that nation's political and economic crises, and their associated anti-Semitism, during the nineteenth and early twentieth centuries. Living descendants of these more recent arrivals include many prominent leaders in contemporary Cabo Verde, including the country's first democratically elected prime minister (Carlos Alberto Wahnon de Carvalho Veiga) and many others. Both for this reason, and because some of these families' descendants retain living memories of their Moroccan ancestors from a couple of generations back, Cabo Verdeans who are aware of the Jewish presence in the archipelago are more likely to know about this more recent wave of immigrants.

In short, this island nation contains a uniquely complicated, multi-leveled history of Jewish presence since the inception of its continued human occupation. That history, however, is only beginning to be adequately documented, publicly acknowledged, and privately incorporated into personal identities.

Identity and Current Ways of Living

What are the consequences of the nation's Jewish history for the lived experiences of Cabo Verdeans today?

Perhaps the most surprising discoveries come from observing the extent to which many Cabo Verdeans today (both on and off the islands) incorporate components of Jewish tradition into their daily lives—while identifying as Catholics (or, in fewer cases, Protestants) and lacking knowledge of the Jewish origins of these practices. Such habits include lighting candles on Friday nights; wearing jewelry with six-pointed stars (including anklets on newborns); avoiding eating pork (on the part of a surprising number of Cabo Verdeans), despite the ubiquity of pork in Portuguese dishes that form a foundation of Cabo Verdean cuisine; and the *nodjadu* style of funeral common in Cabo Verde, which bears many similarities to the common Jewish funeral custom of "sitting shiva" (in contrast to West African funeral customs common on the mainland). Moreover, for many contemporary Cabo Verdeans both on the islands and in the diaspora, secular components of daily life that likely have Jewish origins include common Sephardic family names (especially those derived from words for plants and animals); an entrepreneurial spirit perhaps nurtured by centuries of anti-Semitic exclusion from many government, farming, and other careers across Europe; and a common commitment to a literacy-based learning style, and education in general, that distinguishes these communities from the respect for oral traditions and learning styles that characterizes many mainland West African societies.

If the Jewish origins of these habits are unknown to many contemporary Cabo Verdeans who perpetuate them, other Cabo Verdeans are now developing awareness of the Jewish foundations to their customs, and some have decided to engage actively with that religious and cultural heritage. Among these Cabo Verdeans, some grew up knowing of their (sometimes whispered) Jewish ancestry, while others have only recently become aware of it.

This expanding (re)discovery of Jewish parentage now takes many forms. Some Cabo Verdeans are researching the genetic foundations of their Jewish lineage through DNA tests. Online, lively conversations now abound concerning how to interpret DNA test results, and at least one "DNA Cousins" meet-up has attracted Cabo Verdeans who have discovered each other through their own DNA tests reported on genealogical websites. Other Cabo Verdeans are using social media, historical websites, and archives and other scholarly resources to research their Jewish history.

In the United States, the largest concentration of Cabo Verdeans resides in the New England region (especially the states of Massachusetts and Rhode Island). Here, a group has created a community Passover Seder that has been held annually in Boston since 2006. At this Seder, which now attracts about one hundred Cabo Verdeans and one hundred American Jews every year, many Cabo Verdeans encounter Jewish ritual (and in some cases, white, American Jews) for the first time. The seating plan intentionally promotes conversations that produce curiosity about possible Jewish ancestry on the part of the Cabo Verdeans. On leaving the event, some feel inspired to pursue further knowledge. Many now return regularly and are beginning to feel camaraderie with their Jewish table-mates.

Another influential event was a ritual rededication of a Jewish cemetery held in the Cabo Verdean capital of Praia (on the island of Santiago) in 2013. The event was organized by the Cape Verde Jewish Heritage Project, a non-profit organization dedicated to calling attention to the archipelago's Jewish heritage, especially by restoring degraded tombstones of Jews on several islands.[14] The ritual event rededicating the graves in Praia attracted a small but passionate number of Cabo Verdeans from on and off the islands. From this initiative emerged a new, local NGO, formed by Cabo Verdeans eager to further preserve and publicize the archipelago's Jewish heritage.

Moved by participation in these and other events, some Cabo Verdeans with Jewish ancestry are testing out particular Jewish practices. Some men try on the traditional skullcaps known as *kippahs* or *yahrmulkes* at appropriate times; some try out ways to observe the Sabbath; some begin wearing a Jewish star or displaying a menorah on their mantelpiece; some read books about Jewish history and display them on their coffee tables; and some blog about their newfound knowledge and practice, tentatively performing their new identity in a more public setting. A small number are becoming more committed to their Jewish identity by joining a synagogue, considering themselves fully practicing Jews, and sometimes undergoing the rigorous, formal process of conversion to Conservative or even Orthodox Judaism.

Conclusions

Within Jewish scholarship, an enormous body of literature has long existed addressing the question: "Who is a Jew?"[15] The simple answer of the Orthodox rabbi typically proposes that anyone with exclusively Jewish ancestry through the maternal line may consider her/himself a Jew.

The modern era, however, raises many challenges to this bio-genealogical approach. New community organizations and scholars now attract Jewish groups outside the simplistic dual division of "Sephardic" and "Ashkenazi" Jews that has dominated mainstream Jewish studies for too long.[16] As such, new questions and research paths arise. The present study forms part of a new scholarly trend recognizing a buried history of Jewish activities across the African continent, as attested by other contributions in this volume.[17]

At a broader level, scholars of memory now point to the cultural and political foundations that characterize not only remembering but also forgetting.[18] Adding Cabo Verdeans—and other Africans with documented but partially or even fully forgotten Jewish ancestry—to the conversation allows new questions concerning race and identity to be raised in this contemporary moment of re-thinking geo-religious borders and those who currently experience—and re-evaluate—the effects of their historical crossings.[19]

Works Cited

Acemoglu, Daron, Simon Johnson, and James Robinson. "The Rise of Europe: Atlantic Trade, Institutional Change, and Economic Growth." *American Economic Review* 95, no. 3 (2005): 546–79.

Adas, Michael. *Machines as the Measure of Men: Science, Technology, and Ideologies of Western Dominance*. Ithaca, NY: Cornell University Press, 1990.

Benbassa, Esther, and Aron Rodrigue. *Sephardi Jewry: A History of the Judeo-Spanish Community, 14th-20th Centuries*. Berkeley, CA: University of California Press, 2000 [1993].

Benedictow, Ole J. *The Black Death, 1346-1353: The Complete History*. Suffolk, UK: Boydell Press, 2004.

Bruder, Edith. *The Black Jews of Africa: History, Religion, Identity*. New York, NY: Oxford University Press, 2008.

Connerton, Paul. *How Societies Remember*. Cambridge: Cambridge University Press, 1989.

Corcos, Alain F. *Who is a Jew? Thoughts of a Biologist: An Essay Dedicated to the Jewish and Non-Jewish Victims of the Nazi Holocaust*. Tucson, AZ: Wheatmark, 2012.

de Jong, Ferdinand, and Michael Rowlands, eds. *Reclaiming Heritage: Alternative Imaginaries of Memory in West Africa*. Walnut Creek, CA: Left Coast Press, 2007.

Egerer, Claudia. "Ambivalent geographies: the exotic as domesticated Other." *Third Text* 15, no. 55 (2001):15–28.

Fabian, Johannes. *Memory against Culture: Arguments and Reminders*. Durham, NC: Duke University Press, 2007.

Fagan, Brian. *Fish on Friday: Feasting, Fasting, and the Discovery of the New World*. New York, NY: Basic Books, 2008.

Gerber, Jane S. *The Jews of Spain: A History of the Sephardic Experience*. New York, NY: Free Press/Simon and Schuster, 1992.

Gillis, J. R. *Islands of the Mind: How the Western Imaginary shaped the Atlantic World*. New York, NY: Palgrave Macmillan, 2004.

Gottlieb, Alma. *Africa across the Seder Table: Jewish Identity in Cabo Verde and Its Diaspora*. Book manuscript in preparation, n.d.

Green, Tobias. "Fear and Atlantic History: Some Observations Derived from the Cape Verde Islands and the African Atlantic." *Atlantic Studies: Literary, Cultural and Historical Perspectives on Europe, Africa and the Americas* 3, no. 1 (2006): 25–42.

Green, Tobias. "Masters of Difference: Creolization and the Jewish Presence in Cabo Verde, 1497-1672." Ph. Dissertation, Centre for West

African Studies, University of Birmingham, 2007.
Green, Tobias. "Building Creole Identity in the African Atlantic: Boundaries of Race and Religion in Seventeenth-Century Cabo Verde." *History in Africa* 36 (2009):103–25.
Green, Tobias. *Inquisition: The Reign of Fear*. London: Macmillan/New York, NY: St Martin's Press, 2009.
Green, Tobias. "Beyond Culture Wars: Reconnecting African and Jewish Diasporas in the Past and the Present." In *African Athena: New Agendas*, edited by Daniel Orrells, Gurminder K. Bhambra, and Tessa Roynon, 139–55. Oxford: Oxford University Press, 2011.
Green, Tobias. "Building Slavery in the Atlantic World: Atlantic Connections and the Changing Institution of Slavery in Cabo Verde, Fifteenth–Sixteenth Centuries." *Slavery & Abolition: A Journal of Slave and Post-Slave Studies* 32, no. 2 (2011): 227–45.
Green, Tobias. "Memories of Slavery, Ethnicity, and Forced Labour in Greater Senegambia." *Mande Studies* 16–17 (2015): 169-86.
Halbwachs, Maurice. *On Collective Memory*. Translated by Lewis A. Coser. Chicago, IL: University of Chicago Press, 1992 [1941/1952].
Kamen, Henry. "The Mediterranean & the Expulsion of Spanish Jews in 1492." *Past and Present* 119 (1988): 30–55.
Kaplan, Josef. *An Alternative Path to Modernity: The Sephardi Diaspora in Western Europe*. Leiden: Brill, 2000.
Kaye/Kantrowitz, Melanie. *The Colors of Jews: Racial Politics and Radical Diasporism*. Bloomington, IN: Indiana University Press, 2007.
Kedourie, Elie, ed. *Spain and the Jews: The Sephardi Experience, 1492 and After.* London: Thames & Hudson, 1992.
Litvin, Baruch. *Jewish Identity: Who is a Jew? David Ben Gurion's Query to Leaders of World Jewry and Their Responses*. Edited by Sidney B. Hoenig; 2nd ed. edited by Jeanne Litvin. Brooklyn, NY: KTAV Publishing House, 2012.
Mark, Peter, and José da Silva Horta. *The Forgotten Diaspora: Jewish Communities in West Africa and the Making of the Atlantic World.* Cambridge: Cambridge University Press, 2011.
Martins, Jorge. *Portugal e os Judeus: Volume I – Dos primórdios da nacionalidade à legislação pombalina*. Lisbon: Veja, 2006.
Mokyr, Joel. *A Culture of Growth: The Origins of the Modern Economy.* Princeton, NJ: Princeton University Press, 2016.
Noel, James A. "The Age of Discovery and the Emergence of the Atlantic World." In James A. Noel, *Black Religion and the Imagination of Matter in the Atlantic World*, 15–35. New York, NY: Palgrave Macmillan/St. Martin's Press, 2009.

Oum, Aomar. *Memories of Absence: How Muslims Remember Jews in Morocco*. Stanford, CA: Stanford University Press, 2013.
Paine, Robert. "Columbus and Anthropology and the Unknown." *Journal of the Royal Anthropological Institute* 1 no. 1 (1995): 47–65.
Parry, J. H. *The Age of Reconnaissance: Discovery, Exploration, and Settlement, 1450-1650*. Berkeley, CA: University of California Press, 1982.
Ray, Jonathan S. *After Expulsion: 1492 and the Making of Sephardic Jewry*. New York, NY: NYU Press, 2013.
Routt, David. "The Economic Impact of the Black Death." EH.Net Encyclopedia, edited by Robert Whaples. Economic History Association. July 20, 2008. URL http://eh.net/encyclopedia/the-economic-impact-of-the-black-death/. Accessed August 20, 2018.
Sapega, Ellen W. "Remembering Empire/Forgetting the Colonies: Accretions of Memory and the Limits of Commemoration in a Lisbon Neighborhood." *History & Memory* 20 no. 2 (2008): 18–38.
Sloan, Dolores. *The Sephardic Jews of Spain and Portugal: Survival of an Imperiled Culture in the Fifteenth and Sixteenth Centuries.* Jefferson, NC and London: McFarland, 2009.
Vilches, Elvira. *New World Gold: Cultural Anxiety and Monetary Disorder in Early Modern Spain*. Chicago, IL: University of Chicago Press, 2010.
Yerushalmi, Yosef Hayim. *History of Sephardic Jewry, XIVth-XXth Centuries*. Berkeley, CA: University of California Press, 2000.
Zohar, Zion, ed. *Sephardic and Mizrahi Jewry: From the Golden Age of Spain to Modern Times*. New York, NY: New York University Press, 2005.

Notes

[1] This complex and extended historical moment was surely overdetermined, governed by multiple factors interacting in complicated (and sometimes contradictory) ways. For an emphasis on the role that Atlantic traders played in stimulating economic and political development during this period, see Daron Acemoglu, Simon Johnson, and James Robinson, "The Rise of Europe: Atlantic Trade, Institutional Change, and Economic Growth," *American Economic Review* 95, (2005): 546–79. For discussion of the economic impact of the bubonic plague and its creation of a demand for new labor markets in and beyond Europe, see Ole J. Benedictow, *The Black Death, 1346-1353: The Complete History* (Suffolk, UK: Boydell Press, 2004), and David Routt, "The Economic Impact of the Black Death," *EH.Net Encyclopedia*, ed. Robert Whaples, July 20, 2008. Accessed August 20, 2018. URL: http://eh.net/encyclopedia/the-economic-impact-of-the-black-death/.

On the ways in which gold impelled expansionist dreams, see Elvira Vilches, *New World Gold: Cultural Anxiety and Monetary Disorder in Early Modern Spain* (Chicago, IL: University of Chicago Press, 2010); for an emphasis on the role played by technological and scientific advances in developing maritime exploration, see Michael Adas, *Machines as the Measure of Men: Science, Technology, and Ideologies of Western Dominance* (Ithaca, NY: Cornell University Press, 1990), and Joel Mokyr, *A Culture of Growth: The Origins of the Modern Economy* (Princeton, NJ: Princeton University Press, 2016).
For a focus on religious factors in stimulating international exploration by European navigators, see James A. Noel, "The Age of Discovery and the Emergence of the Atlantic World," in *Black Religion and the Imagination of Matter in the Atlantic World*, James A. Noel (New York, NY: Palgrave Macmillan/St. Martin's Press, 2009), 15–35; for an emphasis on the "yearning for the unusual, the wish to escape one's everyday surroundings", see Claudia Egerer, "Ambivalent Geographies: The Exotic as Domesticated Other," *Third Text* 15, no. 55 (2001): 15–28, and Robert Paine, "Columbus and Anthropology and the Unknown," *Journal of the Royal Anthropological Institute* 1, no. 1 (1995): 47–65; for the conceptual impact of islands, in particular, on European thought, see J. R. Gillis, *Islands of the Mind: How the Western Imaginary Shaped the Atlantic World* (New York, NY: Palgrave Macmillan, 2004).
For multileveled analyses citing technological, economic, political, and religious motives, see, for example, J. H. Parry, Part 1, in *The Age of Reconnaissance: Discovery, Exploration, and Settlement, 1450-1650* (Berkeley, CA: University of California Press, 1982), and Brian Fagan, *Fish on Friday: Feasting, Fasting, and the Discovery of the New World* (New York, NY: Basic Books, 2008).
Finally, for an example of how contemporary memory reinterprets the eras of early global navigation by European sailors compared with more recent soldiers fighting colonial wars, see Ellen W. Sapega, "Remembering Empire/Forgetting the Colonies: Accretions of Memory and the Limits of Commemoration in a Lisbon Neighborhood," *History & Memory* 20, no. 2 (2008): 18–38.

[2] For a cogent synopsis of the mutual impact of the growing slave trade on both Cabo Verde and the Americas, see Tobias Green, "Building Slavery in the Atlantic World: Atlantic Connections and the Changing Institution of Slavery in Cabo Verde, Fifteenth–Sixteenth Centuries," *Slavery & Abolition: A Journal of Slave and Post-Slave Studies* 32, no. 2 (2011)" 227–45.

[3] For one discussion of this era in Portuguese history, see Jorge Martins, *Portugal e os Judeus: Volume I – Dos primórdios da nacionalidade à legislação pombalina* (Lisbon: Veja, 2006).

[4] Although the Spanish Order of Expulsion did not mention conversion as an alternative to expulsion, scholars of this period generally agree that "There can be no doubt whatever that conversion rather than expulsion was the primary objective of the Catholic monarchs". Henry Kamen, "The Mediterranean & the Expulsion of Spanish Jews in 1492," *Past and Present*, no. 119 (1988): 37.

[5] Scholarship about the history of Sephardic Jews both before and after the twin Edicts of Expulsion from Spain and Portugal is now robust; for a few key works, see: Esther Benbassa and Aron Rodrigue, *Sephardi Jewry: A History of the Judeo-*

Spanish Community, 14th-20th Centuries (Berkeley, CA: University of California Press, 2000 [1993]); Jane S. Gerber, *The Jews of Spain: A History of the Sephardic Experience* (New York, NY: Free Press/Simon and Schuster, 1992); Josef Kaplan, *An Alternative Path to Modernity: The Sephardi Diaspora in Western Europe* (Leiden: Brill, 2000); Elie Kedourie, ed., *Spain and the Jews: The Sephardi Experience, 1492 and After* (London: Thames & Hudson, 1992); Jonathan S. Ray, *After Expulsion: 1492 and the Making of Sephardic Jewry* (New York, NY: NYU Press, 2013); Dolores Sloan, *The Sephardic Jews of Spain and Portugal: Survival of an Imperiled Culture in the Fifteenth and Sixteenth Centuries* (Jefferson, NC/London: McFarland, 2009); and Zion Zohar, ed., *Sephardic and Mizrahi Jewry: From the Golden Age of Spain to Modern Times* (New York, NY: New York University Press, 2005).

[6] Tobias Green, *Inquisition: The Reign of Fear* (New York, NY: St. Martin's Press, 2009).

[7] Precise figures are impossible to ascertain, due to ambiguous or missing records. Earlier claims of one hundred and fifty thousand refugees following the two expulsion orders were disputed by Kamen, who estimated the figure to be closer to forty thousand to fifty thousand. Henry Kamen, "The Mediterranean & the Expulsion of Spanish Jews in 1492," *Past and Present*, no. 119 (1988): 44.

[8] Yosef Hayim Yerushalmi, *History of Sephardic Jewry, XIVth-XXth Centuries* (Berkeley, CA: University of California Press, 2000).

[9] Tobias Green, "Masters of Difference: Creolization and the Jewish Presence in Cabo Verde, 1497-1672" (PhD Diss., Centre of West African Studies, University of Birmingham, 2007).

[10] Ibid.

[11] Green, "Masters of Difference".

[12] For a discussion of one case, see Tobias Green, "Building Creole Identity in the African Atlantic: Boundaries of Race and Religion in Seventeenth-Century Cabo Verde," *History in Africa* 36:103-25 (2009).

[13] I have recorded some intriguing exceptions to this normative expectation; I explore their unique circumstances elsewhere – Alma Gottlieb, *Africa across the Seder Table: Jewish Identity in Cabo Verde and Its Diaspora* (book manuscript in preparation, n.d.).

[14] This organization was founded by Carol Castiel, an American Jew who first became aware of the Jewish origins of some Cabo Verdeans while working for a foundation in New York. The organization she created has now attracted significant funding from donors, and attention from the Cabo Verdean government (https://capeverdejewishheritage.org/).

[15] For some recent, conflicting accounts, see, for example, Joyathan Boyarin, *Thinking in Jewish* (Chicago, IL: University of Chicago Press, 1996); Alain F. Corcos, *Who is a Jew? Thoughts of a Biologist: An Essay Dedicated to the Jewish and Non-Jewish Victims of the Nazi Holocaust* (Tucson, AZ: Wheatmark, 2012); Meryl Hyman, *"Who Is a Jew?" Conversations, Not Conclusions* (Woodstock, VT: Jewish Lights Publ., 1998); Morris N. Kertzer, *What Is a Jew? A Guide to the Beliefs, Traditions, and Practices of Judaism that Answers Questions for Both Jew and Non-Jew*, rev. ed. (New York, NY: Touchstone/ Simon and Schuster, 1993

[1953]); and Baruch Litvin, *Jewish Identity: Who is a Jew?* ed. Sidney B. Hoenig, 2nd edition ed. Jeanne Litvin (Brooklyn, NY: KTAV Publishing House, 2012). By contrast, for a warning of the risks incurred in delineating Jews from others, as exemplified by the Inquisition and the Third Reich, see Tobias Green, "Beyond Culture Wars: Reconnecting African and Jewish Diasporas in the Past and the Present," in *African Athena: New Agendas,* eds. Daniel Orrells, Gurminder K. Bhambra, and Tessa Roynon (Oxford: Oxford University Press, 2011), 147.

[16] Melanie Kaye/Kantrowitz, *The Colors of Jews: Racial Politics and Radical Diasporism* (Bloomington, IN: Indiana University Press, 2007).

[17] Two important recent works of scholarship are Edith Bruder, *The Black Jews of Africa: History, Religion, Identity* (New York, NY: Oxford University Press, 2008); and Peter Mark and José da Silva Horta, *The Forgotten Diaspora: Jewish Communities in West Africa and the Making of the Atlantic World* (Cambridge: Cambridge University Press, 2011).

[18] A selective list includes: Paul Connerton, *How Societies Remember* (Cambridge: Cambridge University Press, 1989); Ferdinand de Jong and Michael Rowlands, eds., *Reclaiming Heritage: Alternative Imaginaries of Memory in West Africa* (Walnut Creek, CA: Left Coast Press, 2007); Johannes Fabian, *Memory against Culture: Arguments and Reminders* (Durham, NC: Duke University Press, 2007); Tobias Green, "Memories of Slavery, Ethnicity, and Forced Labour in Greater Senegambia," *Mande Studies* 16–17 (2015); Maurice Halbwachs [1941/1952], *On Collective Memory*, transl. Lewis A. Coser (Chicago, IL: University of Chicago Press, 1992); Aomar Oum, *Memories of Absence: How Muslims Remember Jews in Morocco* (Stanford, CA: Stanford University Press, 2013).

[19] Tobias Green, "Beyond Culture Wars: Reconnecting African and Jewish Diasporas in the Past and the Present," in *African Athena: New Agendas*, eds. Daniel Orrells, Gurminder K. Bhambra, and Tessa Roynon (Oxford: Oxford University Press, 2015) 139–55.

Acknowledgments

A much shorter version of this chapter was first presented at the Third Conference of the International Society for the Study of African Jewry—ISSAJ, "The Surge of Judaism across Africa, the African Diaspora and Asia in the Twenty-first Century" (November 10–11, 2015, Museum of Jewish History and Art, Paris). A short piece derived from that talk appeared as "The Jews of Cape Verde," in *Jews from Elsewhere*. I am grateful to audience members at the original conference for their thoughtful questions and comments, and to Edith Bruder for the invitation to expand on that talk for the present publication.

The research that forms the foundation for this contribution was supported by the US National Endowment for the Humanities, the European Commission/US Department of Education, and several units at the University of Illinois at Urbana-Champaign (European Union Center, Research Board, and International Programs and Studies). I am grateful to each of these agencies and organizations for their financial support.

Most importantly, I am indebted to the many Cabo Verdeans and American Jews who have contributed their time, expertise, memories, and opinions to this project. All interpretations are my own.

CHAPTER EIGHT

CONCENTRIC CIRCLES OF JEWISH/ISRAELITE IDENTITY IN SUB-SAHARAN AFRICA[1]

WILLIAM F. S. MILES

Introduction: The Need for African Jewish Identity Differentiation

The emergence of new Jewish communities in Africa begs an old question: "Who is a Jew?" This question takes on particular resonance where some segments of long-established African ethnic groups increasingly invoke descent from ancient Israelite tribes. Some self-identifying Jewish communities in Africa employ the narrative of Hebrew lineage to buttress a claim of Jewishness that they otherwise advance by Torah-based scriptural study and religious observance. For other supposed "members of the tribe", the mere belief in such historicity suffices to assume the mantle of Jewishness, regardless of current religious affiliation and practice. Yet others advance the "fact" of Israelite ancestry to legitimate their claims to Jewishness while adopting new beliefs or renewing older practices at direct odds with contemporary rabbinic norms of Judaism.

Indiscriminately lumping all three categories together under the rubric of "African Judaism" or "African Jewry" represents a kind of intellectual disfigurement of the subject at hand. It also does real harm to those "core" ring practitioners of Judaism who undertake real sacrifices to practice the Jewish faith and struggle to be recognized as Jews. Some scholarly consensus regarding the legitimacy (and not) of all the wide-ranging claims to Jewish identity in Black Africa is critical to the integrity of the discipline. More important is the ethical imperative of not harming genuine African practitioners of Judaism by contributing to their confusion with "Judaizing" groups who embrace beliefs and practices beyond the bounds of global Jewish consensus. Such confusion invites their (often uninformed) rejection by global gatekeepers of Jewish peoplehood.

This chapter therefore proposes a conceptualization of these differential degrees of historicized Jewish identity in Africa in terms of three concentric circles or rings: "core" (characterized by "orthopraxy," or the embrace of *normative Judaism*), "middle" ("pseudopraxy," characterized by *Hebraic eclecticism*), and "outer" (*vague Israelitism*, which claims Jewishness merely on the basis of putative descent from a lost tribe of Israel). This taxonomy emanates from a review of the extant scholarly literature on the emerging phenomenon of New Jewish Movements (NJMs)[2] as informed by the author's published findings from the geographical antipodes of African Judaism: Nigeria and Madagascar.[3] It also benefits from fieldwork with the original Beth Yeshourun Jewish community in Yaoundé, Cameroon.

From the outset, it should be emphasized that the lines separating the different rings are highly permeable. Individuals commonly shift between the rings; the direction, however, generally tends to be from the outer core towards the middle and then sometimes to the center. The closer to the inner core of the ring sub-Saharan Jews come, the more important maintaining the lines of separation becomes. In the conclusion, I shall address a potential weakness to the position set forth here: that the standard for acceptance as Jews could, at least for the foreseeable future, be more rigorous, and more religion-based, in the African than in Western contexts. The Euro-American notion of a purely "cultural Jew"—one for whom Jewishness, inherited by ancestry, is merely a matter of cuisine, or humor, or social affiliation—does not translate to African societies that take their religions, and religious affiliations, much more seriously than that.

The Concentric-Ring Model

The Outer Ring: Vague Israelitism

The outer ring of the model (see Figure 1) harks back to a kind of orthodoxy in the original sense of Jewish identity: descent from ancient Hebrews/Israelites. "Orthodoxy", with a capital "O" (as in the Orthodox movement of Judaism), further maintains that that descent must be maternal: a Jew is one whose mother is Jewish.

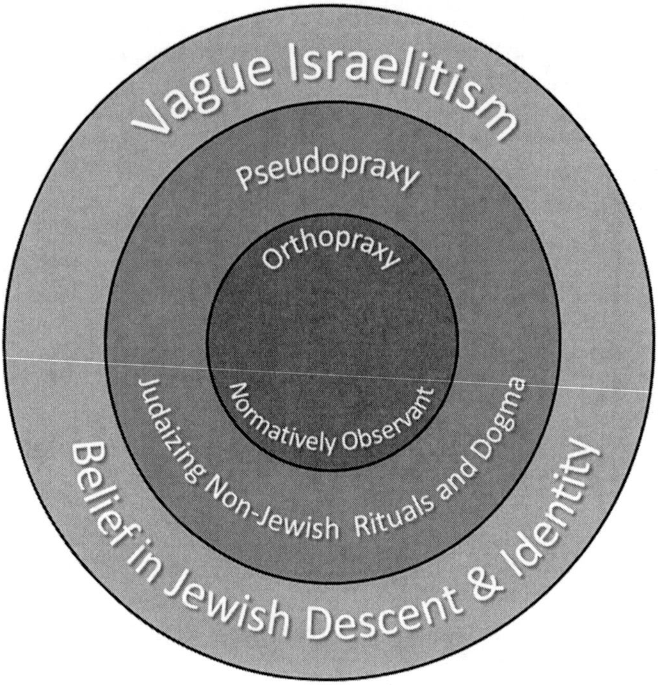

Figure 1. The Concentric Circle-Model of sub-Saharan Israelite/Jewish Identity

Where claimed in the sub-Saharan African context, however, the line of descent is so obscured that immediate or maternal descent is irrelevant. This often takes the Ten Lost Tribes of Israel tack: "We are descendants of the Lost Tribe of…; we are therefore Jews." Often the actual tribe is not emphasized, or even identified: that is why *vague Israelitism* characterizes this outer ring. Note that there is no presumption of exclusivity in this formulation: "We are Jews" can also be followed by "and we are also…s" (some other religion). Both in Africa itself and throughout the African diaspora the wildly speculative colonial-era thesis of British missionary Joseph Williams is still regularly invoked to "prove" West African Israelite (as well as West Indian) tribal descent.[4]

This outer-ring belief in Jewish identity may be generalized throughout the broader society without it implying any further consequence or change in more recently inherited religious belief in practice. "Our forefathers were Israelites; we are Israelites/Jews." Outer-ring belief in Jewish identity is often also reduced to a sense of "DNA Jewry": "I have Hebrew/Israelite/

Jewish blood. I, too, am therefore a Jew." In certain cases, such belief is buttressed by genetic testing, the most famous one being of the Lemba of Southern Africa. According to published peer-reviewed results, Lemba men carry in their DNA a "cohen-associated-genetic-signature" that lies in the Y chromosome. It is a finding that corroborates Lemba oral tradition.[5]

Presumably, many if not most of these genetically-Jewish-connected persons are content with whatever religion they have inherited or adopted and would resent the implication that they are "really" Jews. In short, the thesis of a "Jewish gene" is problematic on several accounts. For their part, most Lemba still prioritize their Lemba customs and traditions and inherited Christian religion over the impetus to rejoin contemporary Jewish religion, observance, and history. That will not prevent them from claiming to be Jews.

The Middle Ring: Pseudopraxy

In the middle ring are those sub-Saharan Africans who adopt practices and rituals that they believe make them Jewish or reinforce their Judaism, even if those practices and rituals have long been abandoned by normative Judaism as it has evolved over the last two millennia. Alternately, they adhere to beliefs that are beyond the pale of contemporary, normative Judaism as it has also evolved over the last two thousand years. In some ways, this is similar to the Middle Eastern cases of the Samaritans and Karaites, who still adhere to Torah-derived precepts and practices while rejecting the Oral Law and putting them outside realm of Jews proper.

The middle ring often serves as the conduit from which core-ring Jews have passed. Acknowledging Saturday as the day of rest, observing Jewish fast days, praying in Hebrew, outwardly dressing as Orthodox Jews—these are hallmarks of a misleading or pseudo-Judaism when adopted simultaneously with belief in Jesus-as-the-Messiah or, indeed, when adopted precisely because this is how Jesus is thought to have lived his life. Levirate ritual sacrifice of heifers and goats as proof of Jewish status is another kind of middle-ring pseudopraxy: It has been millennia, as a result of the destruction of the Second Temple, since Jews have ceased offering such sacrifices, moving to a text-based, rabbinic kind of Judaism instead.

Emulating a Jewish lifestyle in order to bring the African "Jew" closer to Jesus (who presumably lived that same lifestyle) is another form of "Judaizing" non-Jewish belief. Sub-Saharans who either sacrifice animals as did Israelites, or adopt Jewish customs to get closer to Christ, exhibit a kind of Hebraic eclecticism: they carefully choose which ancient Hebrew or Israelite practices to adopt, and they do so religiously. In this, they differ from the outer-ring Africans who maintain beliefs in Hebrew/Israelite/Jewish origin without acting upon them.

Indeed, in certain respects these middle-ring Jewish/Israelite identifiers are more respectful and observant of certain aspects of Jewish law and teaching than are normative Jews themselves. What is nevertheless "pseudo" in their praxis is the affirmation that such beliefs and rituals make them *ipso facto* Jews. It is by their non-normative Jewish practices and beliefs that those in this middle circle remain outside of the inner ring—however much they would like to be regarded as lying within in it.

The Inner Ring: Orthopraxy

Orthopractitioners, according to this model, are observers and practitioners of normative Judaism: Jews *tout court*. Attributes of normative Judaism include recognition of Torah and Talmud as foundational texts; identification with the history of the people who have preserved these texts; Hebrew as common language of prayer; knowledge, if not celebration, of the range of holidays, from the biblically-based (e.g., Yom Kippur, Passover) to the post-biblical ones (e.g., Hanukkah, Purim); and recognition of Israel as ancestral homeland.

Whether they are descendants of ancient Israelites or not; whether they *believe* that they are descendants (e.g., Sefwi Akan of Ghana, Dan of Côte d'Ivoire) or not (e.g., Abayudaya of Uganda, Beti of Cameroon)—these are the communities for which we should, in the African context, reserve the nomenclature "sub-Saharan Jew". Many if not most of these sub-Saharan Jews have crossed over from the middle ring (often at great personal sacrifice; excommunication, divorce, and bachelorhood are not uncommon results). Other sub-Saharan Jews have come from more traditional Christian backgrounds and not from the messianic bridging denominations. (Very few have come to normative Judaism from Islam.)

Regardless of their belief in Hebraic/Israelite origins, orthopraxy takes precedence over orthodoxy for all these inner-core sub-Saharan Jews. It is by their observance and practice of Judaism more than their belief in Hebraic/Israelite origins that they stake their claims as Jews. If genealogy alone sufficed to constitute sub-Saharan Jewry, then there would be no need for Jewish practice—as is the case with the outer-ring believers in Jewish descent and identity.

Belief in Jewish descent is neither necessary nor sufficient for inner-ring status. While its assertion reinforces the impulse to practice Judaism for those who do make the claim, belief in Israelite descent is not the primary driver of sub-Saharan Judaism. The primary driver is the single characteristic that transcends all other differences among sub-Saharan religions, languages, traditions, and histories: taking religion seriously.

A multiplicity of denominations has come to characterize world Judaism. The concentric-circle model for sub-Saharan Jewry therefore begs the question: "What is normative Judaism?" The answer is less definitional than phenomenological and admittedly vulnerable to criticism of being self-referential: "Normative Judaism is the aggregate of religious beliefs, and especially practices, which are recognizable and accepted by most individuals and communities who are themselves recognized as normatively Jewish." In other words, if the overwhelming majority of Jews of all ethno-cultural provenances—Mizrachi, Cochini, Ashkenazi—witness, recognize, relate to, and identify with the worship, study, and teachings undertaken by sub-Saharans, self-consciously as Jews, then those practices and beliefs qualify as normative Judaism.

There are difficulties, of course, with this standard of inner-ring Jewish orthopraxy. Ultraorthodox denominations, for example, reject the Reform movement (among others) as constitutive of normative Judaism. (In fact, the Ultraorthodox do not accept Reform as being an authentic expression of Judaism at all). The inner-core definition put forth here will not satisfy the monopolistic claims of the Ultraorthodox (or even the modern Orthodox); but, in reality, there is no functional gatekeeping monopoly within Judaism as it is.

The next section applies the concentric-circle model to two specific cases: Igbo of Nigeria and Malagasy of Madagascar.

Applications of the Model: Igbo (Nigeria) and Malagasy (Madagascar)

The Outer Ring: Nigerian Covenant Heritage and the Malagasy Secret

Two of the largest ethnic groups in Nigeria maintain parallel beliefs in descent from ancient Semitic, if not outright Israelite, tribes. Court chroniclers of the Yoruba (or at least those of the Oyo), whose ancestral home is in southwest Nigeria, invoke a lineage that follows the Assyrian conquest of ancient Israel.[6] Although Dierk Lange's scholarly compilation (and largely positive assessment) of Yoruba beliefs in Israelite origins does not invoke a specific tribe from which they supposedly descend, other Yoruba assume the mantle of "sons of Ephraim".[7] Linguistic, creedal, and ritualistic parallels are all invoked to prove the Yoruba-Israelite thesis. Yoruba Protestant theologian and linguist Modupe Oduyoye traces his people's origins even further, to the biblical figure Nimrod (a cognate of Lamurudu).[8]

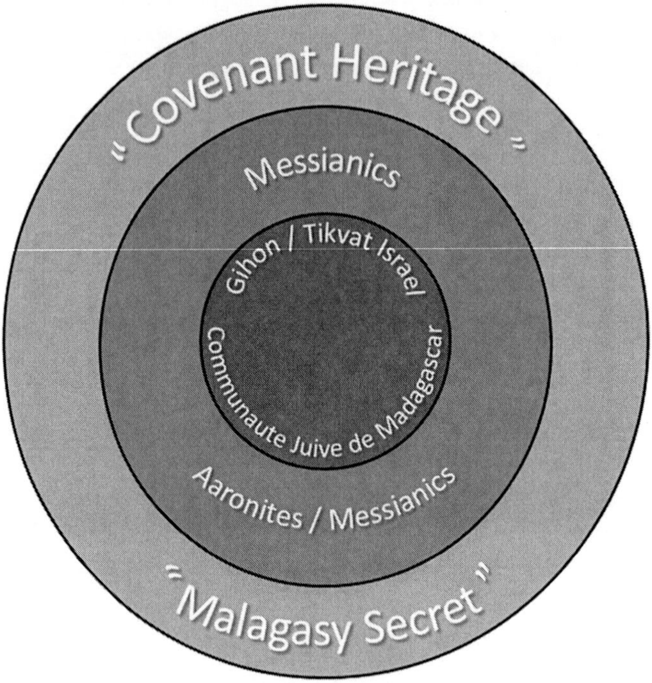

Figure 2. Jubo and Malagasy Applications of the Concentric-Circle Model

More generalized belief in Hebrew/Israelite descent occurs among the Igbo. In the southeast Nigerian homeland of the Igbo, the ancient settlement of Aguleri is believed by many Igbo to be the West African relocation site of the Northern Israelite tribe of Gad. In the palace of the Eze Eri, the traditional chief and custodian of this local Igbo clan, are inscriptions in the floor locally believed to be ancient Hebrew.[9] Numerous similarities between the Igbo and Hebrew languages, and between Igbo traditional practices and ancient Jewish rituals (e.g., infant male circumcision, and New Moon and First Harvest celebrations) are invoked as evidence of Igbo-Israelite ethnogenesis.[10] So why did the Igbos lose their connection to Judaism? The answer is British colonialism: "Cultural imperialism against the Ibos [came] in such a way that all traces of Jewish culture, artefacts [sic], and so on in

Iboland were targeted for destruction."[11] Some colonial-era texts are nevertheless invoked to buttress the claim of Israelite descent of the Igbos. These include the writings of missionary G. T. Basden and the earlier autobiography of Equiano Olaudah.

Chinuaekpwere (who also goes by "Emmanuel") Fakas uses the term "Covenant Heritage" to describe the bond between the God of the Hebrews and the Igbos.

Since the Igbo-led secessionist movement for an independent Biafra in the 1960s, and the characterization of the (Muslim-dominated) federal government's suppression of the rebellion as genocide, leaders of the lost cause have drawn a direct parallel between Biafrans and the victims of the *Shoah*. Although not intended to encourage Jewish-Igbo identification, Israeli support for the secessionists fueled it at the time—and it continues to. Release of a jailed Igbo nationalist in May of 2017 was conditional on the appearance of a religious leader of notoriety to vouch for him. Coming forward to fulfill that role was one Immanuel-El Shalom Oka-Ben Madu, who came to court wearing a Jewish skull cap and a prayer shawl (emblazoned with Star of David emblems). This prompted one local news site to ironically describe him as "An Igbo in Jewish Clothing".[12] Beyond lingering bitterness from the Biafran war, broader tensions between Muslims and Christians in Nigeria contribute to the pro-Israel sentiments of the latter, which leads in varying degrees to identification with the Jewish people.

Like the Igbo of Nigeria, many Malagasy in Madagascar hold to the belief of ancient Israelite migration and descent. General loss of that memory is, even more intensely than in Nigeria, attributed to a concerted campaign by colonialists and missionaries (there, French) to simultaneously govern and convert.

As an island, Madagascar's version of the original Israelite coming is maritime: one legend speaks of Hebrew-speaking marooned mariners from the time of King Solomon who came searching for timber to build the Temple in Jerusalem.[13] For a belief that circulates fairly widely, it is curiously dubbed Madagascar's "secret". A version particular to the kings and scribes in Vatumasina (Vohipeno district), almost 400 miles to the southwest of Antananarivo, the capital, has it that their ancestor was a Jew who fled to Mecca and converted to Islam after the Romans sacked Jerusalem, his original home. This man, though, Ali, still used the Torah; hence his full name, Alitawarat. Consistent with the melding of Israelite identity with anti-imperialism, the elders lamented that the sacred objects proving their Jewish origins were lost during the brutal French colonial repression of the island's pro-independence rebellion in the 1940s.

The most prominent populizer of the Malagasy Israelite descent thesis is a member of one of the royal houses of Madagascar, Prince Ndriana Rabarioelina. On social media and in voluminous writing,[14] Ndriana invokes, as do Igbo Judaizers, extensive ritualistic and linguistic similarities between ancient Israel and his own Malagasy people. He also promulgates the Vatumasina thesis described above; however, in an interview he assured me that the elders of that village dissemble to outsiders regarding the loss of their material proof of Israelite descent, and that they are still secretly preserving both the staff of Moses and a fragment of the Ten Commandments tablet. Others who make similar claims of Malagasy Israelite descent include a German-trained pastor [15] and a controversial Kabbalist.[16]

In both Nigeria and Madagascar, then, there is much "in the air"—particularly in the Igbo and Malagasy air—to provide grist for the mill of Israelite ethnogenesis. What is made of those beliefs is another matter.

The Middle Ring: Igbo and Malagasy Messianics, and Aaronites of Madagascar

Belief in Israelite descent, be it in Nigeria or Madagascar, does not necessarily change religious behavior or affiliation. When it does, however, it leads to the adoption of beliefs and practices that draw the practitioners into the middle ring. That middle ring is characterized by practices and beliefs that approximate some version of Judaism—either ancient or contemporary—without quite equalling it.

Among the Igbo of Nigeria, the portal for entry to the middle ring were North American "Messianic Jewish" evangelizers such as Richard "Aharon" Chaimberlin, self-annointed rabbi of the Petach Tikva Fellowship based in Rochester, New York.[17] African Messianic Judaism grafts core tenets and scriptures of Christianity (Jesus Christ as Messiah, New Testament) onto traditional Judaism. The major theological premise of Messianic Judaism is that, since Jesus was himself Jewish, there is no incompatibilty between Judaism and Christianity, between being Jewish and being Christian.

According to Onwukwe Alaezi, therefore, the "blindness and prejudice" of Jews' rejection of Christ can be overcome in Nigeria by Igbos' acceptance of their Hebrew roots and simultaneously embracing Christianity and Judaism. "How are we to include our Jewishness or Hebraism into Christian way of life under the New Covenant of Christ the Messiah," he asks rhetorically, "rather than the Old Covenant of Moses with its heavy 613 rules and regulations?"[18]

Messianic synagogues and congregations in Nigeria are also concentrated among the Igbo. Igbo are the object of renewed and intensified missionizing efforts by American Messianic Christians in the form of Jewish Voice Ministries International. This has resulted in competition, if not tension, with normatively Jewish US- and Israel-based outreach organizations also present in Nigeria for whom there is a fundamental incompatibility between Judaism and belief in Jesus Christ as Messiah.[19] Messianic activity has sown theological confusion and discord in southeast Nigeria. Perhaps even more disruptive has been the conducting of DNA tests by Messianic Jewish Voice, results of which negated Igbo claims of Jewish descent.[20]

The permeability between Igbo middle-ring Messianism and inner-ring normative Judaism is worth stressing. Many of those now situated in the inner core passed there having learned about Judaism as Messianics themselves. In most cases it was theological dissonance that led them to reject the doctrine of a human God and a Trinity within monotheism, but they still recognize Messianism as the pathway that eventually brought them to "true" Judaism. It was the plan of Hashem (God; literally, "the Name") they believe: how else in such a Christianized part of Nigeria could they have been exposed at all to Judaism, were it not for "Messianics"?

A parallel middle-ring phenomenon exists in Madagascar: Christian or Messianic "synagogues" are sprinkled around the island. Mesirima, for instance, is one accorded recognition by the government in 2007 and self-characterized as closer to "Messianic" than "Zionic" Judaism.[21]

As in Nigeria, "Messianic" churches in Madagascar have also served as portals for those who eventually moved into the inner ring of Judaism without Jesus. In neither case, however, is there inevitability or uni-directionality from Messianism to Judaism. In Nigeria, there are ambivalently related cases of individuals or entire synagogues "backsliding" back to Messianism. Such fluidity is an example of the porousness of the rings that I mentioned earlier.

The Inner Ring: Jubos and the Jewish Community of Madagascar

Whether they transitioned from "Messianic" Judaism or from more mainstream branches of Christianity (i.e., Protestant, Roman Catholic), normative Jewish congregations in both Nigeria and Madagascar take pains not to be confused with their theological forebears or other institutions of "Jesus-followers". A survey conducted on behalf of Edith Bruder identified eighteen synagogues and congregations operating as of 2012 in the Federal Capital Territory of Abuja and five of Nigeria's thirty-six states: Anambra,

Edo, Imo, Lagos, and Rivers.[22] As of 2018, the number of synagogues aligned under the Judaism Fellowship Inititative (functionally, the Jewish federation of Nigeria) is double that originally identified by Bruder. A similar number of synagogues are potential adherents, pending their agreement to join and satisfaction of standards established by the umbrella organization.[23] The vast majority of synagogues are located in the southeast of Nigeria, cradle of the Igbo. They range from standalone structures to synagogues within compounds to parts of homes designated as prayer spaces. Services are held on Shabbat and holidays according to the Jewish calendar. Study sessions of Torah, Jewish history and culture are held. Identification with modern Israel is intense. Bar and bat mitzvah rites of passage are celebrated. WhatsApp groups join Jewish youth across the southern half of the country. Blogs that publicize Nigerian synagogue and community events enliven cyberspace.[24] Depending on size and location, there is formal Jewish instruction for children.

In terms of numbers of practitioners, from the partial data provided in the published table by Bruder one can infer approximately five hundred "regular participants" in the eighteen synagogues. This is a far cry from the estimate of thirty thousand Igbo she provides in the opening line of her chapter as "practicing a form of Judaism".[25] The discrepancy, of course, redounds to the difference between those Igbos inhabiting the core ring of Nigerian Jewry and the middle- and outer-ringers: in the middle circle, Jesus-followers who have adopted some Jewish practices; in the outer, "Hebrewists who consider themselves 'pre-Talmudic' Jews on the basis of alleged Hebraic traditions of their forefathers".[26] Muddying the demographic waters are the "more than two million [Sabbatharians] who practice a kind of Judaism while also reading the New Testament".[27] Afsai estimates the number of core-ring Jubos—that is, Nigerian Igbos adhering to the belief system of and practicing according to normative Judaism—as between two thousand and five thousand.[28]

The normative Jewish community of Madagascar is much smaller than that of Nigeria, numbering in the hundreds rather than the thousands. Only a handful of Nigerians whom I situate within the inner ring have actually undergone ritual conversion to Judaism—some in Uganda under the auspices of the Conservative movement, others in Israel under the state (and therefore Orthodox) rabbinate. In Madagascar, however, over one hundred men and women underwent collective conversion ceremonies in 2016 through a North American *bet din* constituted by three modern Orthodox rabbis.[29] These are the ones who have unambiguously left behind traces of either normative Christianity for some or Jesus-inflected "Messianic Judaism" for others. As in Nigeria (and, to a certain extent, Cameroon), however, traces of the *style* of Christian and "Messianic Jewish" preaching can still be detected.

The *Communauté Juive de Madagascar* (CJM) is the sole Jewish institution recognized by the government of Madagascar. (In Nigeria, offical recognition of synagogues is accorded by the individual states.) As registered, CJM objectives are to promote education, health, and the environment "according to the principles of the TORAH". As of 2015, only one house of worship (a room in a private home) served the Jews of Madagascar. Rented facilities served as locus for Hebrew language and religious study classes. While these classes were open to all Malagasy interested in learning about Judaism, it aimed specifically to prepare for formal conversion.

While there is no Jubo or Malagasy rabbi, proficient cantors serve both the Jewish communities in both countries. Although both profess higher affinity for Sephardic as opposed to Ashkenazi rites, liturgy, and prayer books, as a Francophone community the Malagasy (as well as the Cameroonian) Jews have easier access through French to Sephardic materials in France than (Anglophone) Nigerian Jews do.

Conclusion: Ideographic Overlap and Scholarly Ethics

The concentric rings of Jewish/Israelite identity in sub-Saharan Africa are permeable not only in the sense of individuals moving among the three circles (albeit more commonly from the outer towards the inner rings). There is also overlap in terms of ethnogenetic belief in identity. Belief in descent from a lost tribe of Israel (a foundational belief in the outer ring) is often shared by inhabitants of the middle and inner rings. In Nigeria and in Madagascar, such belief (specifically, descending from the tribe of Gad for the former, and being descendendants of Abraham and David for the latter) legitimates and reinforces the choice among Igbos and Malagasy to assume the responsibilities of covenant that adherence to normative Judaism there requires. The difficulty of adhering to the *mitzvot* (613 commandments) and joining an historically vilified minority people is, in other words, eased by the belief that such actions constitute ancient inheritances of the Igbo and Malagasy peoples. Inner-ring Jews from Nigeria and Madagascar believe that *all* Igbo and Malagasy are descendants of ancient Israel but only some fully assume and re-actualize that long- (colonially) suppressed legacy. Jewish/Israelite ethnogenesis is not the only, or even primary, reason for living as Jews, for these Igbo of Nigeria and Malagasy of Madagascar. In their daily lives, it is their Jewish *praxis*—worship, study, diet, dress—that dominates, not discussion of origins. And it is this that defines them as sub-

Saharan Jews, not their descent (be it actually historic or merely asserted) from ancient Israel.

Cameroon provides a partial exception to this phenomenon. As Nathan Devir writes, “This community is unique [in that] its founding members”—all from the Eton subgroup of the Beti—“do not claim to ever have been ‘lost’ from the hereditary Jewish fold”.[30] Still, he goes on to detail a “geneological trope, after all” among the Bamileke and Bassa linking them to ancient Israel. While the vast majority of these Bassa reside conceptually in the outer ring, a few inner-ring individuals have latched on to Israelite descent legends.

The concentric-circle model of sub-Saharan Jewish identity should not leave the impression that there is staunch unity among all those who dwell within the inner ring of sub-Saharan Judaism. One may utter or write on a synagogue wall in Hebrew (as is the case in Tikvat Israel, Abuja) words to the effect that All Israel is One. The reality is different. From Nigeria to Cameroon to Madagascar and in-between, Jewish community life is riven by factionalization, for reasons of theology as well as personality. This, ironically, only brings sub-Saharan Judaism closer to Jewish life throughout history and in the world today: Jewish Africa is not immune from the “two Jews, three synagogues” allegory. In the context of severe resource scarcity typifying sub-Saharan Africa in general, however, inner-ring factionalization is aggravated by the role of well-intentioned but inadvertently disruptive external Jewish organizations, which intervene by providing scarce liturgical resources.

Related are the ethical dimensions of scholarship that overlooks or minimizes the profound chagrin among inner-ring sub-Saharan Jews when they are conceptually aggregated among, labelled alongside, or simply confused with fellow Africans who call themselves “Jews” for outer- and middle-ring reasons. The fact that they themselves have transitioned from “Messianic” to normative Judaism in no way lessens that sense of grievance. To a certain degree, given the sacrifices they have made as a result of their move from the middle to the inner ring, it even intensifies it. From Nigeria to Cameroon to Madagascar, individuals have unburdened to me the pain they experienced from having a spouse leave them on account of their transition from Christianity (Messianic and not) to Judaism *sans* Jesus. Others have expressed wariness that neighbors fear that they have left a recognizable religion to practice a cult—this, in a nation where cults are widely associated with ritual murder. Most recently, I have had to counsel a Nigerian Jewish friend who was deeply confused, upset and fearful when adversaries insidiously attacked him by invoking *The Protocols of the Elders of Zion*. Normative Judaism in sub-Saharan Africa entails real emotional as well as material costs. Outer- and middle-ring inhabitants do not suffer equivalent rejection or sacrifice.

I conclude by suggesting that the budding phenomenon of sub-Saharan Judaism poses challenges to First World notions of Jewish identity. Western Jews often dispense with the necessity of Jewish religion as a criterion for credibly claiming membership within *klal Yisrael*, the global "tribe" of the Jewish people. At this stage, sub-Saharan Jews do not have a similar "luxury" to claim—or be taken seriously if they claim—that they are ethnically Jewish while dispensing with all obligations or niceties of Jewish religious practice: "secular sub-Saharan Jew" is a non sequitur. Conversely, the seriousness with which sub-Saharan Jews *do* take their Judaism challenges First World Jewry, particularly in a context of declining Jewish affiliation and demographic replacement in the Jewish diaspora. In the long run, then, the model of concentric circles of Jewish identity may not only help clarify the "who is a Jew" question in the context sub-Saharan Africa. Ultimately, the blossoming of Judaism in Africa may force Western Jews to re-examine what "being Jewish" means to them. If that happens, sub-Saharan Jews may no longer remain merely the objects of Western (and academic) Jewish scrutiny but become active definers of what it means for anyone, anywhere, to claim to be a Jew.

Works Cited

Afsai, Shai. "Nigeria's Igbo Jews: Jewish identity and practice in Abuja." *Anthropology Today* 32 (2016) 14-17 and back cover.

Alaezi, Onwukwe. *Ibos: Hebrew Exiles from Israel. Amazing Facts and Revelations*. 2012.

Bruder, Edith. "The Proto-History of Igbo Jewish Identity, 1890-1970." In *African Zion*, edited by Edith Bruder and Tudor Parfitt. Newcastle upon Tyne: Cambridge Scholars Publishing, 2012.

Bruder, Edith. "The Descendants of David in Madagascar: Crypto-Judaism in Twentieth-Century Africa." In *Race, Color, Identity: Rethinking Discourses About 'Jews' in the Twenty-First Century*, edited by Efraim Sicher. New York, NY: Berghahn Books, 2013.

Devir, Nathan. *New Children of Israel. Emerging Jewish Communities in an Era of Globalization*. Salt Lake City, UT: University of Utah, 2017.

Herimanda, R. "Eglise 'Mesirama' à Madagascar." *Madagascar Tribune.com*, August 2, 2007.

Josefson, Deborah. "Madagascar, a new community chooses to be Jewish." *Times of Israel*, June 6, 2016.

Kestenbaum, Samuel. "In Nigeria, Messianic Jews Join Contest for Souls

of 'Lost Tribe'." *Forward*, September 25, 2016.
Kestenbaum, Samuel. "Joining Fabric of World Jewish Community, 100 Convert on African Island of Madagascar." *Forward*, May 24, 2016.
Lange, Dierk. "Origin of the Yoruba and the 'Lost Tribes of Israel'." *Anthropos* 106 (2011): 579-595.
Lidman, Melanie. "Messianic Jews to Nigerians: You're not 'real' Jews. *Times of Israel*, August 11, 2017.
Lis, Daniel. "Igbo Jews – Religious Shift: From Igbo Sabbatharians to Igbo Converts to Judaism in Israel." *Chilufim* 11 (2011): 99-124.
Miles, William F. S. *Jews of Nigeria. An Afro-Judaic Odyssey*. Princeton, NJ: Markus Wiener, 2013.
Miles, William F. S. "Malagasy Judaism: The 'Who is a Jew?' conundrum comes to Madagascar." *Anthropology Today* 33, no. 6 (December 2017): 7–10 and back cover.
Oduyoye, Modupe. *The Sons of the Gods and Daughters of Men. An Afro-Asiatic Interpretation of Genesis 1-11*. Ibadan: Sefer Books, 1998.
Parfitt, Tudor. *Journey to the Vanished City. The Search for a Lost Tribe of Israel*. London: Hodder and Stoughton, 1991/1992.
Ratefy, Tolotra. "Sind die Madagassen Juden? [Are the Malagasy Jews?]" PhD dissertation. Munster: International Royal Academy of Theology, 2017.
Ujah, Charles. *The Origin of Ibos. A Linguistic and Cultural Revelation*. Lagos: Ezbon Communications, 2006.
Williams, Joseph. *Hebrewisms of West Africa. From Nile to Niger with the Jews*. London: Allen and Unwin, 1930.

Notes

[1] The author expresses his appreciation to the Memorial Foundation for Jewish Culture, which supported a portion of the fieldwork (in Nigeria and in Cameroon in 2017–2018) on which this chapter is based. Travel to Madagascar (2015) was made possible thanks to the Franklin Research Grant program of the American Philosophical Society.
[2] "NJMs" is my adaptation of the "New Religious Movements" (NRMs) paradigm, used by scholars of the sociology of religion.
[3] See William F. S. Miles, *Jews of Nigeria. An Afro-Judaic Odyssey* (Princeton, NJ: Markus Wiener, 2013) and William F. S. Miles, "Malagasy Judaism: The 'Who is a Jew?' conundrum comes to Madagascar," *Anthropology Today*, no. 33 (2017): 7–10.
[4] Joseph Williams, *Hebrewisms of West Africa. From Nile to Niger with the Jews* (London: Allen and Unwin, 1930).
[5] Tudor Parfitt, *Journey to the Vanished City. The Search for a Lost Tribe of Israel*

(London: Hodder and Stoughton, 1991/1992).

[6] Dierk Lange, "Origin of the Yoruba and the 'Lost Tribes of Israel'," *Anthropos* 106 (2011): 579–95.

[7] See, for instance, "Yorubas; the lost ancient Hebrew tribe Israelites," Condir (blog), January 9, 2017, http://machpelahcave.website/yoruba-hebrew-israelites/.

[8] Modupe Oduyoye, *The Sons of the Gods and Daughters of Men. An Afro-Asiatic Interpretation of Genesis 1-11* (Ibadan: Sefer Books, 1998).

[9] In my visit to Eri in December 2017, palace guides had only a vague notion of the writing (which appeared like cowry shells embedded in the floor in front of the Eze's throne). The official receiving room of the King is replete with images and symbols reflecting ties to contemporary Jewish and Israeli life.

[10] See Charles Ujah, *The Origin of Ibos. A Linguistic and Cultural Revelation* (Lagos: Ezbon Communications, 2006).

[11] Onwukwe Alaezi, *Ibos: Hebrew Exiles from Israel. Amazing Facts and Revelations*. 2012 (American edition), 52.

[12] "Nnamdi Kanu: An Igbo in Jewish Clothing," *Naijiant*, https://www.naijiant.com/articles/nnamdi-kanu-igbo-jewish-clothing, January 13, 2017.

[13] Miles, "Malagasy Judaism." Bruder, relying on the archives of longtime Madagascar resident Katharine Quanbeck, does specify the time frame or sailing purpose. See Edith Bruder, "The Descendants of David in Madagascar: Crypto-Judaism in Twentieth Century Africa," in *Race, Color, Identity: Rethinking Discourses About 'Jews' in the Twenty-First Century*, edited by Efraim Sicher (New York, NY: Berghahn Books, 2013), 196–98.

[14] Rev. Dr. Prince Ndriana Rabarioelina, "Biblical Relations between Israel and Madagacar" (PhD thesis, Saint-Alcuin House Theological Seminary, 2010).

[15] Tolotra Ratefy, "Sind die Madagassen Juden? [Are the Malagasy Jews?]" (PhD dissertation, Munster: International Royal Academy of Theology).

[16] Professor Rabi, a.k.a. Rivol Lala Cohen, a.k.a. Cohen Bera.

[17] A longer-established theologically aligned organization is the New York City-based Chosen People Ministries.

[18] Alaezi, *Ibos: Hebrew Exiles*, 118–19.

[19] Sam Kestenbaum, "In Nigeria, Messianic Jews Join Contest for Souls of 'Lost Tribe'," *Forward*, September 25, 2016.

[20] Melanie Lidman, "Messianic Jews to Nigerians: You're not 'real' Jews, *Times of Israel*, August 11, 2017.

[21] R. Herimanda, "Eglise 'Mesirama' à Madagascar," *Madagascar Tribune.com*, August 2, 2007.

[22] Edith Bruder, "The Proto-History of Igbo Jewish Identity, 1890-1970," in *African Zion*, eds. Edith Bruder and Tudor Parfitt (Newcastle upon Tyne: Cambridge Scholars Publishing, 2012), 35. The data is provided in a table labeled "Synagogues in Nigeria in 2012". In March 2012, a list of nineteen synagogues was posted under the title "Jewish Synagogues in Nigeria" (https://jewishsynagogues.blogspot.com). There is substantial overlap between the two lists, but they are not identical.

Interview with Daniel Okoli, president of the Judaism Fellowship Initiative and head

of Beth Shalom Knesset (congregation), Awka, December 23, 2018.
[24] See for example, the *Jewish Standards* blog (https://tikvatyisraelsynagogue.blogspot.com.ng).
[25] Bruder, "Proto-History," 31.
[26] Ibid.
[27] Ibid. Referenced for this quote is Daniel Lis, "Igbo Jews – Religious Shift: From Igbo Sabbatharians to Igbo Converts to Judaism in Israel," *Chilufim* 11 (2011): 99–124.
[28] Shai Afsai, "Nigeria's Igbo Jews: Jewish identity and practice in Abuja," *Anthropology Today* 32 (2016): 14.
[29] Deborah Josefson, "Madagascar, a new community chooses to be Jewish," *Times of Israel*, June 6, 2016; Samuel Kestenbaum, [29] "Joining Fabric of World Jewish Community, 100 Convert on African Island of Madagascar," *Forward*, May 24, 2016.
[30] Nathan Devir, *New Children of Israel. Emerging Jewish Communities in an Era of Globalization* (Salt Lake City, UT: University of Utah, 2017), 117–18.

PART THREE:

NEW DIRECTIONS IN LEMBA STUDIES

CHAPTER NINE

LEMBA AND OTHER PERSPECTIVES ON GREAT ZIMBABWE AND MAPUNGUBWE

MAGDEL LE ROUX

The oldest recorded oral tradition of the Lemba holds that their Israelite ancestors came by boat to Africa as traders from a remote place called Sena on the "other side" of the "Phusela".[1] The Lemba cannot remember the name of their country, but they do know that they were *masters of gold, iron and copper smelting and manufacturing*. In their country, they made pots and grew and wove cotton, and they were masters of timber-work because they had to build their own ships for their maritime undertakings. They do not know where "Sena" was or what "Phusela" was, but on their journeys to Africa they erected trading posts at different places, and each time some of their people were left behind to take charge. They were mainly in search of gold and, after each trading expedition, they went back to their country by sea. As "children of Abraham" they kept themselves separate from the native peoples, but after a war broke out in their country they could not return. They had not brought their wives with them and now had to take wives from among the gentiles (*wazendji*), the local peoples.[2] Professor Mathivha, former President of the Lemba Cultural Association in Southern Africa, records that in Africa, they rebuilt Sena—in perhaps more than one place—and helped to construct a great stone city, which they identify as Great Zimbabwe.[3] From there they were led by a star southward to Mapungubwe in the Zoutpansberg area[4] and eventually to Moriah (in the Limpopo Province, Republic of South Africa[5]).

The different names that the Lemba use to describe themselves, as well as terms used by other peoples, also tell a story: "Israelites"; "Jews" or "Black Jews";[6] "children of Abraham";[7] "the chosen people"; the "Good Men," "Mwenye", and the "Basena"—the people coming from Sena. A Lemba of importance is shown great respect when he is addressed as *mušavi* (buyer/trader), *nyakuwana* (the man who finds the things which are bought), or *mulungu*, probably "White man" or "the man from the North".[8] Some informants say the name “Lemba” means “the people who refuse”. Nyamutswa[9] (a Mwenye from Zimbabwe) explains that the Mwenye people include the Lemba and constitute a much larger group. *mwenye* is a Swahili East African word that primarily means “owner” or “lord”. Nyamutswa lists the Muremba (Lemba) as a family name of the tribe of the Mhani or Mani.[10]

Many different theories exist as far as the history of Great Zimbabwe and Mapungubwe is concerned. The interpretations and analyses of historians and archaeologists “have tended to sail with the political and nationalistic winds”.[11] “One perspective is that of the Lemba (or Mwenye) of southern Africa. After it had been neglected for many years, scholars started to investigate the possibility of the influence and presence of traders and skilled workers at Mapungubwe, such as the Lemba (cf. S. Meyer, curator Mapungubwe Museum, University of Pretoria, 10 May 2001, private communication).

The involvement of the Lemba at Mapungubwe was further highlighted in December 2005, when President Thabo Mbeki (of the Republic of South Africa) was “approached” by Dr. Kgalushi Koka, an African traditionalist and head of the African Institute. Koka (a Lemba) was one of President Thabo Mbeki’s personal advisors, and, knowing that he was terminally ill, Koka asked Mbeki to facilitate the return and reburial of the hundreds of Lemba skeletons that had (according to him) been removed from the archaeological site at Mapungubwe in Limpopo (Province) over many years by the University of Pretoria. Mbeki promised to do so and requested “proof” from Samuel Moeti, (then) president of the Lemba Cultural Association (and Member of Parliament in the Northern Province, now Limpopo Province), concerning the Lemba involvement in, or settlement at Mapungubwe. Moeti requested that I assist, as he and the Lemba elders “do not know anything” as far as their involvement at Mapungubwe is concerned, except what (the late) Prof. Mathivha and I wrote about it. I was quite surprised to learn how little they knew about this aspect of their history.[12] Armed with the few pages I compiled from available sources, Moeti and the Koka-sisters went to President Mbeki to state their case.

The next thing I heard was that other African communities close to Mapungubwe in Limpopo were also demanding the return and reburial of the human skeletons—including those of twelve former rulers—removed from the famous archaeological site and transferred to the University of Pretoria. Accordingly, a meeting was organized at the university and all the stakeholders were invited. While the university was not opposed to the repatriation of the skeletons, it seemed likely that controversy over how this should be done could hold up the project. There were concerns over whether golden artefacts, including a gold-plated rhino, scepter, and bowl, would be sufficiently secure if they were kept at the Mapungubwe Park. As far as I know, only one Lemba skeleton was found in a typical Lemba burial place. The skeleton was buried in an outstretched position, notable because other groups bury their dead in a sitting position. Lemba trading beads were also found at Mapungubwe. I personally advised the Lemba that the remains should be "buried" in containers that could be accessed for further research in two or three generations.

Are there any traces of ancient mining and gold working near Great Zimbabwe and Mapungubwe? Who built Great Zimbabwe? And Mapungubwe? In what follows, I will examine the maritime undertakings between the Semitic world and the East Coast of Africa. How do these relate to the Lemba (or Mwenye) and to other perspectives on or memories of Great Zimbabwe and Mapungubwe? All possible biblical and extra-biblical accounts, and reports by traders and observers on the East Coast of Africa, as well as Lemba and other oral traditions, will be used.

Phoenician, Hebrew, Egyptian, Sabean, Arab, and Portuguese accounts and Lemba oral traditions on maritime activities between the Semitic world and East Africa

Some of the earliest documents on maritime undertakings and trade between the Semitic world (Tyre, Israel, and Saba) and Africa are probably the Hebrew Bible and extra-biblical accounts.

According to the Hebrew Bible, it was the *Phoenicians* (or Tyrians) who traded with the Land of Ophir (1 Kgs 10:11–15; Gn 10:29), from whence King Solomon from Israel (approx. 1000 BCE) drew rich merchandise after he had formed an alliance with Hiram, King of Tyre.[13] Ophir could have been in southern Arabia, India, or even East Africa (Sofala, with its merchants and markets), but it seems certain that the Phoenicians (and other Semitic peoples) circumnavigated Africa from east to west (around 600 BCE) and traded with East Africa by at least 110 BCE (Periplus [of the Erythraean Sea, first century CE][14]). The fleet of Solomon took three years to return and brought with it various kinds of items that would be the combined products of the coast of East Africa and of Southern India.[15] Because of the distance, it would nevertheless have been impossible to voyage to and from Ophir (if it was India) without making a principal landfall at Sofala (i.e., Mozambique). Through the archaeological discovery at Tell Qasile (in Israel) of a storage jar inscribed in cursive Phoenician script "Gold of Ophir", historical substance is given to a land hitherto thought to be legendary.[16]

The Egyptian sources provide information about the legendary country named Pwanit, or Punt, from which they obtained *antimony*. Usually, Punt is identified with the northern coast of Somalia, but Lendering[17] is convinced that this is unlikely since antimony was not produced in the Horn of Africa but in modern Mozambique (not far from Great Zimbabwe and Mapungubwe). Daffue[18] mentions that numerous examples of Phoenician and Egyptian pottery, glass beads, coins, idols, and shrines mainly dedicated to the goddess Hathor have been discovered at Great Zimbabwe, Mapungubwe, and related sites in Southern Africa.[19] The hawk (Horus, the companion of Hathor) and emblems of the goddess Hathor nearly always appear as guardian emblems in the mines and quarries of the ancient Egyptians in Africa and in Sinia.[20] Hathor was the miners' patron goddess, and her temples, statues, or inscriptions have been found in many rediscovered mining locations.

The Hebrew Bible similarly refers to the "kingdom of Saba" from which the famous Queen of Sheba came to visit King Solomon (II Chr 9:1ff). It is clear that Saba was a rich merchant nation in the *gold trade*, since Arabia itself is deficient in gold. The Assyrian Inscriptions tell us that Teima, Saba, and Haipá paid Tiglath Pileser III (733 BCE) tribute in *gold, silver, and incense*; similarly, numerous other leaders speak of the wealth and greatness of the Sabaeans.[21] According to the Periplus, the Sabaean colonies were established very early (at the beginning of the seventh century BCE) in Ethiopia.[22]

Lemba tradition records that the Israelite ancestors of the Lemba migrated from "the North" to the South as traders in the seventh century BCE, and that they established a large community at a place called Sena.[23] Here they met Phoenician and Arabian merchants who introduced them to trading with the Orient and Africa.

Folklore of Yemenite Jews similarly bears witness to a migration of their ancient forebears from Palestine to Yemen.[24] An oral tradition from there still exists, namely that a group of Jews left Yemen centuries ago (how long ago is not certain) for Africa and did not return.[25] In addition, Beeston[26] confirms the fact that, in the pre-Islamic times, Judaism was indeed widely practiced in the area (Yemen) and that there were Jews in the Hadramaut even after the rise of Islam. This Jewish community in Yemen was repatriated to the newly founded State of Israel (from 1948–1962). These people formed a large proportion of Yemen's *artisans, gold- and silversmiths, and weavers*.[27]

The Lemba aver that they came from a city on the other side of the *Phusela* called "Sena". Ruins of an ancient city named Sena, "re-built" in Yemen, were found by Parfitt, at the end of the *wadi* Hadramaut, just before the valley turns away towards the sea. It was situated on the trade route from the sea to Terim. Parfitt[28] explains that the valley that leads from Sena, in the eastern Hadramaut, to an old port on the Yemeni coast called "Sayhut" is the Wadi al-Masilah. Parfitt[29] believes that Masilah may be the "Phusela" of Lemba oral tradition. I have learned that Phusela was also "rebuilt" in South Africa by the Lemba, close to the current city of Tzaneen in Mpumalanga.

Interestingly, Nehemiah 7 ,in the Old Testament, refers to all the different groups of Israelites who returned to Israel after the Exile. Verse 38 specifically mentions the return of the "children of Sénaä". Where or who was this place or people? One should perhaps consider the possibility that some of the children of Sénaä and other groups escaped the exile by fleeing into the Arabian Peninsula, such as indicated on inscriptions found in Israel.[30] A Lemba in Soweto once told Parfitt that his grandparents had told him that they had originally come from a place called Sena, "somewhere south of Jericho".

In 1999, Dr. Wapnick (from Pretoria) brought it to my attention that there is a city called "Lemba"—"southeast of Jericho"—indicated on an ancient map of Moab.[31] Apparently, the name "Lemba" does not necessarily mean anything other than a reference to a place where the Lemba came from. Rabbi Richard Newman also "discovered" a place called "Senaah", again "southeast of Jericho" (a short distance away from the place called "Lemba"), on a map in May's *Oxford Bible Atlas*.[32] The site is identified as Khirbet Libba. Parfitt's informant's oral tradition conveyed by his grandparents was confirmed. Will we also find a place called "Phusela" in that vicinity in the future?

The historian Josephus also referred to the city of "Lemba". According to him, *Judaism was imposed* on the cities of ancient Moab by Alexander Janneus in c. 103–76 BCE of which Lemba was one (*Antiquities* XIII). Whether this city has anything to do with the Lemba people here in Southern Africa, one would never know. At least we now have an indication of a city called Lemba, which gives us an educated guess that this is where the Lemba people originally came from. In addition, Josephus refers to a group of priests and Levites who fled from Palestine into Egypt in response to the persecutions of Anthiochus IV Epiphanes almost a hundred years earlier, in 175–163 BCE,[33] and who probably established a kind of Judaistic influence in the north of Africa. Nothing could have stopped some of these priestly groups from migrating further southwards into Africa. If the Lemba left "Israel" in the time of Alexander Janneus it means that this tradition is now more than two thousand years old.

As far as the Christian period is concerned, Boscawen[34] records that, in CE 35, the Sabean (pre-Islamic-Arabian, from what is now the Yemenite) King Kharabit was "to an indefinite extent" in possession of the eastern coast of Africa.[35] This, to my mind, could be significant information since it confirms a very early pre-Islamic-Arabic influence in East Africa.

The last Himyarite ("Homeritic") king, King Dhú Nuwás, who had become Jewish, was notorious for his persecution and massacre of the Christians, which in 399 CE led to the termination of his reign and the invasion by Ethiopians on behalf of their Christian brothers.[36] In turn, the Jewish Arabs were persecuted by the Christians, and, after several conquests and subsequent pressure to migrate, they left for the Himyarite colonies in East Africa and present-day Zimbabwe in ships, of which their merchants had plenty.[37] Did these groups include some of the artisans, gold- and silversmiths, and weavers referred to above?

A further important source of information is the records of *Arab* historians and traders. Marco Polo, the twelfth century (CE) Venetian writer and explorer, made it his business to learn something about East Africa and mainly used the earlier Arab sources. Polo's account again confirms that not only the Arabs, but many other nations as well, were involved in the east coast of Africa and, more specifically, from Mombassa and Kilwa southwards to Sofala (a harbour city on the Zambezi—not far from Great Zimbabwe and even Mapungubwe on the Limpopo), in Mozambique.[38] The entire area between the Zambezi and Limpopo rivers, including Great Zimbabwe, was known at that time as the "hinterland of Sofala".

It was only in 943 CE that one of the Arab historians, Masudi, wrote that the Muslims of Oman in Arabia, of the Al-Azd tribe, sailed on the Zang, Zing, Zenj or Negro Sea (Indian Ocean) as far south as Madagascar and to Sofala (Sufalah) in the land of the Wak-Wak (Khoisan, either "Bushmen" or "Hottentots").[39]

There is every reason to believe that the earlier immigrants from (pre-Islamic) Yemen (ancestors of the artisans), as mentioned above, would soon have associated with those Muslim refugees (newcomers; followers of Zaid or Sa'îd from Yemen) on the coast of Africa. After a short while, there would have been no apparent differences between the two groups and they would be described only as "Moorish" traders by historians and missionaries.[40]

In approximately 1150 CE (nearly a thousand years ago), Idrisi[41] records that the Senzi (Zanji people), possessors of the *ngoma lungundu* ("magic drum"),[42] were forced from their territory in the North and down into the Sena area (at the Zambezi, in the Sofala area). These people of the drum, calling themselves the BaSenzi (probably the Venda), became closely associated with the Lemba in the same area.

Wilmot[43] collected information from letters of early *Portuguese missionaries* preserved in the archives in Rome. Those sources refer to a book from the tenth century, which contains the travels of a merchant, Soleyman, who describes the country of "Zenj". It was a firm Arab tradition that Ophir (cf. 1 Kgs 10:11–15) might well have been situated along the East African coast. Thomas Lopez reported (1502) about Sofala that "the *Moorish merchants* were telling us that in Sofala there is a *wonderfully rich mine* to which, as they find in their books, King Solomon used to send every three years to draw an infinite quantity of *gold*"[44] (italics mine). This same tradition is repeated by the Portuguese missionary João dos Santos (1609; and Senhor Ferão).[45] It is in no way clear who the "Moorish merchants", to whom reference is made here, are. Moreover, the central question is: Who linked the mines of Sofala with the story of King Solomon and, additionally, was this story was merely transmitted from one generation to the next?

In any case, prominent characteristics of those "Moorish" people were that they came as merchants to Africa, already possessing the skills of *goldsmiths, copper miners, potters, cultivators of rice, builders, and men of magic and medicine*, among others. They distinguished themselves from the people of Africa (referring to them as the *vhazendji* "heathen") by their features, rituals, and practices. Furthermore, they were described by Dos Santos as "Moors" (Muslim) only in name since they neither kept nor knew the law of Mohammed and were "very fond of wine".[46] During the barter trade, the "East" provided "beads, Indian pottery, Chinese Ming ware, earrings and cloth, all for use by women and these were traded for gold, ivory, copper, iron and slaves".[47]

The Lemba, Great Zimbabwe, and Mapungubwe

There is plenty of evidence of ancient mining in the area stretching from the northern Limpopo Province to the Zambezi (known as the hinterland of Sofala or the so-called area of Monomotapa). Summers[48] has gone on record with a figure of between four and five thousand pre-European gold workings in Rhodesia (Zimbabwe), and Mason[49] has mentioned several in the former Transvaal (Gauteng). According to Summers,[50] the mining and treatment methods used in Zimbabwe were almost exactly the same as those recorded from Ptolemaic Egypt.[51] The oldest signs of gold ore mining are to be found at the so-called Cradle of Humankind, just north of Johannesburg (RSA). It was possibly the hope of gold (and other minerals) that brought ancient traders to the southeastern coast of Africa.[52] There were no gold mining activities close to Great Zimbabwe, but gold was produced at Manicaland and Mazoe much closer to Sofala.[53] Manyikeni is 350 km from Great Zimbabwe and 52 km inland from the coastal city of Vilanculos (in Mozambique). The settlement established in Sofala by the Lemba (Mwenye) on the mouth of the Zambezi was called "Sena". From there, they carried on their trade by boat up the Zambezi and Sabi rivers or walked inland to mine or trade for other commodities and bring them to the boats on the coastline. It was about a seven days' walk from Sofala to "Monomotapa".[54]

The earliest written mention of the Lemba name, however, is most probably in 1721 and 1726, in the Dutch East India Company's reports from Delagoa Bay on the conditions in the interior. Liesegang[55] published Mahumane's report in 1728, which refers to the "Walembers" in the vicinity of the *Zoutpansberg* as being *rich in gold, traders, and a separate people*. Baines[56] refers to a "Slaamzyn" (Islaams or Mahomedan) group between the Zoutpansberg and the Blouberg (this is exactly where Machemma is located—see below).[57] He also refers to a rock painting in a cave close to Mapungubwe, which depicts light-skinned people with long white robes.[58]

In his search for gold (and other items) for an Austrian agency, Bolts (1777)[59] reported to Pollet, agent for their Imperial Majesties in Mcafûmo River, that "the Natives of this part [Sofala; on the Zambezi], seem to have no knowledge of gold… But…a people called *Malembe…*" (my italics) have many skills as smiths and weavers and know where to find the gold. Later, he wrote[60] about a big and important city called Zimbabwe, where gold was mined and gold articles were manufactured by a tribe known as the Balemba.

Valuable information is also captured in the praise-names and songs of the various Lemba clans and lineages. Mathivha states that the people of Tovakare (also Tovhakale or Thobakgale)[61] lineage were famous for their stone masonry in Zimbabwe. They are also called: "Makudo-a-Zimbabwe" and are referred to as "those who built Great Zimbabwe". In the region between the Zambezi and Limpopo rivers, there are between three hundred and six hundred similar ruins in Zimbabwe, a number in Mozambique, and across the border in South Africa there are over seventy-five hundred similar sites.[62] Mapela is the biggest of them all and is older than Great Zimbabwe and Mapungubwe across the Limpopo in South Africa.[63] Nyamutswa[64] is convinced that Great Zimbabwe was built for the sole purpose of male and female circumcision. The Mwenye are a highly secretive group who did not even tell the "Monomotapa and his people", who took over Great Zimbabwe from them, what it was built for.[65]

By the end of the nineteenth century, Anderson,[66] who travelled to the old Mutapa Empire (also known as: Monomotapa, Benomotapa, Mwene

Mutapa, Mwenye Mutapa, and Mwena Mutapa,[67] vicinity of Mapungubwe, and Great Zimbabwe, and often referred to as the "hinterland of Sofala"), wrote: "The natives state that the gold was worked and the forts built by the White men that once occupied this country whom they call *Abberlomba* (men who made everything)." Later, he reported about broken tribes (clearly not Islamic) who were a separate people who flourished among the Shona and the Venda and asked whether "this remnant be descendants of the Monomotapa people, and those the Mashona call 'Abberlemba'"?[68]

Wangemann[69] recorded that the Lemba near Mberengwa (Zimbabwe) became famous for their "medicine and the magic power" they had over their enemies. Sengani (Sengani, Prof. in African Languages, private communication, 10 August 2017, University of South Africa, Pretoria) opines that the Mavange (in Zimbabwe) or Malange or Malaka (Bhuba and Selamolela in the vicinity of Soekmekaar—in Mpumalanga Province) are the people who were involved in mining activities (mainly diamonds, copper, and gold). He explained that the name *Ramboda* (*u boda*) refers to somebody who crushes (stones/minerals) effectively and thus "makes the stones to flow".

Mathivha[70] recorded that the Sadiki lineage first moved southwards to the Dumbwi (Dumbghe) Mountain (100–50 BCE) and then went into the Limpopo valley (in the Northern Transvaal) in order to be nearer to the copper ore. This group built another big village where they smelted iron, gold, copper, and silver and called it "Mapungubwe" ("the stones [minerals] flowed like a liquid"). According to the UNESCO General History of Africa, Mapungubwe is dated as 1075–1250 CE.[71] From Mapungubwe, Mathivha said, they migrated in an easterly direction until they joined another groups of Basena from Mashonaland and settled at Dzata (50 CE, in Venda).[72] These dates are debatable;[73] however, this information does concur with the "crushers of stone" idea (see above). According to von Sicard,[74] the Sarevu/Sarifu and Chineravhi were the winders of bangles from copper and brass wire. It is also said that they were the first to have discovered the Musina ("People from Sena") copper mines (on the border between Zimbabwe and South Africa).[75]

The Sadiki clan are also known as the "medicine men" since they knew all medicines. Sengani referred to the word "*nganga*" in their praise-song—*Rudzi rwavo vaiva nganga dzokurwa, vaiziva miti yose*[76]—which is often wrongly interpreted as "wizards" or "workers of magic". Sengani is convinced that this word actually refers to this special gift of having knowledge not known to other people (Private communication, November 3, 2017, University of South Africa). Sengani and other Sadiki have the same kind of experiences. It was those of the Madi lineage who were particularly famous as iron workers and goldsmiths but also as medicine men and judges.[77]A few years ago, a Lemba, Johannes Sadiki from the Zoutpansberg (not far from Mapungubwe) area (Louis Trichardt), told me about his special gift of knowing "where to find the gold". Due to space constraints I am unable to share the whole story here, but his son later confirmed that his father had a special gift of knowing things that "normal" people do not know. Even more recently, another Sadiki, this time a Lemba women, Ethel Phillips, told me a similar story: Her father (a Sadiki) was a skilful miner close to a place called Machemma where she was born. Machemma is not far from Mapungubwe and was most probably the place where the Lemba lived while they were involved in the mining, manufacturing, and trading activities at Mapungubwe. Ethel also shared with me that she and her late father (both of them Sadikis) have/had a "special gift to know things" that are not revealed to other people.

Lestrade[78] explains the special technique in the *working with gold and the use of it for plate and bead ornamentation*, as reflected in the gold artefacts found at Mapungubwe, as an "Arab" influence that was presented by Lemba traders acting as "middlemen" (about 900 CE). Lestrade[79] maintains that the Lemba were either Arabs themselves or an admixture of Semitic groups who traded between Mapungubwe, Zimbabwe, and the east coast of Africa (the hinterland of the Sofala/"Monomotapa" area; my insertion).

Many spinning wheels, beads, smelting pots, and utensils, as well as remnants of copper and evidence of other mining activities, were also found elsewhere in the Zoutpansberg (near Tshipese), the Blouberg and other archaeological sites such as Musina,[80] and the "Spelonken" (close to Moeketsi; Wessmann 1908[81]) and Phalaborwa, which are all linked to the Lemba (in Mpumalanga Province).[82]

Junod, writing in 1908, describes the crafts and industries of the Lemba in the Selati district (near Leydsdorp), the skill of women in making earthenware, and the remarkable *metallurgical technique* of the men. Leydsdorp is a former gold-rush town also situated in the Limpopo Province.[83]

Conclusion

Apparently, at a very early stage, continuing influences between the Semitic world and the southeastern parts of Africa had a reciprocal impact on one another. From written sources, it is clear that authors were uneasy differentiating (or, indeed, unable to differentiate) between, for example, Jews and Semites, Arabs and Muslims, as well as Arabs and Swahili-speaking groups.

"Moorish" people journeyed into Africa as merchants looking for gold and other minerals at different stages in the past. They were already skilled as goldsmiths, potters, builders and weavers and were also men of "magic and medicine". They distinguished themselves from the people of Africa by referring to themselves as "the chosen people" and to the locals as *vhazendji* (heathen).

This information might point to these "Moorish" or "Arab" traders being "Jewish", or rather at their being Israelite descendants coming from Yemen, or even Israel or Tyre. It is as difficult to prove this issue, as it is to refute it. Nonetheless, it seems reasonable to assume that, although the "Moorish" or "Arab" traders were not specifically referred to, their traditions and customs were reminiscent of those people that we know today as Lemba. The Lemba/Mwenye/Basena are "an admixture of Semitic groups" who journeyed into Africa as traders, skilled builders, miners and workers of gold and other minerals who acted as middlemen between Mapungubwe (and the Zoutpansberg area), Great Zimbabwe and Sofala. They do not claim to have lived at either Great Zimbabwe or Mapungubwe, but evidence of their presence, influence, and involvement is evident. The oral traditions of the Lemba (and Mwenye) reflect important points of contingence to information from other sources, information which may be as old as two thousand years.

Works Cited

Ahroni, Reuben. *Yemenite Jewry*. Indiana: Indiana University Press, 1986.

Aharoni, Y., and M. Avi-Yonah. *MacMillan Bible Atlas*. New York, NY: Macmillan, 1974.

Anderson, Andrew A. *Twenty-five years in a waggon* [sic]. London: Chapman & Hall, 1974.

Baines, Thomas. *The gold regions of south-eastern Africa*. London: Stanford, 1877.

Beeston, Alfred F. L. "The so-called harlots of the Hadramaut." *Oriens* 5 (1952): 16–22.

Bent, J. Theodore. *Ruined cities of Mashonaland*. London: Longmans Green, 1969.

Culican, William. *The first merchant ventures*. London: Oxford University Press, 1966.

Daffue, Alex E. "The ancient world and Southern Africa." Unpublished conference papers for the Centre of Portuguese Nautical Studies—CPNS, 2006, 5.

Dart, Raymond D. "Foreign influences of the Zimbabwean and pre-Zimbabwe eras." *Native Affairs Department Annual* 1, no. 6 (2) (1955): 19–22.
De Vaal, Jacobus B. N. D. "Ysterbewerking in Vendaland." *Iscor News* 17 (1952): 591–96.
De Vaal, Jacobus B. N. D. "Die ou kopermyne van Messina." *Lantern* 1, no. 5 (1952): 405–8.
De Vaal, Jacobus B. N. D. "Die Lemba: Die Semiete onder die Bantu van suidelike Afrika." *Bantoe* 7 (1958): 67.
Fagan, Brian M. "The Greefswald sequence: Bambandyanalo and Mapungubwe." In *Papers in African prehistory*, edited by John D. Fage and Roland A. Oliver, 337-361. Cambridge: Cambridge University Press, 1970.
Gayre of Gayre, Robert. "The Lembas or Vendas of Vendaland." *Mankind Quarterly* 8, no. 3 (1967): 3-15.
Gayre of Gayre, Robert. *The origin of the Zimbabwean civilization*. Salisbury: Galaxie, 1972.
Goitein, Solomon. D. "The Jews of Yemen." In *Religion in the Middle East: Three religions in concord and conflict*, Vol I, edited by Arthur J. Arberry, 226–35. Cambridge: Cambridge University Press, 1969.
Hall, Richard N. *Pre-historic Rhodesia*. London: Unwin, 1909.
Hendrickx, Ben. "The Lemba and Islam: A contribution to the study of the ancient origin of the Lemba people." *Journal for Islamic Studies* 10 (1990): 32–44.
Hendrickx, Ben. "The ancient origin of the Lemba (Mwenye). A critical overview of the existing theories." *Journal for Oriental and African Studies* 3 (1991): 172-193.
Ingrams, W. H. *Zanzibar: its history and peoples*. London: Frank Cass, [1931] 1967.
Junod, Henri A. "The Balemba of the Zoutpansberg (Transvaal)." *Folk-lore* 19 (1908): 276–87.
Junod, Henri A. *The life of a South African tribe*. London: Macmillan, 1927.
Landström, Björn. *The quest for India*. London: Doubleday, 1964.
Le Roux, Magdel. "Ancient Near Eastern influence in Sub-Saharan Africa." *Ekklesiastikos Pharos* 90, no. 1 (2008): 8–12.
Le Roux, Magdel. "Ngoma lungundu: An African Ark of the Covenant." *Old Testament Essays* 22, no. 1 (2009): 102–25.
Le Roux, Magdel. "The Bhuba. A paternally inherited Jewish priesthood in southern Africa?" *Ekklesiastikos Pharos* 92, no. 2 (2010): 286–304.
Le Roux, Magdel. "Judaism in the Sabaean 'Kingdom': Oral world, material culture and written word." *Graeco-Arabica* XII (2017): 571–

80.
Lendering, Jona. *Herodotus of Halicarnassus*. Amsterdam: Moellerhaus, 2007.
Lestrade, Gérard P. "On certain ethnological investigations in connection with the archaeological discoveries at Mapungubwe." In *Mapungubwe: Ancient Bantu civilization on the Limpopo*, edited by Leo Fouché, 99-126. Cambridge: Cambridge University Press, 1937.
Liesegang, G. "New light on Venda traditions: Mahumane's account of 1730." *History in Africa* 4 (1977):160-183.
Lipiński, E. *Itineraria Phoenicia. Orientalia Lovaniensia Analecta 127. Studia Phoenicia XVIII*. Leuven: Peeters and Dept. Oosterse Studies 2004.
Mathivha, Mashaya E. R. *The Basena/Vamwenye/Balemba*. Môrester: The Author, 1992.
Mandivenga, Ephraim C. "The history and 'reconversion' of the Varemba of Zimbabwe." *Journal of Religion in Africa* 19, no. 2 (1989): 99–102.
Mullan, James E. *The Arab builders of Zimbabwe*. Umtali: Rhodesia Mission, 1969.
Niditch, Susan. *Oral world and written word. Ancient Israelite literature*. Kentucky Louisville KY: Westminster John Knox, 1996.
Nyamutswa, Cosmas. *Great Zimbabwe. Who built it and why?* Harare: Themba, 2017.
Parfitt, Tudor. "Africa and Zion: The case of the Lemba." In *Between Africa and Zion: Proceedings of the first international congress of the society for the study of Ethiopian Jewry*, edited by Steven Kaplan; Tudor Parfitt, and Emanuela T. Semi, 5. Jerusalem: SOSREJ Ben Zvi Institute, 1995.
Peters, Carl. *The Eldorado of the Ancients*. New York, NY: Pearson, 1902.
Prichard, James B. *Ancient Near Eastern Texts*. Princeton, NJ: Princeton University Press, 1969.
Stayt, Hugh A. "Notes on the Balemba (An Arabic Bantu tribe living among the BaVenda and other Bantu tribes in the Northern Transvaal and Southern Rhodesia)." *Journal of the Royal Anthropological Institute of Great Britain and Ireland* 26 (1931): 231-238.
Summers, Ralph. *Zimbabwe.* Johannesburg: Nelson, 1963.
Summers, Ralph. "Ancient mining in Rhodesia and adjacent areas." National Museum of Rhodesia Memoirs 3 (1969).
Summers, Ralph. "The Iron Age of Southern Rhodesia." *Current Anthropology* 7, no. 4 (1966):450-66.
Summers, Ralph. "Ancient mining in Rhodesia and adjacent areas." *National Museum of Rhodesia Memoirs* 3 (1969), [n p].
Theal, George M. *Records of south-eastern Africa*. Vol 7. Cape Town:

Struik, [1898–1903] 1964.
Van Warmelo, N. J., ed. *A preliminary survey of the Bantu tribes of South Africa. Ethnological Publications 5*. Pretoria: Government Printer, 1935.
Van Warmelo, N. J., ed. *The copper miners of Musina and the early history of the Zoutpansberg. Ethnological Publications 8*. Pretoria: Government Printer, 1940.
Von Sicard, Harald. *Ngoma lungundu. Eine afrikanische Bundeslade. Studia Ethnographica Upsaliensia V*. Uppsala: Almquist & Wiksells Boktrycker, 1952.
Von Sicard, Harald. "African tree dwellers." *Native Affairs Department Annual* (1955): 67-69.
Von Sicard, Harald. "Lemba clans." *Native Affairs Department Annual* 39 (1962): 68-80.
Wangemann, Hermann T. *Ein Reise-Jahr in Süd-Afrika: ausführliches Tagebuch über eine in den Jahren 1866 und 1867 ausgeführte Inspectionsreise durch die Missions-Stationen der Berliner Missions-Gesellschaft*. Berlin: Verlag des Missionshauses, 1868.
Wessmann, R. *The Bavenda of the Spelonken (Transvaal). A contribution towards the psychology and folk-lore of African peoples*. London: The African World, 1908.
Wilmot, A. *Monomotapa*. London: T Fisher Unwin, 1896.
Zeitlin, Solomon. *The rise and fall of the Judaean State*. Philadelphia, PA: JPSA, 1962.

Notes

[1] Hermann T. Wangemann, *Ein Reise-Jahr in Süd-Afrika: ausführliches Tagebuch über eine in den Jahren 1866 und 1867 ausgeführte Inspectionsreise durch die Missions-Stationen der Berliner Missions-Gesellschaft* (Berlin: Verlag des Missionshauses, 1868).

[2] Cf. Wangemann, "*Ein Reise-Jahr*"; Henri A. Junod, "The Balemba of the Zoutpansberg (Transvaal)," *Folk-lore* 19 (1908): 276–87.

[3] Mashaya E. R. Mathivha, *The Basena/Vamwenye/Balemba* (Môrester: The Author, 1992).

[4] Mathivha, "*Basena*," 26.

[5] Cf. Magdel le Roux, "The Bhuba. A paternally inherited Jewish priesthood in southern Africa?" *Ekklesiastikos Pharos* 92, no. 2 (2010): 286–304.

[6] Interviews conducted and transcribed: Document: I[1]:10: April 1997, Chief Mpaketsane's niece, India, Sekhukhuneland; Document: M:8-10: July 1997, Zivengwa Mphosi (brother of the late Chief Mposi), Zimbabwe.

[7] Interviews conducted and transcribed: Document: L:8: June 1997, Runesu

Vhimisai, Nyajena, Zimbabwe; Document: K:5: April 1997, John Mpaketsane, India, Sekhukhuneland.

[8] Cf. Tudor Parfitt, *Journey to the vanished city.* Second edition (London: Phoenix, 1997), 18.

[9] Cosmas Nyamutswa, *Great Zimbabwe. Who built it and why?* (Harare: Themba, 2017), 121, 178.

[10] Nyamutswa, *Great Zimbabwe*, 257.

[11] Nyamutswa, *Great Zimbabwe*, 245. The discussion of all the different theories falls outside the parameters of this essay.

[12] In the meantime, I have learned that there are so many different tribes and lineages within the Mwenye group that it could easily happen.

[13] See Magdel le Roux, "In search of the understanding of the Old Testament in Africa. The case of the Lemba" (unpublished Doctoral thesis, University of South Africa, Pretoria, 1999).

[14] Björn Landström, *The quest for India* (London: Doubleday, 1964), 52.

[15] Landström, "*Quest*", 52; Robert Gayre of Gayre, *The origin of the Zimbabwean civilisation* (Salisbury: Galaxie, 1972), 28.

[16] William Culican, *The first merchant ventures* (London: Oxford University Press, 1966), 77–79; E. Lipiński, *Itineraria Phoenicia. Orientalia Lovaniensia Analecta 127. Studia Phoenicia XVIII* (Leuven: Peeters and Dept. Oosterse Studies 2004), 223.

[17] Jona Lendering, *Herodotus of Halicarnassus* (Amsterdam: Moellerhaus, 2007).

[18] Alex E. Daffue, "The ancient world and Southern Africa" (unpublished conference papers for the Centre of Portuguese Nautical Studies—CPNS, 2006), 5.

[19] Carl Peters, *The Eldorado of the Ancients* (New York, NY: Pearson, 1902), 393; W. H. Ingrams, *Zanzibar: its history and peoples* (London: Frank Cass, [1931]1967); Magdel le Roux, "Ancient Near Eastern influence in Sub-Saharan Africa," *Ekklesiastikos Pharos* 90, N.S. 19 (2008): 8–12.

[20] Boscawen, in J. Theodore Bent, *Ruined cities of Mashonaland* (London: Longmans Green, 1969), xviii–xx.

[21] D. H. Müller, *EB*, s.v. "Yemen," 9th ed. (Edinburgh: Black & White 1888), 24, 739, 741; James B. Prichard, *Ancient Near Eastern Texts* (Princeton: Princeton University Press, 1969); cf. Magdel le Roux, "Judaism in the Sabaean "Kingdom": Oral world, material culture and written word," *Graeco-Arabica*, Vol XII (2017), 571-580.

[22] Gayre of Gayre, "*Origin*," 89.

[23] Mathivha, "Basena," 1–7.

[24] Reuben Ahroni, *Yemenite Jewry* (Indiana: University Press, 1986), 25.

[25] Tudor Parfitt, "Africa and Zion: The case of the Lemba," in *Between Africa and Zion: Proceedings of the First International congress of the Society for the Study of Ethiopian Jewry*, eds. Steven Kaplan; Tudor Parfitt & Emanuela T. Semi, 5.C (Jerusalem: SOSREJ Ben Zvi Institute, 1995).

[26] Alfred F. L. Beeston, "The so-called harlots of the Hadramaut," *Oriens* 5 (1952): 16–22.

[27] Solomon D. Goitein, "The Jews of Yemen," in *Religion in the Middle East: Three religions in concord and conflict*, Vol I., ed. Arthur J. Arberry (Cambridge:

Cambridge University Press, 1969), 226–35.
[28] Parfitt, "Africa and Zion," 336.
[29] Parfitt, *Journey,* 336.
[30] Susan Niditch, *Oral world and written word. Ancient Israelite literature* (KY: Westminster John Knox, 1996), 47–48.
[31] Y. Aharoni and M. Avi-Yonah, *MacMillan Bible Atlas* (New York, NY: Macmillan, 1974), map 213, 133; cf. Solomon Zeitlin, *The rise and fall of the Judaean State* (Philadelphia, PA: JPSA, 1962), 332.
[32] Herbert G. May, ed., *Oxford Bible Atlas* (New York, NY: OUP, 1984), 77.
[33] Flavius Josephus, Antiquities of the Jews XIII. Translated by William Whiston [1737]. 2005; cf. Mishnah Menachod 10, 13.
[34] Boscawen, in Bent, *Ruined cities.*
[35] Cf. Robert Gayre of Gayre, "Zimbabwe," *Mankind Quarterly* 5, no. 4 (1965): 212–43.
[36] Ben Hendrickx, "The ancient origin of the Lemba (Mwenye). A critical overview of the existing theories," *Journal for Oriental and African Studies* 3 (1991): 181; cf. Gayre of Gayre, *Origin,* 94.
[37] Ben Hendrickx, "The Lemba and Islam: A contribution to the study of the ancient origin of the Lemba people," *Journal for Islamic Studies* 10 (1990): 32–44.
[38] George M. Theal, *Records of south-eastern Africa*, Vol. 7 (Cape Town: Struik, [1898–1903]1964), 437; cf. Hugh A. Stayt, "Notes on the Balemba (An Arabic Bantu tribe living among the BaVenda and other Bantu tribes in the Northern Transvaal and Southern Rhodesia)," *Journal of the Royal Anthropological Institute of Great Britain and Ireland* 26 (1931): 237; Ephraim C. Mandivenga, "The history and 'reconversion' of the Varemba of Zimbabwe," *Journal of Religion in Africa* 19, no. 2 (1989): 99–102.
[39] Cf. Parfitt, *Journey*; George M. Theal, *Records of south-eastern Africa*, Vol. 4 (London: Clomes, [1898–1903]1964); Richard N. Hall, *Pre-historic Rhodesia* (London: Unwin, 1909); Raymond A. Dart, "Foreign influences of the Zimbabwean and pre-Zimbabwe eras," *Native Affairs Department Annual* 1, no. 6 (2) (1955): 19–22.
[40] Cf. Theal, *Records,* Vol. 7, 253, 348, 289, 371; Stayt, "Notes," 237; N. J. Van Warmelo, ed., *A preliminary survey of the Bantu tribes of South Africa. Ethnological Publications 5* (Pretoria: Government Printer, 1935), 122; Jacobus B. N. D. de Vaal, "Die Lemba: Die Semiete onder die Bantu van suidelike Afrika," *Bantoe* 7 (1958): 67.
[41] In James E. Mullan, *The Arab builders of Zimbabwe* (Umtali: Rhodesia Mission, 1969): 73–76.
[42] Cf. Henri A. Junod, *The life of a South African tribe* (London: Macmillan, 1927), 430; Van Warmelo, *Preliminary*, 122; Jacobus B. N. D. de Vaal, "Die Vhalemba, die Semitiese Bantoes," *Suid Afrika* (Feb 1947): 46; Harald von Sicard, *Ngoma lungundu. Eine afrikanische Bundeslade. Studia Ethnographica Upsaliensia V* (Uppsala: Almquist & Wiksells Boktrycker, 1952); Robert Gayre of Gayre, "The Lembas or Vendas of Vendaland," *Mankind Quarterly* 8, no. 3 (1967); Magdel le Roux, "Ngoma lungundu: An African Ark of the Covenant," *Old Testament Essays* 22, no. 1 (2009): 102–25.

[43] A. Wilmot, *Monomotapa* (London: T Fisher Unwin, 1896), 107–8, 111.
[44] Harold von Sicard, "African tree dwellers," *Native Affairs Department Annual* [s. n.] (1955): 67.
[45] In Theal, *Records*, Vol. 4, 185, 188, 223, 268, 365, 371.
[46] In Theal, *Records,* Vol. 4, 330.
[47] Nyamutswa, *Great Zimbabwe*, 183.
[48] Ralph Summers, *Zimbabwe* (Johannesburg: Nelson, 1963), 54–58; Ralph Summers, "Ancient mining in Rhodesia and adjacent areas," *National Museum of Rhodesia Memoirs* 3 (1969).
[49] In Summers, *Zimbabwe.*
[50] Ralph Summers, "The Iron Age of Southern Rhodesia," *Current Anthropology* 7, no. 4 (1966): 466.
[51] Cf. Le Roux, "Ancient," 11.
[52] Cf. Le Roux, "Ancient," 13.
[53] W. B. Bolts, "To Mr Andrew Daniel Pollet, Agent for their Imperial Majestics, in Mcafumo River," Transvaal Archive number A (1777), 6.
[54] Nyamutswa, *Great Zimbabwe*, 179.
[55] G. Liesegang, "New light on Venda traditions: Mahumane's account of 1730," *History in Africa* 4 (1977): 166, 171.
[56] Thomas Baines, *The gold regions of south-eastern Africa* (London: Stanford, 1877), 71.
[57] I have visited Machemma with its beautiful walls with the name Mah-Chemma (in Hebrew from right to left) spelled out with black stones in the white stones; a conical tower and a monolith.
[58] Jacobus B. N. D. de Vaal, "Die Lemba en hul herkoms," personal notes [s. a.].
[59] Bolts, "To Mr Andrew Daniel Pollet", 497.
[60] In Willem Punt, "The relationship between the pioneer routes in the Transvaal and ancient trade routes." Paper delivered at the South African archaeological society, (unpublished, 1975), 26, 27.
[61] Different spellings are used in different African languages.
[62] Nyamutswa, *Great Zimbabwe*, 17, 18.
[63] Nyamutswa, *Great Zimbabwe*, 17, 18.
[64] Nyamutswa, *Great Zimbabwe*, 228–30.
[65] Cf. Le Roux, "*In search of*," 166–75; H. A. Stayt, "Notes on the BaLemba [An Arab-Bantu tribe living among the BaVenda and other Bantu tribes in the Northern Transvaal and Southern Rhodesia]," *Journal of the Royal Anthropological Institute of Great Britain and Ireland* 26 (1931): 231–38.
[66] Andrew A. Anderson, *Twenty-five years in a wagon in the gold regions of Africa.* Vol. II (London: Chapman & Hall, 1887), 144.
[67] Nyamutswa, *Great Zimbabwe*, v.
[68] Andrew A. Anderson, *Twenty-five years in a waggon* [sic], (London: Chapman & Hall, 1974), 384.
[69] Wangemann, *Ein Reise-Jahr,* 436; Von Sicard, *Ngoma lungundu*, 165; Mberengwa M. Motenda, "History of the western Venda and of the Lemba," in *The copper miners of Musina and the early history of the Zoutpansberg. Ethnological Publications 8*, ed. N. J. Van Warmelo, 62 (Pretoria: Government Printer, 1940).

---

[70] Mathivha, *Basena*, 5.
[71] UNESCO. World heritage list. General history of Africa, Mapungubwe. Updated 2014. https://whc.unesco.org/en/list/1099
[72] Cf. Gérard P. Lestrade, in *Some notes on the ethnic history of the Vhavenda and their Rhodesian affinities*, ed. Van Warmelo (Pretoria: Government Printer ([1927]1960), 24.
[73] Cf. Brian M. Fagan, "The Greefswald sequence: Bambandyanalo and Mapungubwe," in *Papers in African prehistory*, eds. John D. Fage and Roland A. Oliver (Cambridge: University Press, 1970), 173. Mapungubwe "Mountain" was the center of an African empire the size of Swaziland, encompassing about two hundred settlements, between 600 CE and 1300 CE.
[74] Von Sicard, "Lemba," 71–72.
[75] Cf. Van Warmelo, *The copper miners*.
[76] Cf. Von Sicard, "Lemba," 70.
[77] Harald von Sicard, "Lemba clans," *Native Affairs Department Annual* 39 (1962): 69. Mathivha, Basena, 1–6.
[78] Gérard P. Lestrade, "On certain ethnological investigations in connection with the archaeological discoveries at Mapungubwe," in *Mapungubwe: Ancient Bantu civilization on the Limpopo*, ed. Leo Fouché (Cambridge: University Press, 1937b), 124.
[79] Lestrade, "On certain ethnological."
[80]cf. Van Warmelo, *The copper miners*.
[81] R. Wessmann, *The Bavenda of the Spelonken (Transvaal). A contribution towards the psychology and folk-lore of African peoples* (London: The African World, 1908).
[82] Jacobus B. N. D. de Vaal, "Ysterbewerking in Vendaland," *Iscor News* 17 (1952a): 591–96; Jacobus B. N. D. de Vaal, "Die ou kopermyne van Messina," *Lantern* 1, no. 5 (1952b): 405–8.
[83] Junod, *Balemba,* 278.

CHAPTER TEN

PRINCIPALLING IN NAMING AMONG VHALEMBA-BASENA OF SOUTH AFRICA

T. M. SENGANI

Among Black Africans in Southern Africa, the Vhalemba/Basena/ BaMwenye/Vhashavhi or Vhasoni people seem to have drawn more attention of the colonial travellers, missionaries, and scholars than other groups. According to Bryant,[1] Masudi, an Arab scholar who wrote around 943 CE, made reference to Arab settlements in Sofala, Mozambique, where people of Jewish descent were involved in trade. Murdock[2] cites a narrative that appeared in a popular book entitled *Periplus of the Erythraean Sea*, written by an anonymous Greek merchant around 60 CE. He is said to have reported about a flourishing trade of Yemenite merchants along the "Azanian" (now called Indian) coast and ports in East Africa. These people are reported to not only have married local women but also to have spoken and understood the language of the native people of the area. It was, however, the arrival of the Portuguese travellers, and later the missionaries, and the scholars from various European colonial powers, who found them to be rather different from other Africans. These peoples' oral narratives stirred controversies, one of which is a narrative regarding their journey from Judea as children of Senaah, also spelled as "Sena" (Ezra 2:35; Nehemiah 7:38), to Yemen where they built a city they called Sena before migrating to Africa in boats at different periods due to religious and trade wars with the country's Arab rulers.[3] Today, the Vhalemba/Basena people are found in the greater parts of the Limpopo Province, among Vhavenda, Polokwane, and surrounding areas, the Sekhukhune area, and the major cities of South Africa, Zimbabwe, and other regions in Africa, using other traceable clan names that are both Jewish and Arabic.

Contemporary scholars indicate, however, that many researchers have had problems with these groups' claims of their historical narratives of who they are and from where they originate.[4] Despite controversies, Vhalemba/Basena themselves have stuck to their historical narratives, which locate their origins as based in Judea, Yemen, and East Africa.

This study employs the notion of principalling within the theory of dialogism, propounded by Bakhtin,[5] and combines it with Critical Discourse Analysis (CDA) to argue that by using names, titles, and clan names one can trace the Vhalemba/Basena people's origin from Venda, Zimbabwe, East Africa, Yemen, and Judea.

This study will use the notion of principalling, whereby one uses language to take a stand.[6] This means that when a people decided to use language—and, in this case, names—to identify themselves, they do so to endorse who they are and as a way of answering to what others are saying about them. Furthermore, this study will apply CDA, which analyzes and interprets how language is used by powerful people to produce dominance, inequality, and abuse but also how oppressed people use language to emancipate themselves.[7] In this way, through principalling within CDA, Vhalemba/Basena actually declare that they have an origin, identity, and multiple others because they are linked to all others.[8]

Background and literature review

A number of scholars have different views on who the Vhalemba/Basena are and where they originate from. These scholars fall into three major categories: firstly, those whose research demonstrates that the Vhalemba/Basena are of Semitic origin linked to the ethnic group currently called "Arabs"; secondly, those who argue that they are of Jewish origin; and lastly, a small number who claim that the Vhalemba/Basena are Africans.

The Arab- or Muslim-origin argument

The primary group of scholars arguing that the Vhalemba/Basena community originates from the Arabs includes Junod,[9] Stayt,[10] van Warmelo,[11] von Sicard,[12] Bullock,[13] Mullan,[14] Mandivenga,[15] and Buijs.[16] Mullan[17] considers the Vhalemba/Basena to be Muslims from Oman, who fled to Yemen in 684 CE, led by Suleiman and Said in 720 CE. He refers to these people as "Emozaid Arabs", different from a group also referred to as "pure" Arabs.[18] Both groups, according to Mullan,[19] were referred to as "Mouros/Moors", or "Arab Mouros/Moors", which means "foreigners" in Portuguese, based on the fact that members of those groups had traditionally Arabic names such as "M(u)stafa", "Sheba", or "Musa". Mullan, in particular, associates the Vhalemba/Basena with Sunni Muslims because they greet one another with chants of "*Musoni*". He argues that they came to speak an African language, Chisena, and not Arabic, as they travelled in East Africa.[20]

Von Sicard[21] and Hromnik[22] also argue that the Vhalemba/Basena are the descendent(s) of the Emozaids or Baduys. Von Sicard[23] goes on to state that, according to communal tradition, Vhalemba are associated with Madi, the Mwenye of Muhamadi (the Mwenye—people of high status who belong to Muhamadi), and links them with Arabs because of names such as "Hamisi", "Hasani", "Sarifu", or "Sherifi".[24] Velez Grilo[25] argues that in this respect von Sicard confused the Mohammedan sect with what Vhalemba referred to as "MaRamadi", which was a prominent group among them.

Stayt[26] indicates that the Vhalemba were originally Muslim traders in East Africa. Though de Vaal[27] concurs here with Stayt, up to a point, he identifies some similarities between Jewish people and Vhalemba in terms of their customs.

The African-origin argument

Not only do van Warmelo[28] and Mandivenga[29] maintain that the Vhalemba/Basena are Arabs, they also claim that they are Swahili, and therefore of African origin. Mandivenga, in the same article, goes on to claim that the Vhalemba in East and Southern Africa refer to themselves as the "Amwenye", "Varemba", or "Vanwenye" (in what was Southern Rhodesia). Furthermore, Mandivenga also maintains that "Musoni", "Ngavi", "Duma", "Nemanga", and "Chidima" are Chishona or Chikalanga names, which they adopted in Zimbabwe. According to Mandivenga, this is further proof that they have migrated and settled in many areas. Buijs,[30] to some extent, believes that these people are of African origin, mainly because of the African languages they speak.

The Jewish-origin argument

There is, however, a host of colonial travellers and scholars who believe that the Vhalemba/Basena's origins are linked to the Jews, although some have observed that there are some Arabic influences in these peoples' practices and religious beliefs. Ahroni[31] maintains that the Yemenite Jews left Judea in 586 BCE for Yemen. These Jews are believed to have been the children of Senaah (Ezra 2:35 and Nehemiah 7:38), who left their homeland and migrated to Yemen (where they built a big city they named "Sena"—with a different spelling in remembrance of Senaah), east of Sanaa in Yemen, where they were referred to as the Yemenite Jews.[32]

Bryant[33] speaks of Yemenite Jews in Africa, whom he refers to as "a population apparently of Jewish descent, whose ancestors were probably Jews from Yemen". Le Roux[34] cites Beeston,[35] who concurs that there were Jews who became Yemenite Jews in pre-Islamic times and who lived in Yemen after the rise of Islam.[36] According to Hendrickx,[37] the Yemenite Jews arrived in Africa in 684 CE, while another group arrived in 720 led by Suleiman and Said. Hendrickx, like others, confirms that in East Africa the Yemenite Jews were known as the Emozaid Moors, or foreigners. Parfitt[38] speaks of Sena, a city located in Eastern Hadramaut in Yemen, east of the Arabian Peninsula, where the tribal names of Vhalemba are still found.

Doke and Cole[39] report that, according to Duarte Barbosa's writing in 1506, the Moors who spoke Arabic and the languages of the location were different from the "pure" Arabs. The same people are spoken of by De Barros (writing in 1552) as having populated the east coast of Africa. He referred to them as the "Emozaidy", who differed from the Arabs and intermarried with the people in the areas and adopted their customs.[40] These Emozaidy are said to have settled in Sofala, East Africa before 900 CE, but they later travelled to Belingwe, Zimbabwe. Thompson[41] agrees with the period indicated by De Barros, the characteristics of their settlements and their migrations to Zimbabwe where they lived among people who spoke Chikalanga, a language spoken in Zimbabwe.[42] Spurdle and Jenkins[43] conducted tests to determine the origins of Vhalemba, or "Black Jews", and found that their oral history was more likely to be of "Jewish ancestry than of an Arab one".

A few Vhalemba/Bashabi, such as Motenda,[44] Mathivha,[45] Phophi,[46] and Raulinga,[47] argue that the Lemba are of Jewish origin. Motenda[48] and Phophi[49] record that Vhalemba, also referred to as "Basena", migrated from Sena in Nyasaland, ending up in Zimbabwe and South Africa, and have lived with Vhasenzi or Vhavenda for years. Mathivha[50] traces their origin and migration from Judea in 586 BCE through Arabia to Yemen, where these peoples built the city of Sena, another Sena in East Africa, a third in Mozambique, and a fourth in Zimbabwe.

It was the pioneering spirit of the legendary scholars—Motenda, along with Mathivha and many others—that ultimately led to the establishment of the Lemba Cultural Association in South Africa. The major aim of establishing the Lemba Cultural Association by these scholars was to search out and bring together all the other members of the Vhalemba/Vhashavhi group, as they are scattered all over South Africa. These people related their historical narratives in isolated groups in Venda, Zimbabwe, Sekhukhune, Polokwane, and in surrounding areas including Botlokwa, Modjadji, and the cities of Johannesburg and Pretoria.[51]

In addition to interviews I have had with Phophi, Mathivha, and Raulinga from the 1990s, I found it important that in any research one should hear, analyze, and interpret issues from the people themselves, as will be seen in the section below.

Methodology

Over a number of years now I have been interviewing Vhalemba/Basena/Bashabi at their homes in various communities: Venda, particularly parts of the Vhembe district; Botlokwa and Polokwane in the Limpopo Province; Soweto in Johannesburg; Daveyton in Benoni; Atteridgeville, Saulsville, Mamelodi, Soshanguve, and Makaunyane in Pretoria, where most of them are found in South Africa, at events such as familial burial meetings, family gatherings, weddings, and funerals. The interviewees included the elderly and the youth, both males and females. Much of my interaction with them has involved observation at these events in order to conduct more research. Both males and females are referred to in their titles and clan names, as is the case with Vhavenda and other Africans with whom they have lived for centuries, from Ethiopia to South Africa.

This is a qualitative study, and a few strategies have been purposefully selected for analysis and interpretation so that the data can be easy to manage.

Data analysis

Musena/Basena

Vhalemba/Vhashavhi were found at many of the above-mentioned events, referring to themselves as "Basena", and when asked where they originated from they indicated that they are the children of Senaah and cited the Bible, in Nehemiah 7:38 and Ezra 2:35. At Vhalemba/Vhashavhi funerals they make reference to the deceased as "*Muzungu ano ku bva Sena*", which implies that the deceased is "an honorable person from Sena".

Munyai/Banyai

Most men indicated that whenever they visit other Vhalemba/Vhashavhi the womenfolk greet them with praises and chants and refer to them as "Munyai!" to welcome them or show agreement with whatever they are saying. What was surprising, wherever I went, was that the men neither made similar chants nor made any reference to themselves as Munyai;

however, they have over the ages made it clear that they were not Banyai and that it is in fact from Banyai that their ancestors got most of their wives when they arrived in Africa.

BaMwenye

The term "BaMwenye" has been popularly used with other clan names such as Basena, Vhashavhi, Vhasoni, or Vhalemba, especially whenever they relayed their historical narratives.

Vhashavhi/Bashabi

The term "Vhashavhi/Bashabi" is used as a title for men. Wherever I went they told me that "Mushavhi" refers to males, although it is also used to refer to the clan, where it includes women. The title is also used to refer to male children, especially when they are being praised or spoken to when important issues are discussed.

Vhasoni

The term "*Musoni*" or "*Basoni*" is used to refer to the clan, but at cultural events and functions, such as weddings and funerals, it is also used as a title for women. Whenever a male, especially a senior member of the clan, speaks to a female person, she has to respond to him by saying "*Isoni/Soni!*", a contraction of "*Iwe Musoni*", which means "you the weaver"; which in this case means, "I hear you, weaver". I was told that it was used to remind men of their responsibility to provide for their families.

Mulungu

The term "*Mulungu*"—"the honorable one"— tended to be rarely used except to refer to an elderly male. There was a situation in which an elderly male used it to refer to a young professor/academic, and he explained that it was a title of honor since the young man had distinguished himself.

Clan names

Vhalemba always refer to themselves in terms of their clans, such as Buba, Sadiki/Sadiq, Hadzhi/Haji, Bakali, Seremani/Nyakavhi, Hamese/Hamisi, Mhani, Thovhakale/Thobakale, Tshinyaladzi, Nemanga, Hasani, and Sarifu. These terms tend to be employed when Vhalemba are gathered at big events. An observation I have made is that the younger generations have personalized the number plates of their cars by using their clan names, such as the ones above.

Surnames

It was noted that although many Vhalemba families use surnames adopted from other language groups, such as Vhavenda, Northern Sotho/Bapedi, Batswana, and Shona, they also use their clan names as surnames. Among these are: Sadiki/Sadike/Sathekge, Hadzhi/Haji, Bakali/Rabakali/ Phakgadi, Hamisi/Hamese, Seremani, Thovhakale/Thobakale, and many others.

There are some surnames that have links with the clan names, such as Ramaleba (father of the Lemba) and Mulembamuthihi (one Lemba nation, or a staunch member of the Lemba nation). A few surnames showed links with Zimbabwe, such as Mbelengwa, Netshiozwi-Mbelengwa, and Ligavha-Mbelengwa. The explanation advanced for the inclusion of "Mbelengwa" in these surnames is that it is added to enhance the status of the family by reminding them of the mountain they hold in high esteem in Zimbabwe.

Titles

Vhalemba use "*Mushavhi*" to refer to "trader", and this term is used for males. "*Musoni*" is used as a title for females.

It is important to note that males are referred to with their clan titles as shown above, but females acquire the prefix "*Nwa-*", which emanates from "*Nwana wa-*" (daughter of) in Tshivenda, before the clan titles, as in Nwa-Hadzhi/Haji, Nwa-Seremane, Nwa-Sadike, Nwa-Bakali, Nwa-Mhani, Nwa-Hamese, Nwa-Buba, Nwa-Tshinyaladzi, and Nwa-Thobakale/ Thovhakale. Males are also referred to with their maternal clan names, signified by the prefixal "*Mphwa-*", which implies that the male is being referred to from the maternal side, as in Mphwa-Hadzhi/Haji, Mphwa-Bakali, Mphwa-Mhani, Mphwa-Buba, Mphwa-Hamese, Mphwa-Sadike, Mphwa-Tshinyaladzi, Mphwa-Thobakale, and Mphwa-Seremane.

First names

The current trend is that in many families children are given clan names as first names, such as Haji, Nwahadzhi, Bakali, Hamese, Tzadik and Sadiq. There are also those given names from clan names, such as Mushabi and Soni, and Chikalanga/Chishona names, in languages spoken in Zimbabwe, such as Tinae, Rumbidzai, Nyengetere, Hamandiishe, and Ishe.

Institutions

Vhalemba/Bashabi have a number of institutions with names that refer to their clans: Lemba Cultural Association (LCA); Lemba Heritage Foundation (LHF); Netshiozwi-Mbelengwa Burial Society; Bashabi Burial Society; Lemba Lodge; and Buba Lodge.

Mountains

In their praises, Vhalemba/Bashabi make reference to the mountains they associate with in Africa. Phophi[52] refers to them as follows: Masenzhele, the mountain of the Bakali; Bhenga of Benga; Nyaoda of Buba; Mbelengwa of Hadzhi; Bere or Beira of Hamisi; Dongola of Hasane; Tshampfula of Mhani; Dumbwi of Sadiki; Tshilamba of Seremane/Nyakavhi; Tshampfula of Ngavhi; Mavhende of Salifo; Tshamulungwana of Tovhakale; and Mbilayamiswoswe of Nemange.

Repeated reference to these mountains as theirs at important events, and whenever they meet, is a strategy they employ in order to associate themselves with Africa. In Africa, most Africans are associated with certain mountains, while some still reside in the vicinity of the mountains or often visit these areas to perform rituals.

Discussion and Interpretations

In their stance of taking and keeping names, it was observed that Vhalemba/Bashabi, or Basena, Basoni, or BaMwenye, yearn to consolidate their identity at all levels. The name Sena, used as a clan name, serves as a greater link with Judea, as they indicate that they are the children of Senaah, referred to in the Bible, in Nehemiah 7:38 and Ezra 2:35. They further cite what Parfitt[53] refers to as "Sena", which is said to have been in the east of Hadramaut, the vanished city in Yemen, east of Sanaa, where their forebears lived for centuries. As traders, they indicate that among them trading is an age-old tradition, as their forebears, known as the Yemenite Jews, who lived in Yemen, were traders. They also made reference to the village-towns they built in East Africa, named Sena, and Chisena, which became the African language that later carried their name. Reference is also made to Sena in Zimbabwe. Moreover, of great significance is the chant of "*Muzungu ano ku bva Sena!*" (The honorable one from Sena!), which is echoed when they sing their praises at various events. There have been misrepresentations by some scholars with regard to the term "*Muzungu/Mulungu*" where it has been used to refer to "a White person".[54] According to Torrend[55] and

Johnston,[56] "*Mu(l)ungu*" in Kiswahili, Chinyanja, and Chisena, all spoken in East Africa, refers to God, the creator. Van Warmelo[57] adds that among Vhavenda the term "*Valungu*" has been used to refer to kings; and Vhalemba, according to Bullock,[58] have used it as a title of honor. Another misconception has to do with the title "*Musoni*", which Mullan[59] associated with the Sunni Islam religious group. Vhalemba themselves indicate that they became known as *Vhasoni*, which means "weavers", as they used "*u sona*" (in Chikalanga spoken in Zimbabwe)—"to weave"—their wares and sold them.

The terms used to refer to the clan, titles, and surnames, including names that are given to their children, such as Buba, Seremani, Hadzi, Sadike, Bakali, and Mhani, can be traced back to East Africa, Yemen, and Judea, carried by both Jewish and Arab people. Some families carry surnames such as Gangazhe, Nzhalavhane, and Ngwanika, which are of Chikalanga/Chishona origin—that is, languages spoken in Zimbabwe—so as to keep the links with the people and country. Most of their children now go around with first names such as Hadzhi/Haji, Bakali, and Hamese, and Chikalanga/Chishona names such as Nyengetere, Hamandiishe, Tinae, and Rumbidzai, so as to strengthen relations and histories with their Jewish background and Zimbabwe.

Conclusion

From the first group of scholars that suggest that the Vhalemba/Basena are of Arabic origin, even though they place their origin at various locations, it is clear that they are traced from Yemen, where they are associated with Zayidis, and in Africa, where they were called the "Emozaid" or "Baduys". When consolidated, research from these scholars further places the same people in various areas of East Africa where they lived and intermarried with Banyai and other Africans, in Sena and Sofala. These are the same people known as Vhalemba that the researchers found speaking Chisena, Chikalanga/Chishona, and other African languages in South Africa and Zimbabwe.

Unlike the pro-Arab group, research by the pro-Jewish-origin group starts with the children of Senaah in the Bible, in the books of Ezra (2:35) and Nehemiah (7:38), where this group believes that the name Sena/Basena originates. Other researchers, such as Ahroni,[60] make reference to the Jews who were later referred to as Yemenite Jews, who left Judea in 586 BCE for Yemen. Much is written about their stay there, including their trade and wars with the Arab groups and their migration due to wars with the Arabs, famine, and climatic conditions, as well as trade.

Vhalemba/Basena have recounted their historical narratives over the years, yet scholars have ignored their history, and decided to adopt what they believed suited them, in order to arrive at their own desired results. Parfitt[61] did to a point travel and follow their narratives as guidelines, up to the Hadramaut in the Yemen Peninsula. It has also been reported that Vhalemba have indicated that they come from Phusela in Yemen, on the other side of the sea. A closer look at both the names "Masilah" (in Wadi al-Masilah, a port on the Yemen coast)[62] and "Phusela" (the sea that Vhalemba claim to have crossed)[63] gives a clue that "Phusela" could be "Masilah", or even "Peninsula".

It is evident that travellers, as well as prominent scholars from different backgrounds such as colonial and missionary, heard different voices. Vhalemba themselves, including Motenda, Mathivha, Phophi, and Raulinga, who wrote in recent times on their narratives and naming of themselves, their children, and institutions, create dialogic voices that answer to their origin and identity, and researchers should therefore listen to their historical narratives, as they always say: "We have come from a very remote place, on the other side of the sea".[64]

Works Cited

Ahroni, R. *Yemenite Jewry.* Bloomington IN: Indiana University Press, 1986.

Bakhtin, M. *Problems of Dostoevsky's poetics*. Edited and translated by C. Emerson, introduction by W. C. Booth. Minneapolis, MN: University of Minnesota Press, 1984.

Beeston, A. F. L. "The so-called harlots of the Hadramaut." *Oriens* 5 (1952): 16–22.

Bullock, C. *The Mashona and the Matebele*. Cape Town: Juta, 1950.

Bryant, A. T. *Bantu origins: The people and their language*. Cape Town: Struik, 1963.

Bruner, J. *Actual minds, possible worlds*. Cambridge, MA: Harvard University Press, 1986.

Buijs, G. "Black Jews in the Northern Province: A study of ethnic identity in South Africa." *Ethnic and Racial Studies* 21, no. 4 (1998): 661–82. https://doi.org/10.1080/014198798329810.

De Vaal, J. B. N. D. "Die Lemba: Die Semiete onder die Bantu van suidelike Afrika." *Bantu* 7 (1958): 51–74.

Doke, C. M., and D. T. Cole. *Contributions to the history of Bantu linguistics*. Johannesburg: Witwatersrand University Press, 1969.

Fairclough, N. *Language and power*. London: Routledge, 2015.

Fairclough, N., and R. Wodak. “Critical discourse analysis.” In *Discourse as social interaction*, edited by T. A. van Dijk, 258–284. London: Sage Publications, 1997.

Gayre of Gayre, R. “Zimbabwe.” *Mankind Quarterly* 5, no. 4 (1965): 212–43.

Gayre of Gayre, R. “The Lembas or Vendas of Vendaland.” *Mankind Quarterly* 8 (1967): 3–15.

Goitein, S. D. “The Jews of Yemen.” In *Religion in the Middle East: Three religions in concord and conflict*, Vol I, edited by A. J. Arberry, 226–35. Cambridge: Cambridge University Press, 1969.

Hendrickx, B. “The Lemba and Islam: A contribution to the ancient origin of the Lemba people.” *Journal for Islamic Studies* 10 (1990): 32–44.

Hromnik, C. A. “Canarens in the Rios de Cuama, 1501–76.” *Journal of African Studies* 9, no. 2 (1979): 27–37.

Hromnik, C. A. *Indo-Africa: Towards a new understanding of the history of sub-Saharan Africa.* Johannesburg: Juta, 1981.

Jacques, A. A. “Notes on the Lemba tribe of the Northern Transvaal.” *Anthropos* 26 (1931): 245–51.

Junod, H. A. “The Balemba of the Zoutpansberg (Transvaal).” *Folklore* 19, no. 3 (1908): 276–87. https://doi.org/10.1080/0015587X.1908.9719831.

Kamberelis, G., and K. D. Scott. “The coarticulation of texts and subjectives.” In *Uses of intertextuality in classroom and educational research*, edited by N. Shuart-Faris and D. Bloome, 201–50. Greenwich: Information Age, 2004.

Le Roux, M. “African ‘Jews’ For Jesus: A preliminary investigation into the Semitic origins and missionary initiatives of some Lemba communities in Southern Africa.” *Missionalia* 25, no. 4 (1997): 493–510.

Le Roux, M. “‘Lost tribes’ of Israel in Africa? Some observations on Judaising movements in Africa, with specific reference to the Lemba in Southern Africa.” *Religion and Theology* 6, no. 2 (1999): 111–39. https://doi.org/10.1163/157430199X00100.

Le Roux, M. “In search of the origin of the merchant of Sena.” *Religion and Theology* 10, no. 1 (2003): 24–50. https://doi.org/10.1163/157430103X00150.

Le Roux, M. *The Lemba: A lost tribe of Israel in Southern Africa?* Pretoria: Unisa Press, 2003.

Le Roux, M. “Ngoma Lungundu: an African Ark of the Covenant.” *Old Testament Essays* 22, no. 1 (2009): 102–25.

Mandivenga, E. "The history of reconversion of Varemba of Zimbabwe." *Journal of religion in Africa* 19, no. 2 (1989): 98–124. https://doi.org/10.1163/157006689X00134.
Mathivha, M. E. R. *The Basena/Vamwenye/Balemba*. Môrester: privately published, 1992.
Motenda-Mbelengwa, M. M. "The Lemba tribe." *Bantu* 2 (1958): 61–65.
Mullan, J. E. *The Arab Builders of Zimbabwe*. Umtali: Rhodesia Mission, 1969.
Murdock, G. P. *Africa: Its peoples and their culture history*. New York, NY: McGraw-Hill, 1959.
Parfitt, T. *Journey to the vanished city: The search for a lost tribe of Israel*. New York, NY: Vintage Books, 1997.
Phophi, W. M. R. "Vhalungunanguvho-Zaidhi: Vhunzi na Dzithavha, Miano na Mbofhekano." Unpublished manuscript, 1989.
Raulinga, F. C. "Who are the Lembas/Senas?" Unpublished manuscript, c.1996.
Scollon, R., V. Yung, W. K. Tsang, D. Li, and R. Jones. "Voice, appropriation, and discourse representation in a student writing task." In *Uses of intertextuality in classroom and educational research*, edited by N. Shuart-Faris and D. Bloome, 173–99. Greenwich: Information Age, 2004.
Smolka, A. L. B. "Voice hearers: Who does the talk? Who does the listening?" *Culture and Psychology* 9, no. 3 (2003): 330–36. https://doi.org/10.1177/1354067X030093012.
Spurdle, A. B., and T. Jenkins. "The origins of the Lemba 'Black Jews' of southern Africa: Evidence from p12F2 and other Y-Chromosome Markers." *American Journal of Human Genetics* 59, no. 5 (1996): 1126–33.
Stayt, H. *The Bavenda*. London: Oxford University Press, 1931.
Thompson, L. C. 1942. "The Ba-Lemba of Southern Rhodesia." *NADA* 19 (1942): 76–86.
Torrend, J. *A comparative grammar of the South-African Bantu languages: Comprising those of Zanzibar, Moçambique, Zambezi, Kafirland, Beguela, Angola, the Congo, the Ogowe, the Cameroons, the Lake region, etc*. London: Kegan Paul, Trench, Trubner, 1891.
Van Dijk, T. A. "Principles of critical discourse analysis." In *Discourse theory and practice: A reader*, edited by M. S. Wetherell and S. J. Yates, 300–17. London: Sage Publications, 2001.
Van Warmelo, N. J. "The classification of cultural groups." In *The Bantu-speaking people of Southern Africa*, edited by W. D. Hammond-Tooke, 56–81. London: Routledge and Kegan Paul, [1937] 1974.

Van Warmelo, N. J. *Venda Dictionary*. Pretoria: Van Schaik, 1989.
Velez Grilo, V. H. "The dispersion of the 'Wa-Remba' (or 'Vha-Lemba') and tribes related, South of the Zambezi." *South African Journal of Science* 54, no. 5 (1958): 111–17.
Von Sicard, H. "The Lemba ancestor Baramina." *African Studies* 12 (1953): 57–61.
Von Sicard, H. "Lemba clans." *NADA* 39 (1962): 68–80.
Wertsch, J. M. "Narrative tools of history and identity." *Culture and Psychology* 3, no. 1 (1997): 5–20. https://doi.org/10.1177/1354067X9700300101.

Notes

[1] A. T. Bryant, *Bantu origins: The people and their language* (Cape Town: Struik, 1963), 284.

[2] G. P. Murdock, *Africa: Its peoples and their culture history* (New York, NY: McGraw-Hill, 1959), 204.

[3] R. Ahroni, *Yemenite Jewry* (Bloomington IN: Indiana University Press, 1986).

[4] M. le Roux, "'Lost tribes' of Israel in Africa? Some observations on Judaising movements in Africa, with specific reference to the Lemba in Southern Africa," *Religion and Theology* 6, no. 2 (1999):111–39; M. le Roux, *The Lemba: A lost tribe of Israel in Southern Africa?* (Pretoria: Unisa Press, 2003); and T. Parfitt, *Journey to the vanished city: The search for a lost tribe of Israel* (New York, NY: Vintage Books, 1997).

[5] M. Bakhtin, *Problems of Dostoievsky's poetics*, ed. and trans. C. Emerson, intro. W. C. Booth (Minneapolis MN: University of Minnesota Press, 1984).

[6] R. Scollon, et al., "Voice, appropriation, and discourse representation in a student writing task," in *Uses of intertextuality in classroom and educational research*, ed. N. Shuart-Faris and D. Bloome, 194 (Greenwich: Information Age, 2004).

[7] N. Fairclough and R. Wodak, "Critical discourse analysis," in *Discourse as social interaction*, ed. T. A. Van Dijk (London: Sage Publications, 1997); N. Fairclough, *Language and power* (London: Routledge, 2015); and T. A. van Dijk, "Principles of critical discourse analysis," in *Discourse theory and practice: A reader*, eds. M. S. Wetherell and S. J. Yates, 300–17 (London: Sage Publications, 2001).

[8] This statement represents a distillation of various conversations and observations during fieldwork, and cannot be attributed to a single source.

[9] H. A. Junod, "The Balemba of the Zoutpansberg (Transvaal)," *Folklore* 19 (1908): 276–87.

[10] H. Stayt, *The Bavenda* (London: Oxford University Press, 1931).

[11] N. J. van Warmelo, "The classification of cultural groups," in *The Bantu-speaking people of Southern Africa*, ed. W. D. Hammond-Tooke (London: Routledge and Kegan Paul, [1937]1974).

[12] H. von Sicard, "The Lemba ancestor Baramina," *African Studies* 12 (1953): 57–61; and H. von Sicard, "Lemba clans," *NADA* 39 (1962): 68–80.

[13] C. Bullock, *The Mashona and the Matebele* (Cape Town: Juta, 1950).
[14] J. E. Mullan, *The Arab Builders of Zimbabwe* (Umtali: Rhodesia Mission, 1969).
[15] E. Mandivenga, "The history of reconversion of Varemba of Zimbabwe," *Journal of religion in Africa* 19, no. 2 (1989): 89–124.
[16] G. Buijs, "Black Jews in the Northern Province: A study of ethnic identity in South Africa," *Ethnic and Racial Studies* 21, no. 4 (1998): 661–82.
[17] Mullan, *The Arab Builders of Zimbabwe.*
[18] S. D. Goitein, "The Jews of Yemen," in *Religion in the Middle East: Three religions in concord and conflict*, Vol. I, ed. A. J. Arberry, 226–35 (Cambridge: Cambridge University Press, 1969).
[19] Mullan, *The Arab Builders of Zimbabwe.*
[20] Ibid.
[21] Von Sicard, "The Lemba ancestor Baramina."
[22] C. A. Hromnik, "Canarens in the Rios de Cuama, 1501–76," *Journal of African Studies* 9, no. 2 (1979): 27–37; and C. A. Hromnik, *Indo-Africa: Towards a new understanding of the history of sub-Saharan Africa* (Johannesburg: Juta, 1981).
[23] H. von Sicard, "Lemba clans." *NADA*, 39 (1962): 68–80.
[24] Ibid., 73.
[25] V. H. Velez Grilo, "The dispersion of the 'Wa-Remba' (or 'Vha-Lemba') and tribes related, South of the Zambezi," *South African Journal of Science* 54, no. 5 (1958): 114.
[26] Stayt, *The Bavenda.*
[27] J. B. N. D. de Vaal, "Die Lemba: Die Semiete onder die Bantu van suidelike Afrika," *Bantu* 7 (1958): 51–74.
[28] Van Warmelo, "The classification of cultural groups."
[29] Mandivenga, "The history of reconversion of Varemba of Zimbabwe."
[30] Buijs, "Black Jews in the Northern Province."
[31] Ahroni, *Yemenite Jewry.*
[32] M. E. R. Mathivha, *The Basena/Vamwenye/Balemba* (Môrester: privately published, 1992).
[33] Bryant, *Bantu origins*, 285.
[34] M. le Roux, "In search of the origin of the merchant of Sena," *Religion and Theology* 10, no. 1 (2003): 30.
[35] A. F. L. Beeston, "The so-called harlots of the Hadramaut" *Oriens* 5 (1952): 16–22.
[36] Ibid., 123.
[37] B. Hendrickx, "The Lemba and Islam: A contribution to the ancient origin of the Lemba people," *Journal for Islamic Studies* 10 (1990): 35.
[38] T. Parfitt, *Journey to the vanished city: The search for a lost tribe of Israel* (New York, NY: Vintage Books, 1997), 5.
[39] C. M. Doke and D. T. Cole, *Contributions to the history of Bantu linguistics* (Johannesburg: Witwatersrand University Press, 1969), 3.
[40] Ibid., 3–4.
[41] L. C. Thompson, "The Ba-Lemba of Southern Rhodesia," *NADA* 19 (1942): 76–86.
[42] R. Gayre of Gayre, "Zimbabwe," *Mankind Quarterly* 5, no. 4 (1965): 212–43; and

R. Gayre of Gayre, "The Lembas or Vendas of Vendaland," *Mankind Quarterly* 8 (1967): 3–15.
[43] A. B. Spurdle and T. Jenkins, "The origins of the Lemba 'Black Jews' of southern Africa: Evidence from p12F2 and other Y-Chromosome Markers," *American Journal of Human Genetics* 59, no. 5 (1996): 1126–33.
[44] M. M. Motenda-Mbelengwa, "The Lemba tribe," *Bantu* 2 (1958): 61–65.
[45] Mathivha, *The Basena/Vamwenye/Balemba.*
[46] W. M. R. Phophi, "Vhalungunanguvho-Zaidhi: Vhunzi na Dzithavha, Miano na Mbofhekano," (unpublished manuscript, n.d.).
[47] F. C. Raulinga, "Who are the Lembas/Senas?" (unpublished manuscript, c.1996).
[48] Motenda-Mbelengwa, "The Lemba tribe."
[49] Phophi, "Vhalungunanguvho-Zaidhi."
[50] Mathivha, *The Basena/Vamwenye/Balemba.*
[51] M. le Roux, "African 'Jews' For Jesus: A preliminary investigation into the Semitic origins and missionary initiatives of some Lemba communities in Southern Africa," *Missionalia* 25, no. 4 (1997): 493–510.
[52] Phophi, "Vhalungunanguvho-Zaidhi."
[53] T. Parfitt, *Journey to the vanished city.*
[54] Motenda-Mbelengwa, "The Lemba tribe"; and le Roux, *The Lemba: A lost tribe of Israel in Southern Africa?*
[55] J. Torrend, *A comparative grammar of the South-African Bantu languages: Comprising those of Zanzibar, Moçambique, Zambezi, Kafirland, Beguela, Angola, the Congo, the Ogowe, the Cameroons, the Lake region, etc* (London: Kegan Paul, Trench, Trubner, 1891).
[56] H. H. Johnston, *A comparative study of the Bantu and semi-Bantu languages* (Oxford: Clarendon Press, 1919).
[57] N. J. van Warmelo, *Venda Dictionary* (Pretoria: Van Schaik, 1989), 225.
[58] C. Bullock, *The Mashona and the Matebel*e, 22.
[59] Mullan, *The Arab Builders of Zimbabwe.*
[60] Ahroni, *Yemenite Jewry.*
[61] T. Parfitt, *Journey to the vanished city.*
[62] See Parfitt, *Journey to the vanished city*, 336.
[63] See Gayre of Gayre, "The Lembas or Vendas of Vendaland," 15.
[64] Junod, "The Balemba of the Zoutpansberg (Transvaal)," 277.

CHAPTER ELEVEN

A DISCUSSION OF LEMBA JEWISH TRADITIONS (OBSERVED AND ABANDONED)

ODED M. H. DUMAH

In this chapter, I offer a personal testimony and explore a few areas of concern within my Lemba community. I believe that compromise in observing our sacred traditions sabotages our efforts to advance the Lemba community's ideals. I worry about our community when I see our leaders 1) buy non-kosher food, 2) fail to encourage communal gatherings on the weekly Sabbaths, and 3) support community members who follow non-Lemba religious traditions. I suggest approaches to strengthening the Lemba community through Sabbath observance and through traditional dietary practices. These practices could promote economic development, spiritual health, and humanitarianism within our community.

Dietary Practice

Lemba dietary practice is one of the most distinctive features marking our tribe. Since time immemorial, traditional members of our community have avoided eating: the flesh of animals whose hooves are not cloven and who do not chew their cud; the hind quarters of permitted animals; fish without fins and scales; "unclean" fowl and birds of prey; and all insects, except for certain types of locusts. We also follow kosher slaughtering laws. Our licensed slaughterers verify that the animals have no serious disease, especially in the lungs, use a particular slaughtering method, drain the blood, and soak and salt the meat prior to cooking.[1] In contemporary times, our practice has come to include preparing, serving, and eating meat and meat products separately from milk and milk derivatives, using separate utensils and dishes for meat and dairy, and allowing a specified time interval to elapse between the consumption of meat and milk.[2] Today, many Lemba no longer keep these practices. I believe this lack of observance harms our community. The following personal story illustrates the current state of observance. It involves an honorable friend and high-profile community elders; if they read this chapter, I hope they will understand that I am sharing this story with all due respect, out of a desire to address what I see as a problematic situation.

About two years ago, an Ashkenazi friend proposed coming to Limpopo to celebrate Passover with my Lemba kin. He planned to fly from Cape Town and meet me in Johannesburg, where I live. Buoyed by the prospect, I made the necessary arrangements. Passover came, and I arrived at Oliver Tambo International Airport to find my friend and his delegation of about 14 guests, most of them Jewish. As we started off in a minibus, I listened with envy as a woman and her son conversed fluently in Hebrew.[3] We did not arrive at our lodge until midnight, so we decided to go to sleep immediately. We rose early, prepared to meet numerous high-profile Lemba elders. The elders received us and took us to the home of a local Venda tribal chief. He boasted that "thanks to [him] the Lemba Jews bury their dead properly," and he proudly took us to see the cemetery that he supported; it was the only exclusively Lemba cemetery in the area. Along the way, the elders narrated confused versions[4] of our Lemba history.

Afterwards, the Lemba elders and the Venda chief accompanied us back to our lodge, where they asked me to slaughter a goat for our supper. In Zimbabwe, where I am from, we Lemba learn to slaughter livestock in a kosher manner, but I did not have a proper knife. In the past, the community gave every circumcised[5] Lemba man his own knife for hunting, koshering, and other activities. This knife would be buried with its owner upon the latter's death. Unfortunately, I had no such knife. The Lemba elders handed me a blunt, non-kosher knife; time constraint did not permit me to boil it, so I only washed and sharpened it instead. I also washed my feet, lower legs, hands, and forearms, as I had seen my uncle do when I was young. I dug a small hole to gather the animal's blood, which I later covered with earth. Skinning the goat took a long time. Afterwards, I began cutting pieces of meat to soak in order to continue draining the blood. It was now dark outside, and the elders sent word that they were hungry. I asked for more time. About ten minutes later one of the elders returned and said, "Oded, the Lemba elders[6] are saying that they are hungry". I explained that I had not even salted the meat yet, which meant that Lemba rules of kashrut would not let me serve them immediately. He went back to his colleagues with this message. He returned accompanied by the most dignified of the Lemba elders. I feared that I might somehow have shown them disrespect, as they both proceeded to interrogate me sternly about the delay. As though addressing strangers unfamiliar with Lemba dietary practices, I humbly explained the kashering process. I hoped that they, as the custodians and representatives of our Lemba heritage, would appreciate my explanation and accept the delay that our tradition dictated. Instead, they said, "Get over it, Oded! We have no time and we need to eat". My face revealed my astonishment, and the two gentlemen repeated their point. I respectfully told them that I was not going to grant their wish, especially not in the presence of our visitors. The elderly gentlemen finally retreated.

What was at issue for me in this scenario? The media celebrates our beautiful history and distinct practices, and their reports inspire visitors. At the time, I felt ashamed that our elected representatives were displaying behavior so different from the reports. Unfortunately, once elected to office, many official Lemba representatives often seem not to care about Lemba traditions. Many of our leaders eat non-kosher foods and neither keep kosher in their homes nor exhort others to do so. In my view, I wondered whether, had the Lemba elders at least masqueraded as keepers of kashrut in front of our guests, these guests would have appreciated the hard work and dedication our kashrut required, and whether they might have solicited assistance from their networks on our behalf. Additionally, it seems to me that because the Lemba elders do not keep kosher they do not experience or appreciate how difficult it is, and therefore they see no need to establish kosher abattoirs and butcheries in Lemba villages.

Every September, when Lemba gather at the meeting of the Lemba Cultural Association at Sweetwaters (Republic of South Africa), our elders emphasize that our progenitors came from Sena/Lemba, two villages northeast of Jericho, in ancient Israel. They stress that we are a historic people defined by our origins as much as our practices or doctrine. Most religious groups, in contrast, are held together by specific beliefs and must therefore exercise extreme care about defining their shared faith, without which they would lose their identity. Our elders exclaim, "Not so the Lemba!" They explain that we have survived as a historic people over millennia of exile in Africa although we did not work so hard to define our beliefs; that although we have become largely assimilated, the Lemba people still survive.[7] I believe this assimilation has proven more injurious to the Lemba heritage than many of our elders acknowledge. It seems to me that our complacence has misled us into allowing ourselves such latitude that our Lemba nation is disintegrating. Kosher abattoirs, butcheries, and grocery stores would facilitate maintaining our distinct Lemba identity.

Contemplating possibilities for the future, I recall my great-grandfather's fiery love for our Lemba heritage. His non-Lemba friends and relatives kept separate utensils in their homes for him and his family. When he travelled to see people or places he did not know, he roasted groundnuts with lots of salt, which made him drink enough water to fill his belly so that it would be easier for him to refrain from eating non-kosher food. On one occasion, when he unknowingly ate food served from non-kosher dishes, he vomited afterwards. My great-grandfather's level of observance may seem excessive, but a slow return to Torah is possible for my community in our time. If the Lemba do not choose to keep kosher for religious reasons, or for hygiene or humanitarianism, it is my contention that they should still observe these dietary laws as part of the ancient pattern of our community and people, just as one defers to the domestic traditions of a home that one visits. Our dietary practices are an important component in countering assimilation because they remind us of our Jewish heritage and help prevent our being swallowed by other groups among whom we live. Like all minority groups, the Lemba stand in danger of being absorbed into oblivion. Only a strong foundation of group practices can preserve Lemba ideals in their fullest. Maintaining our dietary practices will also likely raise the public profile of the Lemba. If we maintain kashrut, and, for example, request kosher arrangements routinely, others will become accustomed to providing special treatment for the Lemba. This will lead to greater curiosity and respect for us and our unique history and traditions. More important still, if the community as a whole returns to a kosher lifestyle, this will create stable jobs. Job creation is significant in the community at this time of high unemployment (currently 27.2% for South Africa as a whole).[8] If we establish kosher Lemba abattoirs, butcheries, and grocery stores, they will provide employment.

Sabbath Observance

Numbers 15:32–36 speaks of a man stoned for gathering wood on the Sabbath during the Exodus from Egypt. Various Jewish commentaries suggest different reasons why this man ventured to pick up wood on Sabbath. I found it remarkable that some Midrashim, including Targum Yonatan, insist that he acted for the sake of heaven and sacrificed himself to demonstrate the importance of the Sabbath. Maccabees 1:43 compares profanation of Sabbath to idolatry. As contemporary scholar Judith Shulevitz describes it,[9] Sabbath, a "Temple in time rather than space," remains a living tradition among observant Jews throughout the diaspora.

I remember spending Shavuot of 5776/2016 with an Ashkenazi Orthodox Jewish family in Johannesburg. Here I witnessed Judaism being not just talked about but lived; for instance, we walked from their home to the synagogue and back instead of driving. In contrast, for the most part, we Lemba mostly talk about being Jewish and wax nostalgic about our glorious past. We talk about how our ancestors considered one day of the week holy and how, on that day, they praised G-d and nobody was allowed to do any kind of work, and they especially avoided gathering wood, making fire, cooking, trading, and farming on that day.[10]

Both our elderly and young Lemba members pride themselves on the achievements of our tribe, which they say are greater than those of our African neighbors. If they were to prove that the Lemba are doing better than their neighbors, I would also feel proud. The younger leaders among us now have friends from other Jewish communities, such as the Ethiopian, Sephardi, and Ashkenazi, and we compare ourselves to them as we mark our progress as a tribe. Other communities, for example, have an infrastructure with many synagogues so that community members may attend Sabbath services; there are, however, only two traditional synagogues for the estimated seventy thousand to two hundred thousand Lemba people. Modreck Maeresera of the Tovakare clan leads the Harare Lemba Synagogue. Dr. Rabson Wuriga of the Hamisi clan leads the Mapakomhere Synagogue. I would like to see more Lemba people make their way to these synagogues every Sabbath. Currently, it is rare for the total number of attendees to reach 45 on any given week. A few Lemba Messianic synagogues were built in Zimbabwe over the past few years, but I have not observed what their members do. Additionally, some Lemba individuals and families observe the Sabbath privately at home or attend Orthodox or Progressive synagogues close to where they live. Lemba involvement in Progressive synagogues is growing.

In recent years, Dr. Msizi Sadiki brought together members of his Sadiki clan for monthly Sabbath meetings in his Pretoria home. During the few months when he managed this, Dr. Sadiki encouraged his kin to value family unity, start their own businesses, move away from non-Lemba philosophies, and return to Judaism. While offering business lectures to Jews on Sabbath may sound paradoxical, when people become their own bosses they answer only to themselves about how they spend their time and so become free to keep the Sabbath. Additionally, this was the only opportunity Dr. Sadiki had to address his kin in this manner. Periodically I hear of other monthly meetings among the Lemba people in different regions. In most cases, however, even when the meetings happen on Sabbath, they turn out to be burial society meetings rather than religious Sabbath gatherings.

At the yearly Sweetwaters gatherings, a few people have asked about regular Sabbath celebrations; however, as far as I recall, this has never been on the formal agenda of the annual Lemba meeting. Until recently, many of our elders did not acknowledge the young talent that could help turn around the fortunes of the tribe. Influential visitors from Israel and the US also attend some of the Sweetwaters gatherings; their presence could open opportunities, but to my knowledge our leaders have not approached them for support transforming our community. Given this state of affairs, I think that our tribe needs help, but the onus lies with the Lemba themselves to realize that the community owes itself self-respect. In my opinion, as an ethno-religious group, the Lemba should have a framework through which we interact with the world. Like the example of Sabbath observance, unfortunately, we are mainly merely talking about our Jewish identities, when the reality of our day-to-day practices does not reflect any philosophy peculiar to Jews.

Josephus (*Antiquities* Bk.11 Ch.4 Pt.2) relates that the construction of Zorobabel's Temple was completed sooner than expected, due to diligent leadership. Josephus shares a touching story about the grief Israel's leaders expressed on recognizing how inferior the Second Temple, which they had just built, was to the first. In contrast, our Lemba elders show no grief at what seems to me their failure to rebuild the tribe today. In my experience, in the past some of our elders sabotaged and discredited talented young Lemba who had energy and wisdom that could have benefited our tribe. I suppose they suspected us of seeking to take over the leadership.

In the Torah (Shemot/Exodus 3:16) G-d tells Moses to assemble Israel's "elders" to tell them that G-d remembered the Hebrew slaves and their suffering; Rashi says that in this verse the word "elders" refers to those devoted to study, not to chronological elders. This criterion of choosing leadership is advantageous, because scholars are more likely to interact intelligently with stakeholders and to lead more effectively.

Similarly, Josephus (*Antiquities* Bk.11 Ch.3 Pt.1–9) tells of a party thrown in the first year of King Darius' reign, after which Darius talked with his three bodyguards and proposed a public debate contest among them. He promised to reward the wisest and most truthful orator with rich gifts and the honor of sitting next to himself and being called his cousin. After motivating the three guards with the prospect of such splendid gifts, Darius asked the first guard, "Whether wine was not the strongest?" He asked the second, "Whether kings were not such?" and, finally, he asked Zorobabel the Jew, "Whether women were not such, or whether truth was not the strongest of all?" Darius then slept while the guards prepared for their debate, which took place the next morning.

The first debater maintained that wine was the most insuperable of all things. The next debater argued that kings were more powerful than anything else appearing to have force or wisdom. Finally, Zorobabel began to speak. He began by acknowledging the strength of both wine and the king. "But," he continued, "women are superior to them in power". Impressed by his eloquence, the princes and rulers began looking at one another, and then Zorobabel proceeded to demonstrate that women and even the king himself were weaker than truth. When Zorobabel completed his argument, the multitude unanimously declared that he had spoken the most wisely. Darius offered to grant him even more than the promised reward. Zorobabel immediately reminded the king that before ascending the throne he had vowed that, if he did, he would "rebuild Jerusalem, and…build therein the temple of G-d". Darius agreed to fulfill this vow, and Zorobabel headed for Babylon to share his news with other Jewish exiles.

Our current leaders are not well acquainted with our Lemba history and practices; this prevents them from engaging effectively with stakeholders and visitors interested in helping to build a stronger infrastructure for our community. At one Sweetwaters meeting, a visitor took me aside and asked the criteria for electing Lemba leaders. Her question awakened me to the problem with leadership based primarily on age rather than knowledge or competence. While our community has always valued age, it is commendable that our elders have recently started turning to new blood for advice. In my view, the alternative would be additional criteria for leadership.

South African Chief Rabbi Dr. Warren Goldstein recently launched the Sabbath Project, a grassroots movement that has become global and seeks to bring together Jews from across the world. We Lemba may do well to take notice of this initiative. As Milton Steinberg writes, the Sabbath has always helped to maintain the vigor of Judaism and of Jews. Similarly, Ahad HaAm wrote, "More than Israel has kept the Sabbath, the Sabbath has kept Israel".[11] I see increased Sabbath observance among the Lemba today as important for restoring our historic culture and community.

As Ilya Lizorkin argued in his M.A. thesis, the question of whether Jews keep the Sabbath covenant with G-d is never an issue of merely keeping the covenant or not; it is instead an issue of which covenant, which holidays, and which religion and culture to keep. As he explains, people always lead their lives in the context of some culture.[12] I would like to see the Lemba reposition themselves in a Jewish cultural and religious context.

Religious Affiliation

Today, various other religions have won over most of the Lemba. The nature of this current disunity is perplexing; nevertheless, every September our clans flock en masse to Sweetwaters, Limpopo, for the annual Lemba gathering, as though the Lemba affiliation were still strong. Historically, the

Jewish people used to be united through Judaism, as we see in the Maccabean narrative about a king who decreed that any Jew seen following the laws and customs of Judaism would be put to death (4 Macc iv.23). Yet, the Jews persisted; Jewish women even continued to circumcise their sons, although they and their infants were thrown down a precipice in punishment (4 Macc iv.25).

Resolved to enforce his decrees, Antiochus Epiphanes compelled every Jew to taste unkosher meat in hope that his victims would abjure Judaism (4 Macc iv.26). He ordered his guards to seize every Hebrew and compel them all to taste both swine and meats offered to idols under penalty of death by torture. After many Jews had been seized, guards brought a particularly learned and honored elderly priest named Eleazer before the king, who exhorted him (4 Macc v.2–4):

> Old man, I would advise you…to eat of the swine's flesh and save your life…. For why, since nature has freely given you the excellent food of this animal's flesh, do you abhor it? For truly it is absurd not to enjoy things which are agreeable, without conveying any disgrace, and unjust to turn ourselves away from the favors of nature…. And will you not chase away the deception of your reasonings and, having regained a mind worthy of your years, follow a philosophy which unites expediency with truth? And, receiving thankfully my benevolent exhortation, have pity on your old age? For consider this also: that, if there be any Power which watches over this your religious system, it would pardon you for every transgression of the law which was committed through compulsion (4 Macc v.5–13).

Eleazer's approach to the question of whether to eat unkosher food followed clearly from his conviction that Judaism is divinely inspired.[13] Eleazer calmly reiterated his commitment to the sacred Jewish law and explained that eating unkosher food was not a minor offence since transgressing in small matters would mean holding the law at naught (4 Macc v.19–20). Eventually, the guards proceeded to torture and kill Eleazer (4 Macc vi.1–25).

A band of seven brothers and their mother are said to have overcome even severer torments (4 Macc viii.1). Antiochus Epiphanes promised that if they would eat the forbidden meat and adopt the Grecian mode of life they would enjoy his friendship and receive positions of authority in the government (4 Macc viii.9–10). After making this offer, Antiochus Epiphanes ordered his guards to display the instruments of torture (4 Macc viii.14). The sons replied that they would rather die than transgress the commandments (4 Macc ix.1–9). Antiochus Epiphanes ordered the first young man's tongue, hands, and feet cut off, and the skin of his head flayed.

Then, he commanded his guards to heat the rest of the man's body in a cauldron. When the young man was near dying, the king ordered the fire removed to prolong the torture. The remaining family members watched as each faced indescribable pain for the sake of a Jewish way of life (4 Macc ix.10–12).

The dedication of the characters in these stories contrasts starkly with current Lemba practices. Today, Lemba members practice many different religions. At the Sweetwaters gathering in September, one finds Lemba men and women dressed in Venda or Pedi cultural regalia. Others at the gathering wear the badges of a Christian cult. At the last conference, a prominent Lemba elder selected to manage the conference program was wearing this badge, and *National Geographic* filmed this occurrence. The Lemba chaplain from Zimbabwe, part of yet another Christian "sect", knelt down to open our Lemba conference in prayer in the fashion of his church. He then stood and spoke in a Zimbabwean language, although he realized that those gathered were primarily Lemba people from South Africa and did not understand this language. Similarly, the conference DJ opened the event by playing reggae music, and later in the day the same DJ played traditional Zimbabwean music instead of traditional Lemba music.

What is the problem with this situation as I see it? First, it is inappropriate for the program manager at a Lemba conference to wear the badge of a Christian cult and for the conference chaplain to pray in the manner of his church rather than following Lemba tradition; this also suggests a conflict of interest. Second, a Lemba spiritual leader should be called "rabbi" or "rabboni," not "chaplain." Third, I believe that wearing regalia belonging to other cultures jeopardizes both our unique tribal identity and the world's perception of the Lemba people. Fourth, playing reggae and traditional Zimbabwean music at a Lemba gathering led at least one observer to exclaim, "The Lemba culture has now become bankrupt!"[14] Finally, in regard to Lemba people adopting different religions, consider the following analogy. Herod sent his sons to Rome to learn the literature and language of the Romans (5 Macc lviii.20). Conversely, Caesar could have sent his people to Israel to learn the ways of the Jews, but it would not make sense to learn Roman ways from a Jew, or vice versa. As Lemba, we are the descendants of the people who wrote the Bible; the Bible comes from and pertains to our culture as much as to our religion. Why, then, should the Lemba flock to centers of other cultures and other religions to learn about the Bible? On the contrary, those of other nations and tribes should flock to us, the Jewish people, if they wish to understand the Bible.

Of course, the socio-political landscape of Judea under Antiochus Epiphanes is not the same as the socio-political landscape of the Lemba people today. In fact, while I was writing this article, I considered the risk that I might be labelled mischievous for juxtaposing such dissimilar contexts. Jewish martyrs modelled endurance for the sake of Judaism; yet, in South Africa in 2017, the Lemba, facing no persecution for our way of life, seem to take our divine philosophy for granted and not to care what legacy we leave for future generations.

Our elders relate that, during apartheid, it was risky for them to stress their Jewish identity. They tell us, the younger generations, that if they emphasized their Jewishness their African neighbors would associate the Lemba people with Europeans and thus become suspicious as to where Lemba loyalty lay.[15] (Although many European Jews were leaders in the anti-apartheid movement, there was a general presumption that they were on the wrong side of the struggle.) I realize that it is easy for me, as someone born after apartheid, to say that the Lemba should have taken this risk, much as their historical counterparts did, and I empathize with the dilemma they faced; yet now, more than twenty years into democracy, what excuse do we have for avoiding our Jewishness? Our African neighbors saw us fight side-by-side with them for freedom; in such a rainbow nation as South Africa today, who will question our loyalty because we insist on being accepted for who we are?

My Vision for Our Lemba People

Rashi hailed from medieval France and became the foremost Jewish commentator.[16] Nachmanides,[17] a prominent Sephardi thinker, said that this Ashkenazi sage "has the firstborn right".[18] Today Jews of all ages and branches of Judaism take inspiration from Rashi. Rashi's commentary draws not only on his knowledge of Hebrew grammar and Halakhah but also on Midrashic, Talmudic, and Aggadic literature originating in the Middle East.

Growing up, I and the Lemba around me generally considered ourselves a people of Middle Eastern extraction. Nowadays, however, our tribe is facing pressure from outsiders to regard ourselves as Black and to mingle more with other Blacks, even though our practice has always been to keep separate from the other peoples among whom we live.

I believe that the Lemba ought to revive our Middle Eastern heritage as much as possible. We can educate our own Lemba scholars. These new Lemba scholars will study Torah commentaries such as Rashi's and assess what was originally Middle Eastern and what became European. They can determine what in these and other commentaries diverged from the Torah and why and whether it makes sense for the Lemba to follow these teachings. Of course, if Lemba purists want to write their own commentaries, they can. Lemba scholars can then compile their work in a way that will appeal to other Middle Eastern people who have also lived in Africa for centuries.

In educating our own scholars, we will not purge our people of good traditions and traits acquired through exile in Africa. Our African experiences inform who the Lemba are today, and we should maintain all of our traditions that are compatible with our Jewish ways and do not reinforce the assimilation that we are working to reverse. As we revive our own scholarship and interpretations, let us disseminate the teachings of our new Lemba scholars throughout our communities. Let Hebrew become the spoken language in Lemba homes again; let there be a separate Lemba school system; let there be Hebrew mass media, literature, and theatre; and let us celebrate and adopt any other means the Lemba devise for maintaining our distinct identity. These initiatives will aid in the quest to stop assimilation among the Lemba.

I am concerned about much of what I see in the Lemba community today. We no longer avoid non-kosher foods, observe the Sabbath, or maintain ourselves as a distinct people; yet the Lemba wonder why our community is little known, and why those with authority in the Jewish world do not recognize us. There may be several reasons, but in my opinion the Lemba share responsibility for this because of our assimilation. Unless we work to change the trajectory of assimilation and achieve Lemba ideals, we will remain a self-sabotaging community. If we make a real effort, however, we can restore the exalted spiritual heritage the Lemba enjoyed in the past.

Works Cited

Adams, Tzvi H. 2000. "Rambam's Response to the Inclusion of Chicken, Duck and Quail in Qaraite Cuisine." In *Uncensored Judaism* at https://www.uncensoredjudaism.com/en/archives/author/tzviha (accessed October 2018).

Josephus, F. 1980. *The Works of Josephus*. Translated by William Whiston. Complete and unabridged, new updated edition. Peabody MA: Hendrickson Publishers.

Lizorkin, Ilya. 2006. "The Sabbath between Testaments," thesis submitted for M.Phil in Biblical Interpretation, University of Stellenbosch.

Miller, Chaim. 2008. "Rashi's method of biblical commentary" online at Chabad.org. https://www.chabad.org/library/article_cdo/aid/476620/jewish/Rashis-Method-of-Biblical-Commentary.htm (accessed 18 October 2018).

Shulevitz, Judith. 2010. *The Sabbath world: Glimpses of a different order of time*. New York: Random House.
Steinberg, Milton. 1975. *Basic Judaism*. Harvest edition. New York: Houghton Mifflin Harcourt.

Notes

[1] Here Lemba tradition shares similarities with Orthodox Judaism (compare Rabbi Milton Steinberg, *Basic Judaism*, page 125), excepting that the Lemba know how to select kosher locusts, and these are said to possess kickers as well as petticoats the same color as the wings.
[2] I wish to make clear here my favor of Rabbi Bar-Hayim's ruling, which is that one may eat poultry followed by dairy without a waiting period; Rabbi Bar-Hayim is an Israeli Orthodox rabbi who heads the Shilo Institute (Machon Shilo), a Jerusalem-based rabbinical court and institute of Jewish education, which is arguing for increased utilization of the Jerusalem Talmud (which, in regard to Torat Eretz Yisrael and Minhagei Eretz Yisrael, possesses more lucid rulings than the Babylonian Talmud which was given supremacy in "exile-mode" Judaism). For more detail, see https://en.wikipedia.org/wiki/David_Bar-Hayim. Also Tzvi H. Adams, in his "Rambam's Response to the Inclusion of Chicken, Duck and Quail in Qaraite Cuisine," Point a, points to the simple reading of the Talmud (Chullin 104b)—עוף וגבינה נאכלין באפיקורן - בלא נטילת ידים ובלא קינוח הפה—as interpreted by the gaonim and rishonim for five centuries, until Rambam allowed poultry and dairy to be consumed consecutively without even *kinuach ve'hadacha* in between.
[3] Lemba individuals and/or families have completely adopted the languages of the people among whom they live, to the point that Lembas from different localities may have to use English to communicate with each other; this is why a few concerned Lembas are now advocating reviving Hebrew as common language for all Lembas, regardless of geography.
[4] This, according to what I have observed, may be blamed on other black groups, especially those coming from the USA; these are well meaning people, with many of whom I am acquainted, but they have come and "educated" our naïve elders in the villages and pursued an objective to "regularize" Lemba history, so that it relates to or conforms with some bigger picture of other groups in Africa who also claim ancient Israelite/Jewish ancestry.
[5] At the time of initiation, or rite of passage to manhood.
[6] It was for me ironic that this group called itself "the Lemba elders," especially at the juncture they were coercing me to disregard a very important Lemba practice; this was furthermore happening in front of visitors, who had apparently considered themselves privileged with front row tickets to watch Lemba tradition in practice!
[7] This perception of mine found resonance with observations in Rabbi Milton's *Basic Judaism*, p. 33, where he discusses the same evil in respect of the wider Jewry.
[8] eNCA news channel, News Night report, 4 September 2018.
[9] Judith Shulevitz, *The Sabbath world: Glimpses of a different order of time* (New York: Random House, 2010), p. xvi.

[10] In this connection, see also the article by Jewish educator Mickey (Miriam) Feinberg, during her visit to the Harare Lemba Synagogue in 2014. The article, titled "Zimbabwe with love," was published on the *Kulanu* website https://kulanu.org/communities/lemba/zimbabwe-with-love2014 (accessed 18 October 2018).

[11] Steinberg, *Basic Judaism*, p. 128.

[12] Ilya Lizorkin, "The Sabbath between Testaments," thesis submitted for M.Phil in Biblical Interpretation, University of Stellenbosch, 2006, p. 35.

[13] Eliezer here exhibited the tendencies of a Jewish traditionalist, of whom we read in Milton Steinberg's *Basic Judaism*, page 126.

[14] The words of Dr. Msizi Sadiki, expressed at the annual conference of the Lemba Cultural Association, Sweetwaters, [date, i.e. 9 September 2017].

[15] I received this tradition from Professor Tom Sengani, a Lemba elder, who was then based at the African Languages Department, University of South Africa.

[16] Rashi is an acronym for French scholar Rabbi Shlomo Yitzchaki (1040–1105).

[17] Rabbi Moshe ben Nachman (1194–1270), known by the acronym Ramban, was the author of commentaries on the Torah, Talmud, and on Maimonides' *Sefer HaMitzvot*.

[18] As quoted by Chaim Miller, "Rashi's method of biblical commentary" online at *Chabad*. https://www.chabad.org/library/article_cdo/aid/476620/jewish/Rashis-Method-of-Biblical-Commentary.htm (accessed 18 October 2018).

PART FOUR:

POLITICS AND RESISTANCE

CHAPTER TWELVE

POLITICS OF RELOCATION OF ETHIOPIAN JEWS

YVONNE M. CRENSHAW

The recognition of Ethiopian Jews as part of the larger Jewish community began hundreds of years before the massive task of relocating thousands of Ethiopian Jews to Israel. The mass rescue of the Beta Israel, begun with Operation Moses on November 18, 1984, brought eight thousand Ethiopian Jews to Israel. This initiative continued in Sudan on March 28, 1985 with Operation Joshua. Also called Operation Sheba, Joshua was a one-day operation conducted by the United States' CIA and supported by the Israeli Army (IDF) that brought another five hundred Jews to Israel. The rescue culminated with Operation Solomon, bringing 14,324 from Ethiopia on May 24, 1991 to May 25, 1991. This article seeks to answer several key questions regarding the mass move of thousands of Ethiopian Jews to Israel. What factors caused a delay in recognizing this community of Jews and rescuing them from their dire situation? What roles did politics and racism play in postponing recognition and help? What were the motives and reasons for the various responses of larger Jewish communities to this crisis over time?

Again and again, rabbis of note have affirmed that the Ethiopian Jews are indeed Jews. In this chapter we explore why, then, anyone was still questioning their authenticity and right to make Aliyah in 1980. There are many significant questions here; for example: Why was this community of Jews left to suffer as Israel welcomed massive numbers of Jews from Iraq, Yemen, Morocco, and the Soviet Union? When global Jewish communities finally acted, why did they abandon some of the Ethiopians claiming to be Jewish, including many relatives of those already brought to Israel? Why did Israeli Jewish authorities scrutinize the religious practices of Ethiopian Jews, who were following the biblical laws of pre-Talmudic Judaism? Why did the Israeli rabbinate tell Ethiopian Jews that they were not worshipping correctly but at the same time accept Soviet Jews who did not practice Judaism and never had? Here I review government documents, religious writing, and articles from newspapers, journals, and internet sources in order to explore these questions and to establish which countries and political actors played key roles in both the delay and the eventual relocation of the Beta Israel.

Historical Background

Historically, a most important European Jewish advocate for Ethiopian Jewry was Jacques Faitlovitch, a student of Professor Joseph Halevy (one of the earliest European Jewish advocates for these African Jews). Professor Halevy had traveled to Ethiopia in 1867, sponsored by European Jewish organizations to investigate stories relayed by Italian Jewish soldiers returning from war of Jews residing there. Faitlovitch came from a rabbinic family in Lodz, Poland. At 23, he learned Amharic and Tigrinya under the tutelage of Professor Halevy with the goal of helping the Beta Israel community. In the 1900s, Faitlovitch managed to acquire the financial support of Baron Edmond de Rothschild, (characterized by one scholar as: "the Enlightened Head of the French banking house")[1] to finance his first visit to Abyssinia (Ethiopia). Faitlovitch hoped that the establishment of a Jewish State of Israel would benefit Ethiopian Jews. As the Zionist movement and, later, Israel, spoke of taking responsibility for bringing Jews to Israel, Faitlovitch trusted that Israel would absorb and educate Ethiopian Jews.

Faitlovitch was the first to establish support groups for Ethiopian Jews in Britain, the United States, and Palestine. Faitlovitch established schools[2] and took students to Europe and Palestine to meet other members of the European Jewish community. Ultimately, when Faitlovitch died in 1955, seeds of his work grew. Beginning in 1955, Israel's Jewish Agency built schools and a seminary to train teachers in Ethiopia to teach the Beta Israel post-rabbinic Jewish Practices. Israel attempted to secure relations with the Ethiopian government in 1956 and sent teams of public health professionals to Gondar Province to address the health crisis of the Beta Israel that was a result of the Marxist State Campaign against them.

International support for the Beta Israel was not sufficient to fundamentally alter their circumstances, but awareness was increasing. After Haile Selassie regained control and returned to rule in 1961, Israel and Ethiopia began full diplomatic relations. Israel, however, was still concentrating on immigration and support for Jews from European countries who had survived the Holocaust; African Jews were not a focus. David Kessler writes that Ethiopian Jews finally began to receive some assistance after a conference in May 1967, funds primarily raised in Britain by the British OSE Society, The Jewish Colonization Society, Jewish

Agency in Israel, and the pledges from the American Joint Distribution Committee.[3] With the support of these organizations, the Beta Israel were able to operate a few more education and health-care programs in Ethiopia.

In 1969, Dr. Graenum Berger founded The American Association for Ethiopian Jews in order to raise awareness in the Jewish community regarding the situation of Jews in Ethiopia and their need for support. This act became part of the shift from Jewish activism's focus in Europe to the crisis in Ethiopia. At that time, Berger, an American Jew, was a social worker for the Federation of Jewish Philanthropies in New York. He had visited Gondar and was shocked by the Beta Israel's conditions. As the first president of the AAEJ, he managed to raise money and develop his organization into a nationally respected advocacy group working in tandem with the Jewish Joint Distribution Committee and the Jewish Agency. In 1970, at the urging of the AAEJ, the Organization for Rehabilitation and Training founded schools, a vocational training center, and clinics in Ethiopia. During 1970s the Israeli government authorized the IDF to assist in the Ethopican Jewish immigration.[4]

Meanwhile, however, European and American Jews of European heritage continued to deny the historical claims and legitimacy of the Beta Israel as Jews. It was in 1973 that then Rabbi Ovadia Yosef, Israel's Chief Sephardic Rabbi, decided the Jews in Ethiopia (Beta Israel) were descendants of Dan and could obtain Israeli citizenship under the Law of Return. Within two years the Ashkenazi chief Rabbi agreed, and the government made it law on April 25, 1975.[5]

Why did this decision take so many decades, and why did it take almost an entire decade more before the first mass Aliyah of Ethiopian Jews? Why, as of 1976, had only 250 Ethiopian Jews arrived in Israel? Here I argue that we must note the role of ego and complex political concerns on the part of numerous actors. We can, for example, see that the strategic significance of Ethiopia for the US declined at this time.[6] Similarly, we find that the Israeli government was also slow to engage.

Obstacles and Deteriorating Conditions

In Stephen Spector's *Operation Solomon*, he sets the obstacles regarding the removal of the Beta Israel in the context of several factors: the Ethiopian Civil War (September 1974–1991); Mengistu Haile Mariam's attempt to prevent his regime from falling; Russia (who had given over $12 million in financial support beginning in 1977) withdrawing support from Ethiopia in the late 1980s; and the political needs of Ethiopia, Israel, and Western governments for face-saving measures. These matters combined to allow the crisis in Ethiopia to continue.

Throughout this period, Graenum Berger's network of colleagues was frustrated with the "Israeli leaders' overt indifference to the Ethiopian Jews (mid-1970s)…and Israel's subsequent reluctance or even hostility regarding Aliyah."[7] Well aware of Israel's prejudice against Black Jews, they argued that racism was the reason for Israeli inaction in the crisis facing the Beta Israel. In accusing Israel of racism, the AAEJ consciously echoed the language of the United Nations General Assembly Resolution 3379, passed in 1975 by enemies of Israel, which stated that Zionism was a form of racism. The AAEJ acquired a reputation for radicalism as part of its work to bring about a substantial Ethiopian Aliyah, and the organization's work succeeded in putting pressure on the Israeli government.[8]

Although the difficulties facing Ethiopian Jews motivated the AAEJ, political expediency and the potential for economic advantage to Ethiopia and other nations played a larger role in bringing the needs of the Beta Israel to the attention of world Jewry. Mengistu Haile Mariam began his rise to power in Ethiopia in 1974, when a coup unseated Emperor Haile Selassie. After the coup, Mengistu Haile Mariam introduced a policy of "Villagization", resettling more than eight hundred thousand farmers to remote areas of the country. The country had already suffered from drought and famine, and Haile Mariam's relocation policy made the situation significantly worse. A rebellion erupted in the north of the country, where most of the Jews lived. The rebellion caused mass starvation throughout the country.[9] These conditions also critically impacted the Jewish communities there.[10]

The combined conditions of anti-Semitism, civil war, and poverty led the Beta Israel to risk life and liberty to leave their ancient home of Ethiopia. The desire to return to Israel, the holy land of their ancestors, had always remained in the hearts of the Beta Israel. This desire became urgent as local and national conditions deteriorated. Impoverished and vulnerable living conditions and frantic attempts to leave, combined with the campaign of the AAEJ, helped to persuade the Israeli and US governments to look for a way to bring them to Israel.

In 1977, Israeli Prime Minister Menachem Begin took office and sought to obtain the release of Ethiopian Jews from the Mengistu Haile Mariam regime. To maintain a relationship with Mengistu Haile Mariam and persuade him to allow the Jews to leave, Israel began selling weapons to Ethiopia. Mengistu Haile Mariam needed weapons and money to sustain his rule; he used the Beta Israel to achieve this goal. Begin made an agreement with Mengistu Haile Mariam to allow two hundred Jews to leave on an empty military cargo plane that had delivered the weapons and was returning to Israel. The agreement was to relocate more Jews to Israel later. Relations broke down mid-way, however, because the West did not want negative consequences from Ethiopia's use of the weapons. Unfortunately, even though weapons were delivered as agreed, at the last moment the Ethiopian government refused to allow the Beta Israel to depart, and the plane delivering the weapons did not return to Israel with Ethiopian Jews. When Begin's plan fell through, Israel and the United States developed a new plan and began working clandestinely with the Sundanese Government.[11]

Meanwhile, the situation of the Beta Israel was worsening as Mengistu's government enforced stricter regulations on their population. In 1980, Ethiopia's government forbade the practice of Judaism and any teaching of Hebrew or other Jewish subjects. Mengistu passed laws to strengthen his rule; among them was a law conscripting all males into his weakened military. Jews were especially hard hit as, "Numerous members of the Beta Israel were imprisoned on fabricated charges of being 'Zionist Spies,' and Jewish Religious leaders [Kesim] were harassed and monitored by the government.... Forced conscription at the age of 12 took many Jewish boys away from their parents, some never to be seen again".[12]

Members of the Beta Israel community responded by leaving Gondar in droves, walking to nearby Sudan.[13] Given this development, the AAEJ maintained political pressure on the Israeli and US governments to rescue the Ethiopian Jews. As a result of this pressure, in 1984 the Israeli and the US governments began planning Operation Moses with the goal of bringing as many Ethiopian Jews as possible to Israel.

An article in the *New York Times*[14] cites the Ethiopian famine among the primary reasons for the operation. The article stated that the operation "stepped up movement of the Ethiopian Jews to Israel out of concern that Ethiopia might block it, involving an airlift through a third country. Although most of the planes and pilots involved were Israeli, some came from other countries".[15] The United States played a role in the operation, although Reagan administration officials explained that the US was involved only in its humanitarian aspects (the US contributed over $15 million to help support the African immigrants). Most of the Beta Israel had lived in extremely simple conditions in Ethiopia. The people of this community were very poor, had few modern work skills, and did not know how to read, write, or use conveniences such as plumbing.[16]

Because the Ethiopians were one of the oldest Jewish groups known to modern Jewry, Israelis regarded their arrival as significant; however, *The Times* also reported that "Some Jews in the United States and Canada have been highly critical of the Israeli Government for reportedly neglecting

Ethiopian Jews in the famine-stricken area. The critics have publicly charged that racism is a factor in keeping Israel from doing all that it should do to bring Jews out of Ethiopia".[17]

Rescue Operations Underway, Stalled, Re-ignited

While critiques continued, it is estimated that between 1977 and 1984 eight thousand Ethiopian Jews gradually arrived in Israel. Additionally, Operation Moses brought another seven thousand, including fifteen hundred children and young people who arrived without their parents. Most of these children were boys at risk of conscription.[18]

Unfortunately, Operation Moses ended abruptly in January 1985.[19] The Sudanese government succumbed to pressure, closing its doors and resulting in almost two-thirds of the Beta Israel remaining in Ethiopia. The Jews remaining in Ethiopia consisted almost entirely of women, young children, and the sick. This was the result of a concerted plan on the part of organizers, who encouraged only the strongest members of the community to make the harrowing journey to Sudan.

After Operation Moses ended, the AAEJ continued its campaign and the US and Israel sought new ways to rescue the remaining Ethiopian Jews. As a result, later in 1985, US Vice President George H. W. Bush used a combination of political pressure and bribery to persuade the Sudanese government to resume cooperation. The US paid Sudan $50 million, after which Vice President Bush arranged for a one-day CIA-directed mission to retrieve the remaining Beta Israel and take them to Israel. This covert operation, carried out by the United States in collaboration with Israel, was named Operation Joshua and Operation Sheba.

The IDF reports the Joshua/Sheba operation as harrowing: "On March 28, 1985, the operation, codenamed 'Sheba', began with Ethiopian Jews from Israel working for the Mossad identifying the Ethiopian Jews in the camps and taking them by truck to the airstrip. The airstrip itself was eight miles outside of Gedaref, just far enough so that it would be difficult to spot the planes from the town. (United States) Planes designed to hold ninety passengers each were prepared at the American base near Frankfurt, West Germany. Planes filled with food, water, and medical supplies were flown from an Israeli military base near Eilat to the airstrip in Sudan". The IDF report continues to record the conditions of the operation: "These camouflaged US Hercules transports landed at twenty-minute intervals to pick up their passengers. Sudanese security officers cordoned off the area and, by 9:00 a.m., all of the Ethiopian Jews were evacuated. Instead of going to an intermediate destination, the planes flew directly to an Israeli air force base outside Eilat where the passengers were greeted by Prime Minister Shimon Peres".[20]

While it had been intended to airlift approximately two thousand Ethiopian Jews from these Sudanese camps, the organizers found only 494 people. The IDF reports: "Three planes returned from Sudan empty. At the end of Operation Sheba, Israeli officials believed that all of the Ethiopian Jews had been evacuated from the refugee camps in Sudan. In fact, a handful was left in the camps and anywhere from seven thousand to fifteen thousand are estimated to be still living in Ethiopia today".[21]

The *L. A. Times* reported that "the rescue of this persecuted segment of Ethiopian Jewry, is both a shining example of both the United States' and Israel's compassion and commitment to freedom".[22] While this operation was indeed significant, no further rescue missions occurred for the following five years. As before, complex political dynamics and egos interfered with bringing the situation to a successful conclusion; for example, we can note the ongoing intransigence on the part of the Haile Mariam.

As the civil war progressed, Mengistu Haile Mariam became increasingly desperate; he was close to losing control of the government. Eritrean and Tigrean rebels were fighting over the northern part of the country. Russia, which had fninancially supported Mengistu Haile Mariam prior, no longer supported Ethiopia during this time. Civil wars, famine, and Haile Mariam's mismanagement had destabilized the country and brought it to the brink of financial collapse. Mengistu Haile Mariam had made it nearly impossible for the Beta Israel to leave Ethiopia even though they were starving. Still, the Beta Israel, the larger global Jewish community, and Israeli authorities wondered whether Mengistu's weakening position might provide a final opportunity for more Beta Israel to leave Ethiopia.

By this time, however, the Jewish community considered the situation of the Ethiopian Jews increasingly precarious. In 1989, the progress of Aliyah for the Ethiopians was once again moving at a snail's pace. At this point, the AAEJ sent Susan Pollack to Addis Ababa on a tourist visa to assess the situation. Pollack was a thirty-year-old, White, American woman working for the Canadian Association for Ethiopian Jews, associated with the AAEJ. She had been public-speaking and raising money. In February 1989, Pollack traveled throughout the Beta Israel villages in the Gondar region where she smuggled in medicine while investigating conditions. She witnessed abject poverty, desperation, and horrendous sickness among the Beta Israel.

Shocked at what she saw, Pollack wrote to the AAEJ regarding the remaining community's dire situation: "Teenagers with rotting hands or feet, pretty young women with goiters, old men and women (dozens per village) gone blind with milky white eyes…suffering from polio, tuberculosis, malaria, skin fungi, skin ulcers, infected wounds. She spoke of babies with their eyes swollen or crusted shut and covered with flies. Every person in the villages needed medical attention, she said. We are losing people and before we lose them, they suffer".[23]

In Pollack's report, she pleaded for the AAEJ to intensify advocacy by "pressuring Washington, Israel, and Western Europe to insist on human rights in Ethiopia, as well as free emigration and family unification" to save the Jews of Gondar. Two thousand or more Beta Israel walked over four hundred miles from Gondar Province to Addis Ababa, where they arrived sick and malnourished, hoping to receive support from the Israeli consulate to help them make Aliyah. They came to Pollack with no resources left after paying bribes for help getting there. Confident that the US Jewish community would raise whatever funds were necessary to save these lives, Nate Shapiro of the AAEJ responded to Pollack, "Do what you have to do, spend $1 million or $100 million".[24] While this exchange occurred, dangers were increasing as Eritreans and other rebel groups achieved victories that led to increased fighting in the northern region, where most of the Beta Israel lived. Other US Jewish groups joined the AAEJ in raising money and looking for legal ways to help the Beta Israel exit the country.

After many delays and arguments regarding the correct way to manage the Aliyah, in 1990 the US and Israel finally began new negotiations with the Ethiopian government. George H. W. Bush urged the Ethiopian government to allow the Beta Israel to leave Ethiopia and go to Israel. Negotiations began among high-level government officials from Ethiopia, Israel, and the United States. Acting President Tesfaye Gebre-Kidan of Ethiopia made the final decisions in cooperation with Hank Cohen, the US Assistant Secretary of State for African Affairs, who was also working to mediate an end to the civil war. The Ethiopian government wanted engagement regarding Jews to appear to the world as a humanitarian effort instead of as a ransoming of hostages. In reality, the government agreed to allow emigration only in exchange for substantial financial benefit.

There were still many obstacles to the successful Aliyah. In March 1991, the Ethiopians shut down the Aliyah completely. Still, at this time, the negotiations of Operation Solomon led to positive developments for Ethiopia generally; for example, the London roundtable discussions commenced, establishing a joint declaration by Eritrean and Tigrean rebels, who agreed to stop fighting during the airlift and organize a conference to select a transitional government.

When all agreements were finalized, many complications still barred the implementation of Operation Solomon. Exorbitant bribes to Ethiopia's government and facilitation of asylum for the outgoing regime ultimately helped make the airlift happen. After finalizing the terms, American Jewish Groups had the task of raising $50 million in only thirty-three hours so that the airlift could begin on Sabbath eve. In this case, the Israeli government determined that the Israeli national airline would fly on the Jewish Sabbath. In the case of saving lives, breaking the holy Sabbath's restrictions are permissible, as an act of charity.

The timing of the operation was deemed critical as relations among the parties remained strained, and subject to reversal. Operation Solomon's airlift began on Friday, May 24, 1991 at 5:00 pm and continued for thirty-six hours; it ended after Havdalah (the close of the Jewish Sabbath) on Saturday, May 25, 1991. Thirty-six flights by Israeli commercial and military jets and transport planes brought a total of 14,325 Beta Israel men, women, and children to Israel. Some of the details are noteworthy: the Boeing 747 used for the operation had a limit of 760 passengers, but since the refugees were underweight due to malnourishment the pilot chose to allow 1,087 people.[25] Their combined weight was equivalent to that estimated for 760 passengers in ordinary circumstances. In fact, previously during Operation Moses (1984–1985) 1,122 people travelled from Sudan to Israel on one such flight, as some mothers hid children under their dresses.[26]

Operation Solomon came as the culmination of years of negotiations, over $50 million in payment to the Ethiopian government (raised by American Jewish groups) and years of work by determined individuals. There were closed-room arguments among Jewish leaders about whether these ancient people were indeed Jews with a right to make Aliyah to Israel. There were backroom negotiations with unscrupulous government officials using the Beta Israel as pawns in a ruthless chess game. Corrupt autocrats were essentially ransoming innocent lives.

Conclusion

To most observers and analysts, the question as to why the resolution of the case of Ethiopian Jewry took so many decades to resolve is crucial. In *Operation Solomon*, Stephen Spector reviews various instances in which personal ego and national or international politics interfered with the mission of removing these Jews from the volatile situation endangering them. Although it could be argued that each group wanted to help save them, Spector argues that all those involved had differing views on the best way to go about the task. He notes that, for example, Jewish groups that were allegedly working together let their goals about how others would perceive the rescue and their role in it overpower their ability to cooperate in bringing about a successful operation.

As we have seen throughout this analysis, better political processes and love of others, instead of ego and xenophobia, could have allowed the Beta Israel to join their fellow Jews decades sooner. As Teshome G. Wagaw argued: "The reasons for recent mass emigration have to do primarily with the current (post 1974) political, religious, and economic conditions of Ethiopia. Their departure also was facilitated by change in the political situation of Israel and countries in northwest Africa, such as the Sudan, Egypt, and Kenya, as well as the United States and to some extent, Western Europe and what was then the Soviet Union".[27] As the above demonstrates, together with egotism on the part of the leaders of various organizations, governments, and rebel fighting groups, national and international politics formed the basis for this story.

Works Cited

Jochnowitz, George. "*An Act of Mercy in a Merciless World*", review of *Operation Solomon: The Daring Rescue of the Ethiopian Jews*, by Stephen Spector. *Midstream*, September/October, 2005. www.jochnowitz.net/Essays/OperationSolomon.html.

Kaplan, Steven." *The Beta Israel (Falasha) in Ethiopia from Earliest Times to The Twentieth Century*." New York: New York University Press, 1992.

Kessler, David. "*Falashas*". New York: Schocken Books, 1982 (2nd ED); New York: Frank Cass publisher, 1996 (3rd Ed)

The Rescue of the Falashas, LA Times January 16, 1985 http:///articles.latimes.com/keyword/operation-moses.

Murphy, Kim. "*Airlift of Ethiopia Jews End in Joy: Rescue: Operation flies more than 14,500 from embattled Addis Ababa to Israel in just over 33 hours. A plan to whisk them to safety was prepared six weeks ago.*" *L. A. Times*, May 26, 1991.

Naim, Asher. "*Saving the Lost Tribe, The Recue and Redemption of Ethiopian Jews*". NY: The Ballantine Publishing Group, 2003.

New York Times. "*Airlift to Israel is Reported Taking Thousands of Jews from Ethiopia*." December 11, 1984.

"*Operation Moses*." Israel Ministry of Aliyah and Immigrant Absorption. http://moia.gov.il/English/FeelingIsrael/AboutIsrael/Pages/mivtzaMoshe.aspx. (accessed 9.11.2018).

Quirin, James. "*The Evolution of the Ethiopian Jews, A History of the Beta*

Israel (Falasha) to 1920". Philadelphia, PA: University of Pennsylvania Press, 1992.

Spector, Stephen. "*Operation Solomon, The Daring Rescue of the Ethiopian Jews"*. Oxford: Oxford University Press, 2005.

Tenenbaum, Murray. "*Rescue of Ethiopian Jews.*" *L. A. Times*, July 19, 1985.

Wagaw, Teshome. "*For Our Soul, Ethiopian Jews in Israel"*. Detroit, MI: Wayne State University Press, 1993.

Notes

[1] David Kessler, *Falashas* (NY: Schocken Books, 1982): 132.

[2] James Quirin, *The Evolution of the Ethiopian Jews, A History of the Beta Israel (Falasha) to 1920* (Philadelphia: University of Pennsylvania Press, 1992): 28 ["Which had the purpose of redefining their religion to make it congruent to world Judiac patterns, laying a basis for eventual migration to Israel."].

[3] David Kessler, *Falashas* (NY: Schocken Books, 1985):155.

[4] "Today in History," *The Official IDF Blog*, www.idf.il/en/mimisites/humanitarian-missions/today-in-history-idf-airlifts-14-500-ethiopian-jews-to-israel/ 12:00pm 9/11/2018.

[5] Teshome G. Wagaw, *For Our Soul: Ethiopian Jews in Israel* (Detroit, MI: Wayne State University Press, 1993): 57.

[6] Stephen Spector, *Operation Solomon: The Daring Rescue of The Ethiopian Jews* (Oxford: Oxford University Press, 2005):21 Spector notes: "Ethiopia's significance for the United States waned in the late 1960's as American space satellite technology lessened the usefulness of the listening post at Kagnew Station. Then, after Nasser's death in 1970, Sadat formed an alliance with the United States, and Egypt's crucial location on the western shore of the Red Sea further diminished Ethiopia's centrality for Washington."

[7] Stephen Spector, *Operation Solomon*: *The Daring Rescue of The Ethiopian Jews* (Oxford: Oxford University Press, 2005): 28.

[8] Stephen Spector, *Operation Solomon*, *The Daring Rescue of The Ethiopian Jews* (Oxford: Oxford University Press,2005): 28.

[9] George Jochnowitz, "An Act of Mercy in a Merciless World," review of *Operation Solomon: The Daring Rescue of the Ethiopian Jews, by Stephen Spector*, *Midstream Magazine*, September/October 2005, https://www.jochnowitz.net/Essays/OperationSolomon.html., accessed 11/23/14

[10] "The Mengistu Threat," *The Jewish Virtual World, Ethiopia, The Mengistu Threat, The Jewish Virtual World, Ethiopia,* https:www.jewishvirtuallibrary.org/Ethiopia-virtual-jewish-tour, 12:15pm, 9/11/2018. [During the weeks surrounding Mariam's coup, an estimated 2,500 Jews were killed and 7,000 became homeless. Soon Mariam instituted a policy of 'Villagization,' relocating millions of peasant farmers onto state-run cooperatives which greatly harmed the Beta Israel by forcing them to share their villages—though they were

denied the right to own land—with non-Jewish famers resulting in increased levels of anti-Semitism throughout Gondar province."]

[11] Stephen Spector, *Operation Solomon: The Daring Rescue of Ethiopian Jews* (Oxford: Oxford University Press,2005):19-30 "Chapter One, Restoring Diplomatic Relations, Conceiving Aliyah".

[12].Asher Naim, *Saving the Lost Tribe, The Recue and Redemption of Ethiopian Jews* (New York: The Ballantine Publishing Group, 2003) [Naim tells of their travels: "Ethiopian immigrants, who longed to reach Israel, faced numerous dangers along the way. They first had to secretly make their way to the Sudanese border, which they attempted by arranging small groups to journey together. The majority traveled on foot, vulnerable to robbers and other violence along the way. The journey to Sudan typically took between two weeks to a month, and countless numbers perished along the way." Naim continues: "Once across the border, the immigrants languished in camps for long periods until they were able to depart for Israel. The conditions in the camps were harsh, and many people died in them as well.] See also "The Mengistu Threat" www.jewishvirtuallibrary.org/ethiopia-virtual-jewish-tour, accessed 3:18pm 9/11/2018.

[13] "Operation Moses," Israel Ministry of Aliyah and Immigration Absorption, http://moia.gov.il/English/FeelingIsrael/AboutIsrael/Pages/mivtzaMoshe.aspx (accessed 9/28/2018).

[14] "Airlift to Israel is Reported Taking Thousands of Jews from Ethiopia," *New York Times*, December 11, 1984.

[15] *New York Times*, Ibid.

[16] *New York Times*, Ibid.

[17] *New York Times*, Ibid.

[18] https://www.jewishvirtuallibrary.org/ethiopia-virtual-jewish-tour (accessed 9/11/2018).

[19] Operation Moses and Joshua, https:www.jewishvirtuallibrary.org/Ethiopia-virtual-jewish-tour, accessed 9/11/2018; "Under a news blackout for security reasons, Operation Moses began on November 18, 1984, and ended six weeks later, on January 5, 1985. In that time, just over 7,000 Jews were rescued and brought to Israel. But the mission was not without problems. Because of news leaks (blamed primarily on a December 6 article in the *Washington Jewish Week* and full-page advertisements placed by the United Jewish Appeal), the mission ended prematurely as Arab nations pressured the Sudanese government to prevent any more Jews from using Sudan to go to Israel. Almost 15,000 Jews were left behind in Ethiopia."
IDF Reports, *Operation Moses*, https:www.idf.il/en/minisites/operations/Journey to Freedom 25.04.16.

[20] IDF Reports, *Operation Moses,* https:www.idf.il/en/minisites/operations/Journey to Freedom 25.04.16.

[21] https://www.idfblog.com/blog/2011/11/21/today-in-history-the-moshe; http://zahal.com/2016/04/journeys-to-freedom-idf-rescue-operations/.

[22] Murray Tenenbaum, "Rescue of Ethiopian Jews," *L. A. Times*, July 19, 1985.

[23] Stephen Spector, *Operation Solomon: The Daring Rescue of Ethiopian Jews* (Oxford: Oxford University Press, 2005):29.

[24] Stephen Spector, *Operation Solomon: The Daring Rescue of Ethiopian Jews*

(Oxford: Oxford University Press,2005):30.
[25] Murphy, Kim. "*Airlift of Ethiopia Jews End in Joy: Rescue: Operation flies more than 14,500 from embattled Addis Ababa to Israel in just over 33 hours. A plan to whisk them to safety was prepared six weeks ago.*" L. A. Times, May 26, 1991.
[26] Association for Diplomatic Studies and Training, "*How Many People Can You Fit on a 747?- Operations Sheba and Solomon,*"
https://www.adst.org/2016/10/operations-sheba-solomon-israel-ethiopia-human-rights-evacuation/
"Operation Moses," Israel Ministry of Aliyah and Immigration Absorption, http://www.gov.il search operation moses
[27] Teshome Wagaw, *For Our Soul: Ethiopian Jews in Israel* (Detroit, MI: Wayne State University Press, 1993):56-57.

Note: The terms "Falasha", "Beta Israel", and "Ethiopian Jews" are used interchangeably. Ethiopian Jews consider the term "Falasha" ("stranger") derogatory.

CHAPTER THIRTEEN

THE EMANCIPATORY ROLE OF JUDAISM FOR AFRICANS

ALEXANDRE CORNET

The land of Africa serves as the initiatory matrix for both Jewish and African civilizations, having provided the setting and instruments for rites of passage of each towards maturity and their separation-based identity quests. In Egypt, Israelites experienced subjugation and loss of freedom. Africans went through similar ordeals when subjugated in their motherland.

Spiritually multifaceted, Africa has a history shaped by interactions with multiple civilizations. Catholicism, Islam, Protestantism, Buddhism, Mahi Kari, and Yoga all spread throughout the continent. Its ancient roots in the region, and also as a recent addition, Judaism resonates with Africa's political, social, cultural, and indigenous religious traditions. Such resonances make many Africans "feel at home" embracing Judaism.[1] In my experience, when Africans embrace Judaism they reaffirm who they were before the trauma of slavery and colonization. Thus, in this article I argue that Judaism can affirmatively play an emancipatory role for Africans.

There are many similarities between Jewish and African cultures regarding family, community, and eco-friendly orientations. Those in most African cultures, however, are specifically familiar with the Israelites' narrative of slavery and freedom. Therefore, in this chapter I will briefly compare general Jewish and African histories of slavery and resistance, experiences formative for both civilizations. With numerous similarities and differences between them, we can also find interesting nodes of common ground. While there remain challenges, including racism and legacies of trauma, I demonstrate in this article that Judaism holds promise for Africans' continuing struggles for independence.

Slavery in African History

As a brief overview of the lengthy history of slavery in Africa, it is important to note that slavery occurred in different forms at different times across the continent, where traditions of human ownership stem from pre-historic social organization. The anthropologist Harris Memel-Fotê described these practices in his study of nine Ivorian ethnic groups.[2] Early African domestic slavery did not entail total lack of freedom nor did it require express brutality. Enslavement followed excommunication, debt, or capture in war. In contrast, both Western and Arabian slavery treated Africans primarily as economic tools.

Two milestones in the history of the Arabian slave trade were the Bakt Treaty (652 CE) and the conquest of Jarma (666–667). In both cases, new rulers demanded hundreds of slaves in tribute. These milestones laid the foundations for systemic Arabian slave trading, a brutal form of slavery historically, which included male castration.[3] For centuries, the magnitude and violence of both Arab and Western slave trading left indelible social, economic, demographic, and spiritual marks, particularly in sub-Saharan Africa.

In the West, a papal bull issued by Pope Nicholas V helped legitimize the Portuguese slave trade from West Africa, which began around the year 1441.[4] Later, in French colonies, the Royal Black Codes of 1685 and 1724 formalized the transatlantic slave trade practiced by European empires. Significantly, even the British (1807 and 1833) and French (1848) Slavery Abolition Acts did not prevent Western powers from perpetuating slavery. The Berlin Conference of 1884–1885, which partitioned and "pacified" Africa, attempted to sanitize slavery by rebranding it as "forced labor", but the system remained genocidal.[5]

Slavery in the Jewish Tradition

As an overview, ancient Hebrews both held and were slaves. In biblical practice, slaves fulfilled roles akin to those of servants. Biblical accounts describe monetary transactions to acquire slaves/servants (Gen. 17:23) but also depict some integration of these people into the family fabric of the households they served.[6] Hebrews enslaved other Hebrews as well. The Torah differentiated between Israelite and non-Israelite slaves. Torah required humane treatment of both but considered only the latter property. This form of slavery differs from that experienced in Egypt, which Louis Ginzberg describes as violent and genocidal.[7]

In the ancient Middle East, war practices supplied slaves to victors.[8] Post-Sinaitic Jewish history involved captivity and slavery under the Assyrian, Babylonian, and Roman empires. In 931 BCE, King Solomon's death split Israel into two warring kingdoms, Israel in the North and Judah (or Judea) in the South. Assyria destroyed Israel and enslaved its population in 722 BCE. In 586 BCE, Babylonia did likewise to Judah. The Assyrian exile caused entire Israelite tribes to disappear, leading to legends of the ten lost tribes. The Persian victory over Babylonia in 530 BCE enabled the Israelites to return to their homeland.

After their return and reconstruction of the Temple, Jews enjoyed a brief period of autonomy followed by invasion and rule by the Persian (538–322 BCE), Hellenistic (322–164 BCE), and Roman (60 BCE–395 CE) empires. In 168 BCE, the Seleucid Antiochus IV Epiphanes (r. 175–164 BCE) quelled a Jewish rebellion. In the first Roman-Jewish war (66–73 CE), according to Josephus Flavius, Titus put [the Jews] into bonds and sent them to the Egyptian mines. Titus also sent a great number into the provinces to be destroyed and those younger than seventeen to be sold as slaves. The Romans destroyed the Temple and razed Jerusalem, as well as destroyed and renamed Judea during the Roman-Jewish wars (132–135 CE).

Fighting for Freedom in the African Tradition

The history of slavery and colonization prompted Africans to organize resistance across the continent and in the diaspora. Born of a deep-seated desire for freedom, self-determination, and equality, these struggles produced such great leaders as Kimpa Vimta (Congo), Frederick Douglass (US), Toussaint Louverture (Haiti), and Nelson Mandela (South Africa). The African struggle for emancipation saw resistance to both slavery and colonization including uprisings, protests, and revolutions, as well as the development of the maroonage system. In addition, these forms of oppression and resistance ignited African independence movements.

Resistance to Slavery and Colonialism

Despite the complicity of certain African leaders profiting from the slave trade, many Africans resisted fiercely.[9] Toyin Falola and Amanda Warnock note of the African resistance: "African resistance had been noted along the slave-trading ports in varying degrees, from threats…and keeping a watchful eye on the coast to prevent European slave ships from docking…to wars against European slave traders and their African collaborators".[10] Overall, the military, technical, and organizational superiority of the Arabs and

Europeans generally allowed them to suppress African resistance and to shackle and deport millions.

Physical shackles, however, could not squelch the ideas of African captives. African captives were able at times to rebel onboard ships, inflicting losses on slave traders. Revolting slaves often preferred death to slavery. Historians have documented more than five hundred shipboard rebellions.[11] Many slave ships reached their destination, of course, uprooting Africans and forcing them into slavery marked by dehumanizing ill-treatment. Still, Africans found ways to express their vehement opposition to this plight.[12] Revolts of varying scales and intensity marked the entire history of African slavery.[13]

European colonization also spawned African resistance ranging from protests to war. These acts of resistance provided fertile ground for African nationalism and independence struggles. A fundamental refusal to accept foreign rule underlay this resistance,[14] which swept across Africa as colonization and slavery spread. Africans sustained long military campaigns against better-equipped European armies.[15] When colonizers' use of technology overpowered resistance at the level of empires and kingdoms, the hinterlands continued the opposition.[16]

Africans and their descendants launched other successful revolts against slavery in the Americas as well. Most notable among them was the Haitian Revolution (1791–1804) in which voodoo—derived from some maroons' African religion—played a key role.[17] The Haitian Revolution had unprecedented social, political, and economic repercussions throughout the Americas, Europe, and Africa. In the United States, it inspired Frederick Douglass (1817–1895) and other Black activists to fight against slavery. The work of Douglass and other freedom fighters, notably Sojourner Truth (1787–1883), David Ruggles (1810–1849), and Harriet Tubman (1822–1923), contributed to stamping out slavery in the US and encouraged others to oppose slavery. In the US, emancipation for slaves finally came at the end of the Civil War (1861–1865); thus, the ripple effects of the Haitian Revolution helped to dismantle slavery throughout the Americas from 1808–1888. Additionally, revolts staged by enslaved Africans also inspired resistance to the European exploitation of the entire African continent, including both natural resources and human beings (since in the name of "civilizing" Africa the Berlin conference [1884–1885] set rules for partition, occupation, and colonization of the continent).

In the new civilizations being developed in the West by Europeans, many enslaved Africans fled to indigenous communities or secluded locations where they often set up maroon communities.[18] The word "Maroon"—"runaway"—derives from the Spanish *Cimarron,* meaning "wild" or "untamed". The practice of fleeing slavery and surviving became known as "marronage". Wherever slavery existed, there were Maroons. In Mexico in 1570, Gaspar Yanga led a band of escaping slaves to the highlands near Veracruz. He later came to be called the "first liberator of the Americas".[19] The Yanga settlement took in other escaped slaves; they survived through agriculture, hunting, and raids. The Spanish colonial government made several unsuccessful attempts to annihilate it but instead, in 1618, signed a treaty granting the settlement self-rule, albeit with some strings attached. This eventually led to the establishment in 1630 of San Lorenzo de los Negros de Cerralvo, the first free Black settlement in the Americas. In 1739–1740, British colonists fought against Jamaican Maroons. Unable to eliminate them, the British instead signed a treaty[20] affirming their right to stay in their primary settlements: Accompong, Trelawny Town, Moore Town, Scott Pass, and Nanny Town, with a superficial form of self-rule under British supervision. Dissatisfied, the communities continued their war in 1795–1796. In 1880, the British relocated the inhabitants of Trelawny to Nova Scotia and then deported them to a British settlement in Sierra Leone.[21]

African Struggles for National Independence

Africans never accepted European colonization. The long history of colonization over time also spurred African struggles for independence, including intellectual, political, and military components. Europeans responded with a triple strategy of missionaries, merchants, and military action. Missionary churches and colonial schools sought to spread Western values based on Christianity while educating Africans. The two World Wars exacerbated colonial exploitation, as European countries forced indigenous populations into their armies. Conscription gave Africans modern military skills; missionaries and colonial schools gave them education. Additionally, colonial trade and agriculture taught colonized Africans commercial skills, including modern administration, marketing natural resources, and international business practices. These skills fueled new independence movements following both world wars.[22] Thus, the triple strategy of European colonization ultimately backfired. As Benedict Anderson wrote, "The 19th century colonial states engendered the nationalism that eventually rose to combat it".[23] An important feature of the relationship between oppression and the development of independence movements is that many African national leaders studied in colonial universities or otherwise spent formative years in Europe. Thus, many who would become founding fathers of African nations achieved political maturity while abroad.[24]

African encounters with Afro-Caribbean and Afro-American Pan-Africanist intellectuals also stimulated African nationalism and Pan-Africanism (an ideology emphasizing the common heritage of people of African descent worldwide and their obligation to collaborate).[25] Marcus Garvey and W. E. B. Dubois pioneered the development of Pan-Africanism, Garvey through his tri-lingual newspaper, *The Negro World,* and Dubois through organizing international Pan-Africanist conferences with other African intellectuals to discuss African self-rule and the emancipation of Africans and their descendants in the diaspora. These conferences inspired African activists to found or re-invigorate youth associations, trade unions, and welfare organizations, as well as religious, ethnic, and other associations. Many of these associations evolved over time into political parties that fought for African independence.[26] Some former French colonies, notably Côte d'Ivoire, Senegal, Mali, Burkina Faso, Benin, and Togo, achieved independence relatively peacefully in 1960. Despite growing international pressure, colonial powers were often reluctant to emancipate their colonies. Due to French reluctance to divest of its colonial presence in much of Africa, many countries, including Algeria in 1962 and Madagascar in 1960, relied on guerrilla warfare to achieve independence. In addition, many European colonizers granted only superficial independence, leading to ongoing weaknesses in African political institutions. African states still struggle to overcome liabilities from their history of slavery and colonialism.

Fighting for Freedom in the Jewish Tradition

The Jewish community has stood the test of time, despite persecution and tragedy. Additionally, the Jewish people have continued to struggle for freedom. Rabbinic Judaism has nurtured this resilience over time, as Jews have provided mutual aid, succeeded in trade, waged war, and engaged in political struggles inspired by nationalism.

Resistance Warfare and Nationalism

Three categories of armed conflicts comprise Jewish resistance warfare: 1) the wars of antiquity against Assyria, Babylonia, Greece and Rome, 2) armed resistance in exile, and 3) contemporary warfare for the state of Israel.

The ancient Israelites' conquest of Canaan resulted in the creation of a new kingdom, later divided into the separate kingdoms of Israel and Judah.

Israel and Judah fought against far larger armies to protect their borders and spiritual heritage from the Assyrian, Babylonian, Persian, Greek, and Roman Empires. The last of three rounds in the Assyrian-Israelite conflict finally broke Israel's resistance.

The kingdom of Judah stayed ahead of the Assyrian army through battles and diplomatic alliances. Babylonia defeated the Assyrians and became the new regional force, turning other nations into vassals. The Judeans resisted but ultimately succumbed to destruction and exile. Josephus writes about ongoing military campaigns for national autonomy, which ended only when Roman legions ruthlessly crushed the resistance and forced the Jews from Judea. The Romans occupied Judea from 70 to 313 and renamed it Palestine.[27] This "Roman" exile, as it was initially termed, lasted from antiquity until 1948. However, tempered by precarious moments of peace, stability, and affluence, this exile entailed constant persecution, and survival required resilience. The worst persecution came in the Nazi Holocaust.[28]

Shoah survivors joined Zionist nationalists returning to their homeland, where they confronted British colonists with a deliberately ambiguous policy regarding permitting Jews to return. The Jewish Zionist organizations Ha-Shomer, Lehi, Irgun, Etsel, Betar, Hagganah, and Mista'arebim fought against both the British and Arabs who opposed Zionist activity. Wars have riddled Israeli stability, and Israel maintains high military standards to deter terrorists. This continues a history of Jews drawing resilience from political and religious nationalism as they defend their national territory and their identity.

The Israelites first experienced nationalism when leaving Egypt. Unlike modern US Americans, who left from within their homelands to wrest independence from European empires, Moshe and his generation had no direct knowledge of Canaan, the land they sought for the expression of their religious and political sovereignty. Nonetheless, they united in nationalism. The power of this passion accounts for the survival and striking geographic portability of Jewish nationalism throughout the exile.

The revelation on Mount Sinai and the subsequent covenant form the climax of early Jewish nationalism. In the wilderness, Jewish nationalism acquired the military, theological, and social organization necessary to defeat Amalek, Basha, the Amorites, and Moav. After Moshe's death, Israelite theocratic nationalism reached a maturity that enabled it to transcend space and time. Joshua and subsequent leaders conquered Canaan and eventually established a monarchy based on theocratic nationalism. Emblematic Jewish nationalist political figures (David, Solomon, Omri, Mattathias, Simon Bar Kochba) and movements (Maccabbees, the Zealots) fought relentlessly for their kingdom until the Romans defeated them.

Exile tested Jewish nationalism, but its geographical transposability produced large-scale organized communities in Babylonia, Africa, Europe, Asia, and the Americas. As these communities were in foreign lands, they faced endless danger, including ostracism, libels, forced conversions, expulsion, massacres, and pogroms. These difficulties inspired early Zionists, such as Moses Hess and Leon Pinsker; early settlement organizations, such as Bilu, Hibbat Tziyon, and Hovevei Tziyon; and, ultimately, Theodore Herzl and the movement that he founded in 1897. To end the cycle of discrimination and fatalities, these leaders advocated and planned a Jewish return to the land of Israel and the creation of a Jewish homeland. Zionism evolved to include socialist, revisionist-nationalist, cultural, and religious divisions. It achieved its major goal in 1948 with Israeli independence, some 1813 years after the annihilation of Judea and the expulsion of the Jewish population by Roman legions in 135.

Although the centrality of the land of Israel remains constant, it is one of the four matrixes (exiles in foreign lands, wanderings in the wilderness, Israel, diaspora experience) in which Jewish nationalism developed. Jewish spirituality and Judaism unify these matrixes by inspiring the social, political, and military actions of Jewish history.

Nationalism and Jewish Religious Resistance

What is called in modernity "religion" is particularly significant in Jewish history because the relationship of B'nei Israel with their ancestral God has been the foundation for the national concept of Israel since antiquity. Jewish intellectual and spiritual work served both a religious and a national purpose, enhancing Jewish memory and protecting the community from alienation and assimilation.

Jewish religion began in antiquity as Hebrew monotheism,[29] and it then acquired a body of laws to become Judaism and eventually rabbinic Judaism. These iterations managed to resist repeated attempts to annihilate them. Such traits made of Judaism a sociological peculiarity and enabled it to resist socio-spiritual phagocytosis.[30]

Judaism preserved its authenticity largely given the prophetic tradition, the *soferim* (scribes), and the rabbis. Moses was the Hebrew prophet *par excellence*. The social, spiritual, and political activism of such prophets as Deborah, Samuel, Nathan, Amos, Elijah, Elisha, Isaiah, Jeremiah, Ezekiel, and Daniel marked Israelite history from the early settlement in Canaan to the reconstruction of the Temple. The prophets strove to prevent the dilution or destruction of Israelite national, social, moral, and spiritual identity.[31] Teachers and incubators of Jewish faith, they protected B'nei Israel from both internal weaknesses and external forces. These made their last contributions to national restoration and reconstruction of the Temple after the Babylonian exile.

The *soferim* succeeded the prophets and committed to compiling the spiritual heritage passed down by earlier generations.[32] Last prolix heirs of a long and unbroken chain of Torah transmission, the rabbis bestowed timelessness on Judaism, ability for self-renewal, and adaptability in exile through the Talmud codification, Kabbalah mysticism, and philosophal reflection.[33] When in history Jews were dispossessed of their religious shield by powerful Christian or Muslim assimilatory currents and forced into conversion, they either escaped or sought refuge into crypto-Judaism contextually called "marranism"[34] in Spain and "donmeh sectarism" in Turkey.[35]

Jewish Social Strategies

Jewish cultural erasure first began following the Assyrian-Israeli war. Just as Torah scholars protected the Jewish community from cultural assimilation, relative social and financial success in the diaspora sometimes allowed Jews to improve their circumstances. Jews in exile often responded to the threat of disappearance of their culture by seeking either affluence and social elevation or balanced social integration into resettlement lands as early Haskalah (Jewish enlightenment movement) advocated it in Germany.[36] When social achievement failed to protect Jews but instead stirred jealousy, Jewish lifestyles, social solidarity, and ability to network allowed Jews to make it through exilic tragedies. Thus, Jewish solidarity has reinforced Ashkenazi, Sephardi, and Mizrahi communities' survival skills throughout the ages.

Conclusion

A scene in *Case Dépabrt*, a 2011 French comedy about slavery directed by Lionel Steketee, Thomas Ngigol, and Fabrice Eboué, highlights the altruism of Isaac, a Jewish merchant who hides and feeds two African slaves on the run. Surprised by such benevolence from a white man, Gedeon and Gaspar question him. Isaac explains that he is a Jew and Jews are called the "Negroes of Europe". He tells them that Jews and Africans experienced significant suffering and should show solidarity. When slave hunters arrive, Isaac helps Gideon and Gaspar escape. Isaac's statements could serve as our conclusion: Jews and Africans share a legacy of slavery, suffering, and a struggle for liberation based on nationalism. With the differences between them, the similarities create a recognizable past and a potentially empowering future for Africans through relationship to and within Jewishness.

Of course, slavery and the fight against oppression are universal themes, and Jews and Africans have no monopoly on suffering. At the same time, historical analysis shows us that these peoples' experiences have been core to the creation and longevity of their communities. Their reactions to long exposure to suffering were dramatically different, though. African resistance was basically mono-strategic and apparently more physical, often prioritizing confrontation. Jewish resistance was multi-strategic and more subtle; it is likely related to the roles Jews have played in the economic production system of the civilized worlds. Jews have often succeeded in moving from the situation of being economic tools to stakeholders. Africa and diaspora countries are still largely struggling against their situation of being economic instruments.

With these differences and beyond the universalism of human suffering, there are also striking similarities common to African and Jewish histories. Although Israel is basically a monotheistic people, and sub-Saharan Africa is polytheist, both cultures are multiethnic. Their histories share the centrality of their land, the multiculturalism generated by exile and colonialism, intellectual, spiritual, political paths of resistance, and dynamics generated by long and recurrent exposure to trauma.

Paradoxically, some scholars suggest that Africans and Jews may share some mutual culpability for each other's enslavement. Cheikh Anta Diop argues that Black Africans populated and ruled ancient Egypt.[37] We may thus posit that Black African Egyptians enslaved the Israelites and subjected them to abuse. Both Max I Dimont and Jacques Attali maintain that Jews played an active role in the African transatlantic slave trade.[38] It is possible this new approach of incriminating both Africans and Jews for slavery may help each to redefine their communal history and grasp the profound bonds between them.

Another historical link between Jewish and African history comes from the story of Germany's colonization of Namibia, where the concepts of concentration camps, racial purity, and human experimentation first gained a foothold. We can trace the industrialized professionalism of the Shoah to the experience the German colonial administration gained when suppressing the Herero and Nama rebellions.[39] These links between African and Jewish experience in the modern period can also point the way to a productive future relationship.

At the same time, questionable Jewish interpretations of *midrash* suggesting that Africans are cursed descendants of Ham and destined for slavery or menial labor undermine any African embrace of Judaism. Similarly, Africans themselves undermine their potential partnership with the Jewish world when they emphasize economic advantages and fabricate religious commitment. Partnerships between Africans and Jews can, however, be quite fruitful if both sides overcome these challenges.

With these histories of trauma and resilience, including various similarities as well as differences, we find an interesting contemporary convergence. When Africans venture into the Jewish world, they enter an emotionally familiar environment. Similarly, though structurally different, Jews' marranism and African slaves' maroonage shared much in common. Africans have much to learn from Jews about transcending history. Jews managed to return from exile and rebuild their nation-state because Judaism provided a unifying force. Africans historically have lacked this unity, but they share the same legacy of suffering as do Jews. Because the Torah facilitated cohesion among scattered Jewish communities, perhaps the Torah may help African communities achieve similar cohesion. Christianity and Islam aided the development of European and Arab civilizations but so far have proven inadequate to meet the needs of Africa. African empires were initially based on social organizations rooted in mystical pantheist and polytheist religions. Judaism offers a much-needed combination of structure and mysticism while nurturing Africans through its parallels to African experience. While not homogenizing, Judaism may motivate Africans seeking sustainable development in both Africa and the diaspora.

Works Cited

Alpert, Michael. *Crypto-Judaism and the Spanish Inquisition*. Basingstoke, UK: Palgrave, 2001.

Anderson, Benedict. *Imagined Communities: Reflections on the Origin and Spread of Nationalism*. London: Verso, 1983.

Attali, Jacques. *Les Juifs, le Monde et l'Argent*. Paris: Fayard, 2002.

Attias, Jean-Christophe, and Esther Benbassa. *Judaïsme: Religion, Cultures, Identités*. Paris: Le Nouvel Observateur, 2007.

Conan Doyle, A. *The Crime of the Congo*. New York, NY: Double Day Page & Company, 1909.

Dallas, Robert Charles. *The History of the Maroons: from their origin to the establishment of their chief tribe in at Sierra Leone*. London: Longman, 1803.

Diop, Cheikh Anta. *Nations Nègres et Cultures*. Translated from the French by Mercer Cook. NY: Lawrence Hill Books, 1974.

Dubnow, S. M. *Jewish History: An Essay in the Philosophy of History*. Philadelphia: The Jewish Publication Society of America, 1903. http://www.gutenberg.org/files/7836/7836-h/7836-h.htm. Accessed 10/01.18.

Epstein, Isidore. *Le Judaïsme: Origines et Histoire*. Paris: Petite Bibliothèque Payot, 1969.

Falola, Toyin, and Amanda Warnock. *Encyclopedia of the Middle Passage*. Westport, CT: Greenwood Publishing Group, 2007.

Fassassi, Assani. *Le Péché du Pape Contre l'Afrique*. Paris: Al Qalam, 2002.

Feiner, Shmuel. *The Jewish Enlightenment*. Translated by Chaya Naor. Philadelphia, PA: University of Pennsylvania Press, 2004.

Firmin, Antenor. *Bookman and the 1791 Slaves Revolt in Haiti: The Beginning of the Haitian Revolution*. Amazon Kindle Edition, 2015. Accessed 10.20.18. https://www.amazon.com/Bookman-1791-Slave-Revolt-Haiti-ebook/dp/B00TZ7CTUI.

Flavius, Joseph. "The Wars of the Jews," Book 6, Chap. 9:2. In *The Works of Flavius Josephus*. Translated by William Whiston. https://books.google.com/books/about/The_Works_of_Flavius_Josephus.html?id=TI5DAAAAYAAJ&printsec=frontcover&source=kp_read_button#v=onepage&q&f=false. Accessed 10.01.18.

Gershaw, Robert, and Stephan Malinowski. "Hannah Arendt's Ghosts: Reflections on the Disputable Path from Windhoek to Auschwitz." *Central European History* 42, no. 2 (June 2009): 279–300.

Ginzberg, Louis. *The Legends of the Jews*. Miami, FL: Hardpress, 2012.

Kahn, Rabbi Zadoc. *Esclavage Selon la Bible et le Talmud*. Paris: France, Louis Guérin, 1867.

Khapoya, Vincent B. *The African Experience*. Upper Saddle River, NJ Prentice Hall, 1998.

Bernard, Kira. "100 ans après la révolte des abbey, pourquoi le colon Rubino a été mange." *Revo-ivoire*. Accessed 10.21.18. http://www.rezoivoire.net/cotedivoire/patrimoine/274/100-ans-apres-la-revolte-des-abbey-pourquoi-le-colon-rubino-a-ete-mange.html#.W8zHwHdFzIV.

Knight, Franklin W. "The Haitian Revolution." In *The American Historical Review* 105 (February 2000): 103–15.

Landers, Jane. "Slavery in Colonial North America." Race, Development and Inequality Project. http://www.erudito.fea.usp.br/PortalFEA/Repositorio/1181/Documentos/leitura_1_1_2.pdf. Accessed 10.01.18.

Memel-Fotê, Harris, Joseph Brunet-Jailly, and Emmanuel Terray. *Esclavage dans les Sociétés Lignagères de la Fôret Ivoirienne XVII-XXe Siecles*. Paris: IRD Editions and Abidjan: Cerap, 2007.

Ndiaye, Tidiane. *Le Génocide Voilé*. Collections Continent Noir Gallimard, 2008.
http://www.gallimard.fr/Catalogue/GALLIMARD/Continents-Noirs/Le-genocide-voile. Accessed 10.01.18.

Orchardson-Mazuri, Elisabeth. *N'zinga: The Warrior Queen*. Nairobi: Jomo Kenyatta Foundation, 2015.

Pélissier, René. "De la Résistance en Afrique Lusophone." In *Recherche, Pédagogie et Culture* 3, no. 39 (1979): 35–39.

Popovic, Alexandre. *The Revolt of African Slaves in Iraq in the 3rd/9th Century*. Princeton, NJ: Markus Wiener Publishers, 1999.

Rabaka, Reiland. *The Negritude Movement: W.E.B. Du Bois, Leon Damas, Aimé Cesaire, Leopold Senghor, Frantz Fanon, and the Evolution of an Insurgent Idea*. Lanham, MD: Lexington Books, 2015.

Reiddel, Heidi. "The Maroon Culture of Endurance." *Americas*. 1990. Volume: 42,1: 46-49. Accessed 10.01.18.

Rodriguez, Junius P. *Encyclopedia of Slave Resistance and Rebellion*. Westport, CT: Greenwood Press, 2007.

Saint-Exupéry, Antoine de. *Lettre à un otage*. Paris: Gallimard, Collection Blanche, 1944.

Serbin, Sylvia. *Reines d'Afrique et héroïnes de la Diaspora noire*. Saint-Maur des Fossés: Éditions Sepia, 2004.

Scholem, Gershom. *Encyclopedia Judaica*. Vol. 6. Edited by Cecil Roth and Geoffrey Wigoder. Jerusalem: Macmillan, 1971.

Taylor, Eric Robert. *If We Must Die: Shipboard Insurrections in the Era of the Atlantic Slave Trade*. Baton Rouge, LA: Louisiana State University Press, 2009.

Thornton, John. *The Kongolese Saint Anthony: Dona Beatriz Kimpa Vita and the Antonian Movement*. Cambridge: Cambridge University Press, 1998.

Welbourn, F.B., and B. A. Ogot. *A Place to Feel at Home: A Study of Two Independent Churches in Western Kenya*. London: Oxford University Press, 1966.

Wondji, Gabriel. "Résistances Africaines Noires à la Colonisation." In *Recherche, Pédagogie et Culture* 3, no. 39 (1979): 30–31.

Yerushalmi, Yosef H. *Zakhor (Histoire juive et mémoire juive)*. Paris: La Découverte, 1984.

Notes

[1] F. B. Welbourn and B. A. Ogot, *A Place to Feel at Home: A Study of Two Independent Churches in Western Kenya* (London: Oxford University Press, 1966).
[2] Harris Memel-Fotê, Joseph Brunet-Jailly, and Emmanuel Terray, *Esclavage dans les Sociétés Lignagères de la Fôret Ivoirienne XVII-XXe Siecles* (Paris: IRD Editions and Abidjan: Cerap, 2007).
[3] Tidiane Ndiaye, *Le Génocide Voilé* (France : Collections Continent Noir Gallimard, 2008).
[4] Assani Fassassi, *le Péché du Pape Contre l'Afrique* (Al Qalam, 2002).
[5] A. Conan Doyle, *The Crime of the Congo* (New York, NY: Double Day Page & Company, 1909).
[6] As examples, Hagar, Bilhah, and Zilpah supported the matriarchs in their marital and maternal duties (Gen. 16:2 and Gen. 30:1–22); Eliezer negotiated Isaac's marriage for Abraham (Gen. 24); and Abraham's concerns in Genesis 15:3 imply that slaves could inherit their masters' estates.
[7] Louis Ginzberg, *The Legends of the Jews* (Miami, FL: Hardpress, 2012), 279–80; also Ex. 1:22. As examples, see note 6.
[8] Rabbi Zadoc Kahn, *Esclavage Selon la Bible et le Talmud* (Paris: France, Louis Guérin, 1867), 76; and Monette Bohrmann, "L'Esclavage dans la Religion Juive," in *Dialogues d'Histoire Ancienne* 24, no. 2 (1998): 25–39.
[9] For example, Anna N'zingha (1583–1663) of Matamba waged a relatively successful military and political campaign against the Portuguese in Angola. Elizabeth Orchardson-Mazuri, *N'zinga: The Warrior Queen* (Nairobi: Jomo Kenyatta Foundation, 2015); and Sylvia Serbin, *Reines d'Afrique et héroïnes de la Diaspora noire* (Saint-Maur des Fossés: Éditions Sepia, 2004). Similarly, the Congolese see-er Kimpa Vita (1684–1706), often compared by Europeans to Joan of Arc, led mass movements against both Portuguese rule and the slave trade in Angola and the Congo. John Thornton, *The Kongolese Saint Anthony: Dona Beatriz Kimpa Vita and the Antonian Movement* (Cambridge: Cambridge University Press, 1998).
[10] Toyin Falola and Amanda Warnock, *Encyclopedia of the Middle Passage* (Westport, CT: Greenwood Publishing Group, 2007), 395.
[11] Eric Robert Taylor, *If We Must Die: Shipboard Insurrections in the Era of the Atlantic Slave Trade* (Baton Rouge, LA: Louisiana State University Press, 2009).
[12] For example, as Jane Landers notes, "The first large contingent of African slaves brought to the present-day Unites States arrived from Hispaniola in 1526 with the ill-fated colonizer, Lucas Vazquez de Ayllon. [H]is settlement, San Miguel de Guadape, was quickly undermined by disease, starvation, and Ayllon's death. Mutiny ensued, and disaffected elements took control of the failing colony. Finally, slaves set fire to the compound of the mutineers and the Guale indians attacked. This episode marked the first known alliance of Indians and Africans against Europeans in what came to be the United States." Jane Landers, *Slavery in Colonial North America* (Vanderbilt University), Race, Development and Inequality Project, 1–2. Accessed 10.01.18.
[13] For example, three Zendji slave revolts almost overthrew the Abbasid dynasty.

Alexandre Popovic, *The Revolt of African Slaves in Iraq in the 3rd/9th Century* (Princeton, NJ: Markus Wiener Publishers, 1999).

[14] Gabriel Wondji, "Résistances Africaines Noires à la Colonisation," *Recherche, Pédagogie et Culture* 3, no. 39 (1979): 30–31.

[15] For example, Toucouleur El Haj Omar (1857–1860), his son Ahmadu (1883–1893), Mandinguo Almamy Samory Tourey (1882–1898), and King Gbeanzin (1890–1894) of Dahomey (Benin) fought against French expansion in West Africa. In South Africa, England faced many wars, including clashes with Chaka Zulu (1786–1828), legendary for his military skill and charisma, and with Basotho fighters in Basutoland (Lesotho), who in 1881 achieved independence. Likewise, the Portuguese encountered fierce resistance in the Gaza Empire (Mozambique). René Pélissier, "De la Résistance en Afrique Lusophone," *Recherche, Pédagogie et Culture* 3, no. 39 (1979): 35–39.

[16] For example: in the southern Ivory Coast, the Abbays (1909–1911) sabotaged railroads, train stations, and telephone facilities. Legend maintains that they killed and cooked the French colonial officer and trader Rubino and served him to French settlers coming to vandalize their villages. The Ivorian town of Rubino continues to commemorate this incident, reminding both French and Ivorian descendants about European brutality and local resistance. Kira Bernard. "100 ans après la révolte des abbey, pourquoi le colon Rubino a été mange." *Revo-ivoire*. Accessed 10.21.18. http://www.rezoivoire.net/cotedivoire/patrimoine/274/100-ans-apres-la-revolte-des-abbey-pourquoi-le-colon-rubino-a-ete-mange.html#.W8zHwHdFzIV.

[17] Antenor Firmin, *Bookman and the 1791 Slaves Revolt in Haiti: The Beginning of the Haitian Revolution* (Amazon Kindle Edition, 2015). Dutty Boukman, Jean-Francois Papillon, Georges Biassu, Toussaint Louverture, and Jean-Jacques Dessalines led this massive war of self-liberation that defeated the French. On January 1, 1804 Jean-Jacques Dessalines declared Haiti's independence and became governor-general. Franklin W. Knight, "The Haitian Revolution," *The American Historical Review* 105 (February 2000): 103–15.

[18] Reiddel, Heidi. "The Maroon Culture of Endurance." *Americas*. 1990. Volume: 42,1: 46-49. Accessed 10.01.18.

[19] Junius P. Rodriguez, *Encyclopedia of Slave Resistance and Rebellion* (Westport, CT: Greenwood Press, 2007).

[20] Treaties obliged the Maroons to return newly escaped slaves to their owners, and sometimes also to provide free labor to the colony and accept some Europeans into their community.

[21] Dallas Robert Charles, *The History of the Maroons: from their origin to the establishment of their chief tribe at Sierra Leone* (London: Longman, 1803).

[22] Vincent B. Khapoya, *The African Experience*, 4th ed. (New York, NY: Routledge, 2016), 150–80.

[23] Benedict Anderson, *Imagined Communities: Reflections on the Origin and Spread of Nationalism* (London: Verso, 1983).

[24] For example, Leopold Sedar Senghor, first president of Senegal, graduated from the Sorbonne; Milton Margai, first prime minister of Sierra Leone, graduated from King's College London; Ghana's first president, Kwame N'kruma, graduated from Lincoln University in Pennsylvania; before becoming the first president of the Ivory

Coast, Félix Houphouet Boigny served in the French Parliament where he fought successfully to abolish forced labor in French colonies.

[25] Vincent Khapoya, *The African Experience.* (Upper Saddle River, NJ: Prentice Hall, 1998), 163.

[26] One can see this in the growth of the Negritude cultural literary movement, a derivative of Pan-Africanism, was instrumental in combating racism and colonialism in French colonies. Reiland Rabaka, *The Negritude Movement: W.E.B. Du Bois, Leon Damas, Aime Cesaire, Leopold Senghor, Frantz Fanon, and the Evolution of an Insurgent Idea.* (Lanham, MD: Lexington Books, 2015).

[27] Other occupations followed: Byzantines (313–636), Arabs (636–1091), Seljuks (1091–1099), Crusaders (1099–1291), Mameluks (1291–1516), Ottoman Turks (1516–1917), and finally, the British (1917–1948).

[28] Jean-Christophe Attias and Esther Benbassa describe Jewish armed resistance to the Reich: "Une résistance apparait dans plusieurs camps et ghettos, entrainant des répressions violentes. Au ghetto de Varsovie, elle est organisée à la fin du mois d'Octobre 1942 par des groupes affiliés aux mouvements de jeunesse sioniste et à des parties politiques. Dans la révolte, qui éclate le 18 Janvier 1943, environs 40,000 juifs trouvent la mort." Jean-Christophe Attias and Esther Benbassa, *Judaïsme: Religion, Cultures, Identités*, (Paris: Le Nouvel Observateur, 2007): 72.

[29] Isidore Epstein, *Le Judaïsme: Origines et Histoire* (Paris: Petite Bibliothèque Payot, 1969).

[30] Saint Exupéry described such faith-based resistance: "L'homme est gouverné par l'Esprit, je vaux dans le désert ce que valent mes divinités." ("Man is governed by Spirit; in the desert I am worth what my deities are worth.") Antoine de Saint-Exupéry, *Lettre à un otage* (Paris: Gallimard, Collection Blanche, 1944).

[31] Isidore Epstein, *Le Judaïsme: Origines et Histoire* (Paris: Petite Bibliothèque Payot, 1969).

[32] S. M. Dubnow assessed their significance: "Without the…compilation achieved by the *Soferim*, of which the uninstructed… speak slightingly, mankind to-day had no Bible, that central sun in world-literature. These two centuries may fitly be called the school-days of the Jewish nation; the Scribes were the teachers of Jewry…. It was then that the Jews first earned their title to the name, 'the People of the Book'." S. M. Dubnow, *Jewish History: An Essay in the Philosophy of History. http://www.gutenberg.org/files/7836/7836-h/7836-h.htm. Accessed 10.01.18.*

[33] Yosef H. Yerushalmi, *Zakhor (Histoire juive et mémoire juive)* (Paris: La Découverte, 1984), 67.

[34] Michael Alpert, *Crypto-Judaism and the Spanish Inquisition*, (Basingstoke, UK: Palgrave, 2001).

[35] Gershom Scholem, *Encyclopedia Judaica*, eds. Cecil Roth and Geoffrey Wigoder. Vol. 6 (Jerusalem: Macmillan, 1971).

[36] Shmuel Feiner, *The Jewish Enlightenment*, trans. Chaya Naor (Philadelphia, PA: University of Pennsylvania Press, 2004).

[37] Cheikh Anta Diop, *Nations Nègres et Cultures* (Translated from the French by Mercer Cook. NY: Lawrence Hill Books, 1974).

[38] Jacques Attali, *Les Juifs, le Monde et l'Argent* (Paris: Fayard, 2002).

[39] Robert Gershaw and Stephan Malinowski write: "The German colonial wars

against the Herero and Nama represent, [Jurgen Zimmerer] argues, a 'decisive link to the crimes of the Nazis' and were 'an important source of ideas' for Germany's war of annihilation in eastern Europe after 1939/41…. [T]he campaign against the Herero was therefore 'paradigmatic for the Nazi war of extermination': 'even the murder of the Jews' would 'probably not have been possible without Germany's colonial experience'." Robert Gershaw and Stephan Malinowski, "Hannah Arendt's Ghosts: Reflections on the Disputable Path from Windhoek to Auschwitz," *Central European History* 42, no. 2 (June 2009), 279–300, 282.

CHAPTER FOURTEEN

THE TRADITION OF ISRAELITE DESCENT AMONG THE PASHTUNS IN INDIA AND ITS CONTEMPORARY RAMIFICATIONS

NAVRAS J. AAFREEDI

This paper explores the tradition of Israelite descent of Pashtuns/Pathans. Here I also examine levels of awareness and ignorance among tribe members in India. I then look at the Jewish and scholarly interest in this tradition, as well as the Pashtun/Pathan response to the Jewish and scholarly attention.

The standard view among scholars across the world is that even if the tribes of Israel, ten of which are allegedly lost, ever existed, assimilated into the general populations of the regions where they were settled, now it is just not possible to trace their descendants. This has, however, neither discouraged groups across the world claiming descent from the lost tribes of Israel nor has it deterred several Jewish organizations from not only welcoming their claims but to also trying to engage with such claimants and persuading them to settle in Israel. Among all these claimants of Israelite descent, one group that stands out is the Pashtuns/Pakhtuns/ Pathans.[1] In spite of having been recognised as the best contenders for the status of the lost tribes of Israel by eminent anthropologists such Shalva Weil,[2] a senior researcher at the Hebrew University of Jerusalem, based on a number of factors discussed below, neither has a Judaizing movement emerged among them nor do they have any desire to emigrate to Israel, unlike other claimants of Israelite origin. In fact, they are just as antagonistic towards the State of Israel as, perhaps, many other Muslims, generally speaking. Additionally, this tradition of their descent from the lost tribes of Israel is rapidly eroding due to the growing Wahabi/Salafi influence among them. Still, there have been a few exceptions. There are individuals among them who have shown genuine interest in exploring their putative Israelite roots. There is also an organization, Anjuman al-Pathan, which claims to represent all Pashtuns in India; this group has even led a five-member delegation to Israel in 2015 at the invitation of religious nationalist Jewish organization Amishav.

Tradition of Israelite Descent among the Pashtuns/Pathans

The Pashtuns are not the only Muslim group in India that has not developed a Judaizing movement in spite of having a tradition of descent from the lost tribes of Israel. Other examples are: the Kashmiris, the Qidwais and the Bani Israil clan of Aligarh and Sambhal, who have similar (not identical) traditions.[3] Still, no other group has attracted as much attention internationally as have the Pashtuns in the recent past.

Pashtuns form the world's largest conglomeration of warlike tribes in northeastern Afghanistan and northwestern Pakistan. No reliable estimates of their population are available due to the prevalence of Islamist militancy in their territories,[4] yet it could be somewhere around forty-one million, conservatively speaking.[5] They are divided into sixty tribes,[6] which are subdivided into four hundred clans. Pashtuns have a large diasporic population also in India[7] where they settled in different waves of migration. Tribe members found employment with Muslim rulers in India from the thirteenth century onwards. Many Pashtun tribes are of Turkish origin, with ancestral roots north of the River Oxus (Amu Darya), with no traditions of descent from the lost Israelites; however, those who are not of Turkish origin traditionally claim descent from the lost tribes of Israel, considering themselves part of *Bani Israil* (Persian/Pashto/Urdu variant of the Hebrew *Bene'i Yisrael*).[8]

Jewish Religious Nationalist Interest in the Tradition of Israelite Origin of Pashtuns/Pathans

I hail from one such diasporic settlement, Malihabad in District Lucknow in Uttar Pradesh, India. This settlement is home to approximately twelve hundred Pashtuns[9] (2002 estimate). Locally, we are called Pathans, half of whom are members of the Afridi tribe. Although I never came across any custom among my fellow Afridi Pathans that even remotely resembled Jewish/Israelite customs, my interest in the subject was triggered by the mention of the Pathan tradition of Israelite descent to me by an uncle of mine when I was still a teenager. Several years later when I reached the tertiary level of education, I got in touch with Amishav.

The Israeli religious nationalist Jewish organisation Amishav is devoted to the search for the remnants of the lost tribes of Israel and aims to convert to Judaism and settle in Israel all those who either claim descent from the lost tribes of Israel, are spiritually attracted to Judaism, or have practiced Judaism in secrecy for generations in hostile environments.[10] The organization came into existence as part of the "Messianic fervour ignited in Israel by the victories of the Six Day War and the Greater Israel Movement".[11] Amishav's work is driven by the belief that the ingathering of the lost tribes will bring about the dawn of the messianic era. Amishav believes it to be every Jew's responsibility to search for the lost tribes and help them return to *Eretz Yisrael* (the land of Israel). This belief emerges from their understanding that helping return Jews to Israel will hasten God's intervention in the coming of the messiah as humans' deeds on earth are believed to be metaphysically linked to God's actions.[12]

Jochanen Shareth indulged in correspondence with me on behalf of Amishav. He recognised my people, the Pashtuns, as descendants of lost Israelites. Shareth was also affiliated with Beit Zur, an organisation devoted to building Jewish settlements in the West Bank. My correspondence with Shareth, took place from 2000 to 2002, culminated in his inviting me to settle in Israel. I could not accept his invitation.

Genetic Research

Later in 2002, I invited anthropologist Tudor Parfitt from SOAS, University of London to collect DNA samples of my fellow Afridi Pathans in Malihabad to confirm their Israelite origin, just as he had done for the Bene Israel.[13] Parfitt collected mouth swabs of fifty paternally unrelated Afridi males. Geneticists Neil Bradman and Mark Thomas at University College London analyzed the swabs. The results were neutral: "They did not say anything one way or the other", as Parfitt noted in an interview with *The Sunday Indian* in 2009.[14] In my view, the inconclusiveness of the testing was perhaps due to the dilution of tribal purity resulting from intertribal marriages among the Pathans in Malihabad. Considering their small numbers, it was just not possible for these tribe members to remain as endogamous in their diaspora in India as they had been and continue to be in their homeland: northeastern Afghanistan and northwestern Pakistan. In 2008, Shahnaz Ali, a geneticist then working at the Central Forensic Science Laboratory in Kolkata, conducted another study to assess Pashtun Israelite descent through a genetic study. Ali collected blood samples, instead of mouth swabs, of fifty-three subjects from Malihabad. In 2009, she took these samples to the Israel Institute of Technology/Technion, in Haifa,

Israel, to analyze them under the supervision of Karl Skorecki.[15] As reported by GeneWatch, an American publication devoted to "monitoring biotechnology's social, ethical and environmental consequences", however, the aim of the analysis was purely medical in nature and not ethnological. GeneWatch reported that although Ali was awarded a fellowship by the Israeli Foreign Ministry to conduct an "ancestry study at Technion University in Israel which would compare Afridi Pashtun and modern Jewish blood samples for ancestral links", it never took place. According to Ali's advisor Skorecki, Ali changed the project as she found it too controversial for the Pashtuns.

These initiatives, however, have not brought an end to the interest in confirming the Israelite origins of Pashtuns through genetics, as evident from the messages that I have been receiving from both Pashtuns themselves and Jews; for example, I received the following e-mail message from M. Naeem Yousafzai from Khyber Pakhtunkhwa, on September 27, 2011:

> I spotted one study about Malih Abad Afridis with DNA data (of 44 persons) available at www.yhrd.org (an organization for maintaining data about human Y-DNA). I myseld [sic] tested that data for haplogroup classification using an online haplogroup utility and most of the haplogroups came out to be G2c/c*, which is found at high frequencies in Ashkenazi Jews. I thought it to be a sampling error but lately two other studies about Pashtun DNA have been published (both in 2011)—one finds a 10% presence of G2c/c* in Pashtuns of Southern Afghanistan while the other discovers about 15% G2c/c* presence in Pashtuns of Khyber Pukhtunkhwa (former NWFP) and FATA. Of FATA Pashtuns, 36 persons were sampled in which the most common haplotype was found to be G2c/c* observed in 4 individuals. Probably, this sample also included a significant number of Afridis.

It would certainly be better to analyze DNA samples of the Pashtuns from their homeland in Afghanistan and Pakistan rather than from their diaspora, considering what the medical doctor Amtul Razzaq Carmichael points out. According to her, the theory regarding Pashtun Israelite descent is supported by evidence from genetic diseases common to Jews and Pashtuns. An example is retinoblastoma, a hereditary cancer of the eye. This eye disease was found to be genetically different in ethnic Pashtuns when compared to the general Pakistani populace, suggesting that the origins of Pashtuns are different from other Pakistanis.[16] Additionally, Carmichael does not consider the Pashtuns indigenous to Pakistan. The territory inhabited by Pashtuns did not belong to India until it was conquered by the British in the Second Anglo-Afghan War (1878–1880). Later, in 1947, when Pakistan was carved out of India, that territory became part of Pakistan by default.

Pashtun/Pathan Response to the Research on the Tradition of their Israelite Descent

My doctoral research on the tradition of Israelite origin among Pathans attracted much attention in the press, triggering the interest of several lost tribes' explorers in the tiny quiet hamlet of Malihabad and alarming its Pathan inhabitants. The study was misrepresented in the Urdu[17] press as a Zionist conspiracy against Islam aimed at depriving it of its bravest followers, the Pathans (as the Pathans see themselves). My work was presented as aiming to convince Pathans of their putative Israelite descent and then to persuade them to convert to Judaism and settle in Israel.[18] The Pathans in their diaspora, largely ignorant of the Pathan tradition of descent from the lost tribes of Israel (with a few exceptions), easily fell for this anti-Semitic propaganda and became increasingly suspicious of all studies focused on this Pathan tradition. Israeli scholar Ari Z. Zivotofsky recounts his experience with the Pathans in Malihabad from his December 2014 visit. At this time, Zivotofsky was asked why Israel intends to prove that the Pashtuns are of Israelite origin and, if proven to be so, would Israel be willing to take in all forty million as immigrants. Zivotofsky interpreted these questions to mean that Pashtuns take offense to, and resent, any scholarly attempt to link them to the ancient Israelites. He concluded that for this research to continue, scholars would need greater involvement of the Pashtuns and heightened sensitivity to tribe members' feelings.[19]

Pashtun/Pathan Delegation's Visit to Israel

From November 15–25, 2015, Amishav organized a five-member Pathan delegation visit to Israel. Amishav noted that the aim of this visit was "to strengthen ties with ancient Israelite brethren, and to show them the current Israel".[20] To facilitate granting visas to each member of the delegation, Uri Ariel extended an official invitation.[21] In response to queries regarding the purpose of the delegation's visit upon arrival at Ben Gurion Airport, delegation head Abdul Rasul Khan (President of Anjuman al-Pathan and a retired colonel from the Indian army) offered: "We have come to learn about our history as Sons of Israel".[22] It is hard to confirm the veracity of Khan's statement. In my view, it is possible that he took this trip for the purpose of tourism or to explore avenues of employment in Israel for the Pashtuns from India, many of whom are already working in a number of oil-rich Middle Eastern countries. While Khan is known for his demand for reservations in government jobs for Pashtuns in India, he has never been heard drawing attention to the putative Israelite origins of Pashtuns. During their stay in

Israel, the delegation was given a tour of Judea and Samaria (West Bank), the alleged ancient homeland of the ten lost tribes of Israel.

After a January 2017 meeting between Abdul Rasul Khan and Uri Ariel at the Hotel Taj in New Delhi, Ariel sent Khan a warm letter on May 26, 2017, thanking him for the visit. Ariel noted that he appreciated the "deep knowledge of their genealogical roots relating to the Israelites" held by the members of the delegation who accompanied Khan to this meeting. Ariel added that it seemed correct to deepen the connection with brothers (Pashtuns) in India, particularly at a time when there are a number of Muslims who turn their back towards Israel when she stretches out a hand for peace.

Since the Pathan delegation's Israel visit in 2015, Israel television's Channel 20 (Arutz Esrim) telecast a two-episode documentary film on the putative Israelite origins of Pathans. The documentary included Rabbi Eliyahu Birnbaum, a judge on the court of the Chief Rabbinate of Israel, visiting the Pathan diaspora in Rajasthan.[23] Rabbi Birnbaum also published a Hebrew article on the subject.[24] Additionally, MyHeritage has launched a project aimed at translating the sixteenth-century manuscripts that were written in a dialect of Rajasthani and contain genealogical accounts of the Pathans of Rajasthan referring to their putative Israelite origins.[25] The MyHeritage project is an online genealogical platform with web, mobile, and software products.[26] Amishav is fundraising to bring more Pathan delegations to Israel for ten-day trips patterned on Taglit's Birthright Israel Trips.[27] Amishav is driven by the vision of its founder, Rabbi Eliyahu Avichail, who said in 2007 that it was his dream to help the Afridi, whom he identified with the lost Israelite tribe of Ephraim, to return to their roots in Israel, just as the lost tribe of Menasse (identified with the Bene Menashe from Manipur and Mizoram in India) had.[28]

Long-term Jewish and Christian Interest

There is a long-standing and growing interest in the putative Israelite origins of Pashtuns. Jewish organizations devoted to the search for the lost tribes of Israel such as Kulanu and Shavei Israel also have sections of their websites devoted to Pathans/Pashtuns.[29] If these organizations succeed in bringing even a few Pathans to settle in Israel, these Pashtuns would not be the first Muslim claimants of Israelite descent to emigrate there (there were some Kashmiri villagers who emigrated to Israel many years ago but soon disappeared).[30]

Additionally, this recent activism is not the first time that Amishav established contact with Pashtuns; for example, Amishav sent an exploratory team on British passports to Afghanistan in 1975, the year the organization was founded, and to Pakistan in 1983. The teams returned convinced of the Israelite descent of Pashtuns based on alleged similarities between some Pashtun and Jewish customs. The delegations' considering the Pashtuns to be descendants of lost Israelites puts Amishav explorers in line with Christian missionaries and British adventurers and scholars preceding them.[31]

Historically, Christian missionaries have been enthusiastic in reaching this conclusion, convinced that it would assist in converting these peoples to Christianity and in this Christian view, "believing that such a conversion would have a double benefit. Not only would it add members to the church, but these new members would be of Israelite—or Jewish—origin, as no specific distinction has been made between the two. Moreover, not only would such a conversion be a great achievement to the Christian Church, which has tried for centuries to convert the Jews, but these converts would be innocent of the heavy sins of the Jews.... If these sinless Israelites recognized Jesus, it would...open the way to the Second Coming of Christ".[32] Christian missionaries have not successfully converted Pashtuns and other Muslims of Israelite descent in India. It remains to be seen what will emerge from the recent involvement of Jewish organizations with Pashtuns in India.

Conclusion

Regardless of Jewish organizational involvement, it is unlikely that a Judaizing movement similar to ones which have emerged among the Bene Menashe in Manipur and Mizoram and the Bene Ephraim in Andhra Pradesh will develop among the Pashtuns/Pathans in India. Unlike the Bene Menashe, Pathans in India have lost their tribal characteristics as a result of acculturation, making them indistinguishable from the rest of the non-Pashtun Muslims in the areas where they live. Pashtuns in India have a strong affinity with the general Muslim population of India (there are approximately 140 million Indian Muslims). Unlike the Bene Menashe, Pashtuns are not geographically isolated. Additionally, Pashtuns are better integrated than both the Bene Menashe (tribals from northeastern India) and the Bene Ephraim (who are all Dalits). The Bene Menashe and the Bene Ephraim were also both Christian before they started practicing Judaism. In contract, Pashtuns are Muslim and sympathetic to Palestinians and fellow Muslims.

Also of note, Pashtun perceptions of Jews and the state of Israel are strongly influenced by anti-Israel views of the Arab-Israeli conflict and are a deterrent to their growing affinity with Jews and Israel; however, even if a Judaizing movement does not develop among them, it is likely that closer interaction with Jewish organisations may soften their anti-Israel stand. Involvement of Jewish organizations with Pashtuns might bring about a change in some Pashtuns' attitudes towards Jews. In my view, this would be a significant development for the promotion of Jewish-Muslim amity.

Works Cited

Aafreedi, Navras. "Traditions of Israelite Descent Among Certain Muslim Groups in South Asia." *Shofar* 28, no. 1 (2009): 1–14.

Barmazid, Khan. "Pashtun Tribes", History of Pashtuns (a blog maintained by Khan Barmazid). n.d., http://www.barmazid.com/p/pashtun-tribes.html

Be'eri, Eyal. "Impressions from the Visit of the First Ever Pathan/Pashtun Delegation to Israel." *Café Dissensus*, January 7, 2016.

Carmichael, Amtul. "The Lost Tribes of Israel in India: A Genetic Perspective." *The Review of Religions* (March 2012), http://www.reviewofreligions.org/6107/the-lost-tribes-of-israel-in-india-a-genetic-perspective/

Cooper, Alanna. "Conceptualizing Diaspora: Tales of Jewish Travelers in Search of the Lost Tribes." *Association for Jewish Studies Review* 30, no. 1 (April 2006): 95-117.

Crooke, W. *The Tribes and Castes of the North-Western Provinces and Oudh*. Vol. IV. Office of the Superintendent of Government Printing, India, 1896. Reprint, New Delhi and Madras: Asian Educational Services, 1999.

Freedman, Shalom. *Learning in Jerusalem: Dialogues with Distinguished Teachers of Judaism*. Northvale, NJ and Jerusalem: Jason Aronson Inc., 1998.

Gonen, Rivka. *The Quest for the Lost Tribes of Israel to the Ends of the Earth*. Northvale, NJ: Jason Aronson Inc., 2002.

Graham-Harrison, Emma. "Afghan census dodges questions of ethnicity and language." *The Guardian*, January 3, 2013.

Kamal, Hasan. "Chāi kī pyālī méin tūfān uthāné kī bachkānā koshish." *Roznama Rashtriya Sahara*, May 26, 2007. Urdu.

Lis, Jonathan. "Right-wing NGO Exposes Extent of Israel's Support of West Bank Settlements." *Haaretz*, November 24, 2011.

Nadia Abu, El Haj. "'A Tool to Recover Past Histories': Genealogy and Identity after the Genome." Institute for Advanced Study School of Social Science, Paper No. 19, December 2004.

Parfitt, Tudor. *The Lost Tribes of Israel: The History of a Myth*. London: Weidenfeld & Nicolson, 2002.
Puja, Awasthi. "Lost & Found." *The Sunday Indian*, May 10, 2009, 50.
Rashmee, Ahmed. "Marathi Jews are Moses' kin says study." *Sunday Times of India*, July 21, 2002, 1.
Scheinberg, Sy. "The Jews of India." In *Jews in Places You Never Thought Of*, edited by Karen Primack. Jersey City, NJ: KTAV Publishing House, Inc., in association with Kulanu, 1998, 19-20.
Weil, Shalva. "Our Brethren the Taliban?" *The Jerusalem Report*, October 22, 2001, 22.

Notes

[1] An historically warlike people, divided into sixty tribes and four hundred clans, inhabiting eastern Afghanistan and the Federally Administered Tribal Areas of the North West Frontier Province of Pakistan. There are also a few Pathan settlements in India. "Pathans", "Pashtuns", "Pakhtuns", and "Afghans" are names used interchangeably. Those who inhabit plains and plateaus are entitled to the name Afghan, which has a far wider connotation than that of a subject of the modern state of Afghanistan, founded only in 1747 CE. The northern highlanders call themselves Pakhtuns; the southern highlanders are known as Pashtuns. The appellation Pathan is the Indian variant of Pakhtanah, the plural of Pakhtun. The overwhelming majority of Pathans are Sunni Muslim. Only some of the border tribes (such as the Turis of Kurram, some Orakzais of Tira, and certain Bangash clans) are Shia.
[2] Shalva Weil, "Our Brethren the Taliban?" *The Jerusalem Report*, October 22, 2001, 22.
[3] Navras Aafreedi, "Traditions of Israelite Descent Among Certain Muslim Groups in South Asia," *Shofar* 28, no. 1 (2009): 1–14.
[4] There are no reliable figures available on the Pashtun population in Afghanistan due to many problems involved in conducting a census. Guardian correspondent Emma Graham-Harrison, "Afghan census dodges questions of ethnicity and language," *The Guardian*, January 3, 2013, accessed on March 15, 2013, http://www.guardian.co.uk/world/2013/jan/03/afghan-census-questions-of-ethnicity.
[5] According to the US Central Intelligence Agency, Pashtuns are 15.42% of the population of Pakistan and 42% of the population of Afghanistan. In 2012, the United Nations estimated the population of Pakistan at about 179 million and Afghanistan at 33.4 million. From this we note that the Pashtun population in Pakistan was 27.60 million and in Afghanistan was 14.02 million in 2012; thus the total Pashtun population from the two countries in which most Pashtuns live was 41.62 million that year.
[6] Khan Barmazid, "Pashtun Tribes," *History of Pashtuns*, n.d., accessed on November 8, 2017, http://www.barmazid.com/p/pashtun-tribes.html.
[7] The Pathan population in Oudh (most of the modern Uttar Pradesh) was estimated

to be 700,398, according to the Census of 1891. This figure seems too large considering that the total Pathan diasporic population in India in 2009 was estimated to be only thirteen thousand (*Wikipedia*, s.v. "Pashtuns", last modified August 26, 2018, Accessed September 9, 2018, https://en.wikipedia.org/wiki/Pashtuns). The total population of only the Afridi tribe in Oudh was estimated to be 12,840 in the Census of 1891. W. Crooke, *The Tribes and Castes of the North-Western Provinces and Oudh*, Vol. IV (Office of the Superintendent of Government Printing, India, 1896, Reprinted by Asian Educational Services, New Delhi and Madras, 1999), 170–71.

[8] The highland Pathan tribes of Afridi, Bangash, Dilazak, Jadran, Jaji, Khatak, Khostwal, Mahsud, Mangal, Orakzai, Turi, Usman Khel, Wardak, and Wazir do not claim descent from Qais (Kais or Kish), believed to be thirty-seventh in descent from the biblical character Saul or Talut, unlike the Pathan/Afghan tribes of plains and plateaus, yet they also have the tradition of Israelite descent and call themselves *Bani Israil* (Children of Israel). They are presented in genealogical legend as descended from a common ancestor, a foundling named Karlanri or Karlan, who had two sons, Koday and Kakay. The northerners who speak the hard variety of Pakhto are the descendants of Koday and the southerners who speak the soft variety of Pashto are the descendants of Kakay. Karlan or Karlanri is believed to have been adopted by a grandson of Sarbanr, one of the three sons of Qais or Kais (see Olaf Caroe, *The Pathans: 550 B.C.–A.D. 1957* [London: Macmillan, 1958, Reprint 1964]). The tradition finds mention in several medieval Persian texts, dating from the thirteenth to the eighteenth century: *Hayāt-é-Afghāni* of Muhammad Hayat Khan, *Khulāsāt-ul-Ansāb* of Hafiz Rahmat, *Majmā-ul-Ansāb* of Hamidullah Mustawfi, *Mirāt al-Afghāni* of Qutb Khan, Sarmast Khan Abdali, Hamza Khan, Umar Khan Kakarr, and Zarif Khan, the five historians commissioned by Khwaja Ni'matullah, courtier of the Mughal emperor of India Jahangir, to investigate the origin of Pathans in 1621 CE, *Mirāt ul-Ālam* of Bukhtawar Khan, *Rauza ul-Bāb Twārīkh ul-Akbar-wal-Ansāb* of Abu Sulayman Daud (1310 CE), *Tarikh-i-Guzīdāh* of Hamidullah Mustawfi (AH 730/1326 CE), *Tadhkirat al-Awliya* of Sulayman Maku (13th c.), and *Tadhkirāt al-Abrār* of Akhund Darwiza (1611 CE).

[9] The Pathan population in District Lucknow stood at 13,977 in 1896, according to the census conducted that year, of which 1,421 were of the Afridi tribe.

[10] Shalom Freedman, *Learning in Jerusalem: Dialogues with Distinguished Teachers of Judaism* (Northvale, NJ and Jerusalem: Jason Aronson Inc., 1998), 35.

[11] Tudor Parfitt, *The Lost Tribes of Israel: The History of a Myth* (London: Weidenfeld & Nicolson, 2002), 141.

[12] Alanna Cooper, "Conceptualizing Diaspora: Tales of Jewish Travelers in Search of the Lost Tribes," *Association for Jewish Studies Review* 30, no. 1 (2006): 101.

[13] Rashmee Ahmed, "Marathi Jews are Moses' kin says study," *Sunday Times of India*, July 21, 2002, 1.

[14] Puja Awasthi, "Lost & Found," *The Sunday Indian*, May 10, 2009, 50.

[15] Skorecki, with the publication of his paper "Y chromosomes of Jewish priests" in the journal *Nature* in 1997, "launched a new field of historical studies, one that attempted to reconstruct the origins, relatedness and migration patterns of Jewish communities on the basis of evidence of patrilineal origin and descent". Nadia Abu

El-Haj, "'A Tool to Recover Past Histories': Genealogy and Identity after the Genome," Institute for Advanced Study School of Social Science, Paper No. 19, December 2004, 1, accessed on December 3, 2017, https://www.sss.ias.edu/files/papers/paper19.pdf.

[16] Amtul Carmichael, "The Lost Tribes of Israel in India: A Genetic Perspective," *The Review of Religions*, March 2012, accessed March 15, 2014, http://www.reviewofreligions.org/6107/the-lost-tribes-of-israel-in-india-a-geneticperspective/.

[17] The lingua franca of most of the South Asian Muslims even if they speak other languages as their mother tongues.

[18] Anonymous, "Aṅdhé ko badī dūr kī sūjhī: Malihabadi Pathānoṅ ko Israel āné kī dāvat," *Nai Duniya*, November 13–19, 2003, Urdu.
Hasan Kamal, "Chāi kī pyālī méin tūfān uthāné kī bachkānā koshish", *Roznama Rashtriya Sahara* (May 26, 2007) [Urdu]

[19] Ari Zivotofsky and Ari Greenspan, "Pashtun Pride, Israel Denied," *Jewish World Review*, May 6, 2015, accessed November 8, 2017, http://www.jewishworldreview.com/0515/pashtun_jews.php3.

[20] Michael Gross, e-mail message to author, June 10, 2015.

[21] Jonathan Lis, "Right-wing NGO Exposes Extent of Israel's Support of West Bank Settlements," *Haaretz*, November 24, 2011, accessed November 9, 2017, https://www.haaretz.com/israel-news/right-wing-ngo-exposes-extent-of-israel-s-support-of-west-bank-settlements-1.397485. In 2011, the settler NGO Mattot Arim recognized Ariel, Member of the Knesset and Minister of Agriculture and Rural Development, as the most effective Member of Knesset.

[22] Eyal Be'eri, "Impressions from the Visit of the First Ever Pathan/Pashtun Delegation to Israel," *Café Dissensus*, January 7, 2016, accessed on November 9, 2017, https://cafedissensus.com/2016/01/07/impressions-from-the-visit-of-the-first-ever-pathanpashtun-delegation-to-israel/. Be'eri, a member of Amishav and a doctoral candidate at Ariel University, was instrumental in organizing the Pathan delegation's visit and played their local guide.

[23] "World Jewry Episode Seven: The Mystery of the Pathans in Rajasthan", *Channel Twenty (Arutz Esrim) News*, September 11, 2017: https://www.inn.co.il/News/News.aspx/353503.

[24] Eliyahu Birnbaum, "True Pathan is from the Bnei Yisrael", *Musaf* Sabbath supplement, December 26, 2014, accessed on September 8, 2018, https://musaf-shabbat.com/2014/12/26/%D7%A4%D7%AA%D7%90%D7%A0%D7%99-%D7%90%D7%9E%D7%99%D7%AA%D7%99-%D7%94%D7%95%D7%90-%D7%9E%D7%91%D7%A0%D7%99-%D7%99%D7%A9%D7%A8%D7%90%D7%9C-%D7%90%D7%9C%D7%99%D7%94%D7%95/#comments

[25] Eyal Beeri, e-mail to the author dated November 7, 2017.

[26] Within a decade of its establishment, MyHeritage was selected by Globes in 2013 as the most promising Israeli startup for 2013–2014. The same year Deloitte ranked MyHeritage among the top ten fastest-growing companies from Europe, the Middle East, and Africa (EMEA) on the Deloitte Fast 500 list (*Wikipedia*, s.v. "MyHeritage", last modified August 15, 2018, Accessed September 9, 2018,

https://en.wikipedia.org/wiki/MyHeritage).

[27] "Taglit" is Hebrew for "discovery". According to its website, "Taglit is the largest educational tourism organization in the world." The organization's mission "is to give every Jewish young adult around the world, especially the unaffiliated, the opportunity to visit Israel". Taglit hopes that its "trips motivate young people to continue to explore their Jewish identity and support for Israel and maintain long-lasting connections with the Israelis they meet on their trip". Taglit reports that: "Since its inception in December 1999, 600,000 participants took part in TAGLIT, nearly 100,000 of which are Israelis". They came from 67 countries. (Taglit - Birthright Israel, Accessed September 9, 2018, https://int.birthrightisrael.com/about_us_inner/52?scroll=art_1) Information on the Pashtun connection: Eyal Beeri, e-mail message to author, November 7, 2017.

[28] Rabbi Eliyahu Avichail's message to the Afridi Pathans of Malihabad, video recorded by the present author at the rabbi's Jerusalem residence on June 14, 2007. Rabbi Eliyahu Avichail was denied a visa twice by the Indian government as he was suspected of being involved in mass conversions to Judaism in the predominantly Christian states of Manipur and Mizoram in northeast India. The Indian government feared that mass conversions to Judaism could pose a threat to the social stability of the predominantly Christian northeast India, where evangelists had been vehemently opposing these mass conversions.

[29] http://kulanu.org/india/index.php; https://shavei.org/spotlight-on-other-communities-the-pathans-of-india-and-afghanistan/.

[30] Sy Scheinberg, "The Jews of India," in *Jews in Places You Never Thought Of*, ed. Karen Primack (Jersey City, NJ: KTAV Publishing House, Inc., in association with Kulanu, 1998), 19–20.

[31] For instance, M. W. Bellew, J. P. Ferrier, A. K. Johnson, Sir William Jones, Captain Riley, John Chamberlain, Sir Alexander Burnes, William Care, John Marshman, J. Samuel, and Theodore Pennel.

[32] Rivka Gonen, *The Quest for the Lost Tribes of Israel to the Ends of the Earth* (Northvale, NJ: Jason Aronson Inc., 2002), 186–87.